The Pants of Perspective

by Anna McNuff

Contents

Prologue

Part I

Contents

Epilogue

To Mum and Dad: my heroes in life, love and sport

The Pants of Perspective

Copyright © 2017 by Anna McNuff

The Pants of Perspective
by Anna McNuff

Te Araroa Trail

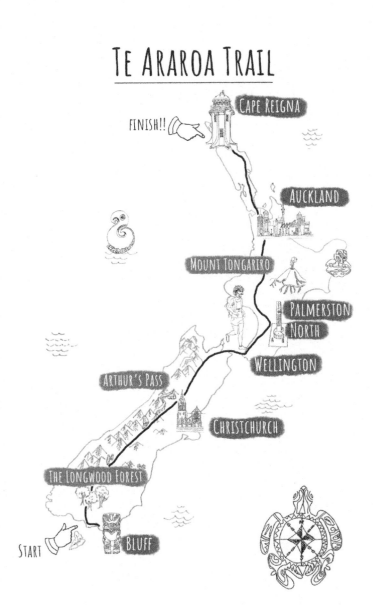

Cape Reigna

FINISH!!

Auckland

Mount Tongariro

Palmerston North

Wellington

Arthur's Pass

Christchurch

The Longwood Forest

Start

Bluff

PART I

Prologue

I'm clinging to a rock face on the north-west coast of New Zealand. A wave slams into my body from the left, and I know I've got 10 seconds until the next one hits. I take the chance to creep just that little bit further around. Months of scrambling over rocks and through bush have worn the soles of my shoes to a pulp, and so every footstep on the slick black rocks beneath them is a game of chance. Sand has mixed with salt water in my shoes and rubs on what once were blisters, and are now red, raw flaps of skin.

'Christ!' I yelp, feeling the final blister pop, closely followed by the inevitable release of warm liquid into my sock.

Pausing for a moment, I catch my breath. I feel like an idiot, a prize plum to be precise. Locals warned me that this section of the trail would be impassable at high tide, but I didn't listen. I couldn't listen. I have run 3,075 kilometres to this point, and have just one kilometre left to go. These waves, this rock, my burst blisters – just like the hundreds that have come before them – are just one more hurdle to overcome. They are now all that stands between me, and turning what was the most ridiculous dream into a reality.

South Island

1

The Dropper

I was three years old when my godfather dropped me on my head. I remember the event as if it were yesterday. I am standing at the top of a royal-blue slide, now heavily faded from exposure to the sun over the summer months. My podgy little toddler fingers are wrapped tightly around the white coated metal rails and I'm feeling rather proud, having negotiated my way, entirely unaided, up the three treacherous steps to the top. I look down at my thick white tights, noting how they wrinkle as I flex my legs, and swing the first, and then the second leg onto the slide. I nudge myself forwards to begin the ride. I'm off! Whoosh!

Sweet and pure delight for a matter of what seems like hours but must have been seconds. Nearing the bottom of the slide, the velocity from my glide carries me straight into my godfather's arms. He scoops me up under the armpits, laughing, and holds me aloft as if he were Bobby Moore and I the Jules Rimet trophy. Alas, in all the excitement my godfather is ill-prepared for the catch. His hands fumble and my nylon top slips through his loose grasp. The world now moves in slow motion, as I tumble, free-falling from far above his head. Everything is the wrong way up and there's a rush of air

7

passing my ears before the inevitable thud as my infant head collides with the soft earth. Then come the tears, and a transfer to the kitchen into the arms of someone with a far superior grip, my mum.

I'd like to argue that the significant early-life bump to the head was to be held entirely responsible for my desire to stand out, to be different. To be noticed, loved, and adored. But this is something that must, in fact, be accredited to an unorthodox family life. My upbringing was not what you would call normal. My godfather, the 'dropper', as he shall be known from this point on (real name: Martin Cross), is an Olympian. The dropper is in fact a quadruple Olympian, winning a gold medal in a boat with Steve Redgrave in Los Angeles in 1984 and a bronze medal in a boat with my dad in Moscow in 1980. Yes, my dad is an Olympian too. And naturally my dad is married to my mum, who, as it turns out, is also an Olympian. If life were a game of Olympic bingo we would have a full house.

Growing up in the McNuff household, life was never dull. I was raised in an environment where I was told I could be anything I wanted to be, if I just tried. As a result, I had a clear vision of the person I wanted to become from an early age. I wanted to be a princess, or an astronaut... or a trucker. Truth be told, I favoured the trucker. The lure of the open road, a chequered shirt and a handlebar moustache was just too much for a young girl to resist.

Being the middle sibling between two brothers I quickly

learnt that in order to get along in life, I must simply do what the boys did. And if I could do it better than them, faster than them, last longer than them, then that earned me something called respect. And I liked respect. I liked how it felt. I liked the swell in my chest when onlookers at the Saturday games in the primary boys' football league cheered as I slide-tackled an unsuspecting young male to the ground.

'Would you look at number seven go?! And she's a girl,' the crowd would coo.

So that's just what I did. I did things as hard and as fast and for as long as I could. I followed as much in my older brother Jamie's footsteps as I could, and I confess, I tried to beat up my younger brother Jonty far more times than was absolutely necessary. Until he got bigger than me, of course, then somehow starting a fight seemed entirely pointless.

Football went from strength to strength for a while, as did trampolining, hockey, athletics, county netball and county judo. Once, when I came away from a trampolining competition with yet another bronze medal, I overheard one parent say to my mum, 'Always the bridesmaid, never the bride.'

Those words stuck like glue. I had started to understand that I was good at many things, but stand-out-great at none. At 16 years old I was playing football for Wimbledon Ladies. Sixteen was the age that players moved into the senior team, and it was then that I realised one crucial thing – you needed to be really rather good, and football must become the sole focus of your life if you were to join the senior team. I just wasn't ready to make that commitment to football. I just didn't love it that much. There was nothing football could do to save the relationship, and so we split.

It followed that I found myself in the market for a new sport, so naturally my parents softly suggested that I give rowing a go. To my surprise, I at last found a sport that I could really get my teeth into.

Robustness and strength were not fortes, but what I did have was good technique. I would spend extra time out on the water when others had gone into the changing rooms. And in that extra 30 minutes out there, alone, I would think about a little secret I had – a secret I hadn't even told my parents. I wanted to be an Olympian too, more than anything. It made my stomach turn and my toes buzz every time I even thought of the possibility of making it happen. I saw the respect and admiration it had earned my parents, and I wanted that for myself. Rowing fitted perfectly with my work ethic, and I could put to use everything I had been brought up to believe: 'If you work hard enough, you will get what you want.' And boy did I work. I threw myself into it heart and soul. I trained as hard as humanly possible and in my final few years at school I was training ten times a week, including before and after school on many days, and all while studying for my A levels.

Things progressed well – I moved from representing England in a single scull to making it into the Great Britain squad.

I won a gold at the World University Championships in 2006 and followed that with a bronze at the European Championships in 2007. There was just one problem. The closer I moved towards the Olympic dream I had been striving for – that thing that I thought was going to make me happier than anything I had ever experienced before – the more I realised that it looked nothing like I thought it would.

I found that I was susceptible to injury and illness. I'd frequently tear things, bruise things, and wiggle bones out of place. I didn't make the cut for the team going to the Beijing Olympics, and so I was facing another four years of struggle and strife to make London in 2012. Four years of a sport that I had now fallen completely out of love with. Rowing had begun to batter my self-esteem, or rather I had allowed it to, and it now made me miserable, day in and day out. I realised it just wasn't ticking enough 'life boxes' any more. But most of all I was tired, so very tired, of the injuries that were impacting on my ability to compete. A shocking life lesson was beginning to dawn on me – if you work hard for something, you don't always get what you want. And that's okay, but it stings like a bitch.

From that point, I made one of the hardest decisions of my life. I dragged my dream of being an Olympian like my parents kicking and screaming from the closet where I had kept it so quietly for all those years, I looked it square in the eyes and I let it go. Everyday happiness just had to take precedence over a dream that may or may not make me happy in the long run.

Did I feel like I had failed? Absolutely. I had let myself down, I had let my parents down and, worse than that, I wasn't just giving up a sport, I was giving up a whole identity. When people asked me who I was, I couldn't tell them that I was a rower any more. I couldn't tell them I was… anything. Life was a Rubik's cube, and it would take some time to get the now scrambled colours back into place.

Five years later, I was sitting at my desk at the 'normal' job I had thought would be a lifelong career, when the realisation hit me: I had lost my way. Where was the girl who lived for the outdoors? For the playing field, for challenges and for doing what the boys did, only better? She had become buried under a stack of PowerPoint presentations and personal development reviews. She could now be found crying on the end of her bed or in the office toilets because she just didn't know where life was going any more.

The thought of stepping away from a good job, a steady pay cheque and a defined career path was terrifying at first. By all accounts, and in the opinion of others, I had a great life. But I just couldn't shake the feeling that there was something more out there. Another life in which I felt truly fulfilled. Once that thought took hold of me, there was no turning back. The compulsion to leave grew so great, that all fears about what on earth I would do when I came home evaporated into thin air. And so I had my 'ah-ha' moment. I negotiated a sabbatical from the big corporate I was working at and I set off to cycle 20,000 kilometres through every single state of America. From Alaska to Hawaii, the long way around. I hadn't a clue what I was doing. I hadn't cycled much and I knew nothing about wild camping or navigating across the wide, open roads of an unfamiliar country, but by God I knew it would be an adventure.

In those seven months riding high atop a bright pink bicycle named Boudicca, I met new people every day, I revelled in the ever-changing landscapes and the chance to take my body to hell and back, daily. On that bike, on the open road, I at last felt like me. Like the me I wanted to be, one I had never met before. I realised I didn't want to be an astronaut-cum-princess-trucker anymore. I wanted to be an adventurer. I knew then that with that first big adventure, I had just opened up a whopping big can of worms.

Having spent seven months of 2013 riding a bike around North America, and now back at the workplace I'd been granted a sabbatical from, I was looking for a new challenge. The original plan had been to hike the length of the Israel National Trail. I was all set to spend two months journeying through one of the most religiously significant countries in the world. I had the maps and everything. Alas, just as I was about to book my flights, the situation worsened and the Foreign Office began advising against travel. After a plea from my long-suffering mum – 'Please, Anna. Do you have to go to Israel right now?' – I decided that it would have to wait. But that left me

13

with a gap and a well of wanderlust so damn deep I feared I may in fact drown in it and stop breathing entirely if I didn't address it.

In my frequent Googling, which is what the eternal fidget does when they cannot actually leave the country, I came across a Wikipedia page which listed all of the long-distance hikes around the world. It is a very dangerous page and should have been approached with caution. I'd worked my way through researching them all: The Baekdudaegan (Dragon's back) Trail in Korea, the GR20 in Corsica, the TransPanama Trail – all of them had left me dribbling with delight and sent the tips of my fingers scurrying back to Google in a frenzy. And then there it was, nestled quietly at the bottom of the Wikipedia page: Te Araroa, 3,000 kilometres (1,900 miles), stretching from Cape Reinga in the north of New Zealand to Bluff in the south.

'Oh, New Zealand,' I swooned. 'Land of the Long White Cloud,' I murmured, dribbling faster still onto the keyboard.

I'd been thinking about a walking journey until this point. And then a crazy side-thought entered my mind. What if I ran this trail? Ran it with all my equipment on my back. Entirely solo and unsupported. I stopped for a moment, and bit down hard on the end of the biro that was in my hand. 'Nah... that's a bloody long way,' I told myself, and I pushed the idea aside.

But it just wouldn't leave me. Every evening on the cycle home from work, every morning over breakfast and every time I moved from my desk to take a break, this idea popped back into my head. The idea, the dream, as I realised it had now become, just wouldn't let me alone. It hung out in the corner of every room I entered. It lay in wait just beneath my eyelids, so that every time I shut my eyes it was there. It manifested itself into emails from Lonely Planet, which would include features on trail running and New Zealand, side by side.

It took me a while, and a good few evenings of staring at my bedroom ceiling to figure out what it was about this notion of running a country that just wouldn't let me be, and then it hit me. It was that the thought of it scared me. It was that I did not think I was capable of it. Cycling, yes, of course, that wasn't a problem. The 50-state ride had taught me that, but running adventures – they were for runners, real runners, and I'd just never felt like a runner before. The problem at its most basic level was that I wanted to do this thing so very badly, but I was afraid. Afraid to fail. Afraid that if I worked hard for it, I wouldn't necessarily get what I wanted. Afraid it would end up like my dream to be an Olympian. I would announce what I intended to do to all my friends and family, and then embark on a journey which I didn't know I could complete. I was afraid I wouldn't finish, and that made me too afraid to start.

Eventually, sense prevailed. I reasoned that being afraid to begin things was no way to live my life, and so I thought 'Stuff it.' It was September 2014. I would be self-funding the trip, and figured I needed as long as possible to save up some money and get my body into some kind of shape. I also knew that the latest I could start running was January, if I hoped to make the journey before Old Man Winter descended on New Zealand. January was four months from now. In four months' time I would begin running the trail. I'd get myself as ready as I could, and if disaster struck while out there, I'd figure it out along the way.

I resolved that running a long way was rather serious stuff. I thought again about not feeling like a 'real runner.' I was rather more muscular than any runner should be. I'd once done a weights session in the English Institute of Sport gym next to Mo Farah and realised that his calves were the size of my upper arms. I'd never gone in search of personal bests or split times while running – perhaps my rowing career had beaten out of me any kind of desire to do that. When I ran, it was for pleasure. Not for times, not to win, not to impress, I ran for me. When I ran my bum cheeks rubbed together, so much so that if I was going on a long run I'd have to 'lube up'. I ran to eat cake. I ran to be free. I ran to freely eat cake. I ran to remind myself what it was like to be a kid – exhilarated and entirely immersed in the moment.

2

Where are all the People?

At last January arrived, and I now had four months of training under my belt. Four months of getting up at 4.30 a.m. to begin a 3-hour shuffle along the River Thames towpath from Hampton to my place of work in the Paddington Basin, or of dashing out of the office at lunchtimes to squeeze in the scheduled mileage for the day. I ran everywhere. To my nephew's first birthday party, to dinners with friends, to the supermarket. You name it, I ran there. What I learned in those four months was not how to make my body move faster, but instead how it would break down and which parts would begin to crumble. I learned the difference between pain and injury, when to rest and when to push on. By the time it came to boarding the plane to Auckland, I knew my body better than a cabby knew the backstreets of London.

I waved goodbye to my mum at Heathrow airport – a fare-well more fitting of a weekend away in Europe with friends than six months across the other side of the world, alone. That was just our way of coping with goodbyes; I know that now. The more 'normal' it all seemed, the less frightening it all was.

The plan was to fly to Auckland on New Zealand's North Island and spend a week there staying with an old friend –

making all the last minute preparations and buying all the crap I had failed to buy in the pre-departure tornado I found myself swept up in. From Auckland, I would take two flights south, first to Christchurch and then on to Invercargill. From there I would make my way 30 km south to the town of Bluff, the most southern point of mainland New Zealand, and the start of the trail. I had allowed myself six months to run the 3,000 km trail, although I hoped to average 32 km a day and do it in five. Six months was what my New Zealand visa would allow for, so I definitely had to be done by June 2015.

To add an extra layer to the challenge, I'd also decided that I would visit schools along the way. Speaking to youngsters about adventure and the great outdoors was something I'd become hugely passionate about over the past few years. I'd first taken to doing it during the bike ride through America and it was a trend I was eager to continue on this adventure.

Sitting on a bed in Mission Bay, in the suburban Auckland apartment of my good friend Becky, I was feeling, perhaps understandably, overwhelmed. It was now T-minus two days until I caught my flights south and the moments of self-doubt were frequent and crippling when they took a hold. I had far more attention from friends and family for this journey than for the American 50-state adventure. No one had been taking much notice of my antics back then, but now I had followers who would actually interact with my social media posts and even invite me into their place of work to speak about my adventures. They would ask me questions about my preparation and what gear I was taking with me – often long before I'd had the chance to figure any of that out myself. I felt that with this attention came a certain level of responsibility, or so I told myself. One thing I wasn't telling anyone was that I had a niggle that I'd been unable to shake. Plantar fasciitis had plagued my right foot for the past three months. I'd taken two weeks off running in a bid to ease the pain, which had worked, but now, with three days to go until I started the run, plantar fasciitis was back, and it seemed angry.

'How the hell have I got an injury before I've even started a five-month run?' I asked myself. 'It's manageable,' I repeated, 'totally manageable…'

I frequently played with the hard stretch of tendon under my heel. I prodded it, jammed my thumb into the grainy strands of collagen, and ran it painfully over a tennis ball in a bid to relieve the pressure. This would ease it just enough to allow me to walk around pain-free for an hour or two, before it'd tighten up again and I'd be back at square one.

'I'd be totally fine if I only didn't have this niggle,' I told myself. Then I wondered if I was projecting all my fears for the trip onto my foot, and that's why it was hurting more than usual. Was fear projection even a thing, I wondered. A far-fetched notion, but I'd take any explanation for the pain at this point.

During that week in Auckland, I read the trail guidebook aghast. 'Do not enter this section of the trail without advanced backcountry skills.' My backcountry skills extended as far as being able to navigate my way across Richmond Park in London without upsetting any deer. I was also well-equipped to get home from a nightclub in Piccadilly Circus at 4 a.m. to Twickenham, but I'm not sure that counted either. I looked at the distances between towns, or between water sources, and bit my nails as I read. I was fast realising that I'd have to carry more food and water than I thought. Always a great thing to realise right before you leave.

That evening, I was standing outside the Mission Bay Starbucks, stealing their free Wi-Fi, when my phone buzzed. A video call from Jamie McDonald. I picked up and stared down at the screen.

'Hello.' I was in darkness. He could only just see my face, but he could see enough to know I was nervous. I could barely speak and when I did, I would stop mid-sentence to bite my lip. This was a far cry from the bouncy, confident, excited Anna he was used to speaking to. I felt uncomfortable with someone I hardly knew seeing just how nervous I was.

'You can do this, Anna. This is going to be AMAZING!' He liked to use the word 'amazing' a lot. Ordinarily I was a fan of that word too, but I was feeling far less than amazing right now. 'I know you're scared, but being scared is natural – it's beeauu-if-fuwl.' He informed me in his West Country accent. 'I can see how scared you are. Can you share this?'

'No, Jamie, I'm not bloody sharing this.'

He looked disappointed and a little hurt. 'People need to

see this, Anna. This is the start of your journey.'

I didn't want to share anything. In fact, I wanted a gigantic hole to appear at the side of the street and swallow me up into it. I couldn't bring myself to tell him or anyone else that my right foot hurt like heck and that I hadn't been able to run for longer than 40 minutes that week without it becoming too painful to carry on. Why had I told so many people? Typical – mouthing off, shouting things from the rooftops without a clue about what I was doing.

I signed off from the call promising to write a blog post about how I was feeling, because I found it easier to write things down than to record them on a video. I strolled back to the apartment and sat on my bed. A message appeared on my phone:

Jamie Mc: 'We'll be looking out for an update on you being scared. Literally just as you were on the phone, that's what you need to share. People need to see it. Keep being AMAZING!!!'

I groaned and threw the phone onto the bed. I turned over, pulled out my laptop, and started a blog post: 'And so, it begins…'

Departure day from Auckland arrived, along with a renewed sense of determination. This was happening. The response to the blog post had been incredible. I had a lovely message from a girl called Faye, who loved what I was doing and said that I had inspired her to fly over from the UK and cycle the length of New Zealand. I also had a message from my friend and seasoned adventurer, Dave Cornthwaite, which read, 'This made me beam. And now I'm a man in an airport lounge beaming at his laptop. Looking around, everyone else with a laptop is stern. This is your power.'

Those messages made me realise that the run wasn't really about me anymore. I needed to shove my nerves, my fears and my ego aside, and get out of my own way, so to speak. There was good to be done, a trail to be run and a whole host of kids to speak to in the process. All I needed to do now was to get going.

Arriving at Auckland airport, I congratulated myself for having already checked in online. Preparation wasn't my forte. I was a needs-must kind of girl and the effort of logging in, filling in my name and checking in online was usually just one step too far.

I strolled joyfully up to the baggage belt, handed the nice smiling man my backpack for the next five months, nodded, smiled back, watched it disappear off around the corner and ambled through to the gate. Had you walked behind me on that short stroll to the gate you would, in fact, have found yourself engulfed in a cloud of smug. I was smug. I'd done it. I'm here. I'm off to run the length of New Zealand.

My train of smug thoughts rumbled to a halt, as I sat down at the gate and looked up at the departures screen. Dunedin. Christchurch. Hastings. I had no idea you could go to so many places from Auckland… so many places… oh, so many places… Anna! So many places. Oh no. I didn't put a tag on the bag. Did I? But the baggage man had smiled at me. He had *smiled* at me. Why hadn't he said something? How are they going to know which flight my bag is for? Anna, you idiot! I launched myself from the chair and lunged at the nearest flight attendant.

Cue being removed from the flight list, a fitful hour in which I located Martin (badass baggage man), who found Vanessa (helpful airport lady), who went and found Colin (sorcerer of suitcases) who found the bag. Bag safely labelled and re-checked, Vanessa somehow managed to get me on a flight that allowed me to pick up my original southbound connection at Christchurch. What a great start. My cloud of smugness disappeared never to be seen again.

Sitting on the flight bound for Christchurch, I found an inner calm at last. I began to think about what lay ahead. Five months of running. Just running. Nothing but running, and through mind-blowing scenery at that. I'd start slow, allowing my body time to adjust and go easy out of the blocks. I reminded myself of what I constantly told other people – that the body has an incredible capacity for change and if you guide it firmly in one direction for long enough it'll work things out.

I watched a little girl in a pink T-shirt and denim skirt run past me, up and down the aisle. A hotchpotch of ladybirds, butterflies and the word 'love' emblazoned across her chest.

She squealed and giggled, toppling, on the verge of control from one foot to the next, her haphazard ponytail swinging wildly from side to side, wearing an expression of sheer uninhibited joy. This is how I would be in the months that followed, I thought. Free, happy and full of wonder, albeit minus the ladybird shirt.

After a change of plane in Christchurch, I touched down on the tarmac at Invercargill airport and was met by a good friend, Jon. 'You made it!' Jon exclaimed.

'Pssssh,' I replied. 'Of course I made it! What else did you expect?'

As Jon and I left the airport I told the tale of my baggage debacle. Jon's response was: 'Welcome to New Zealand, Nuffers. It's not a very big place, we tend to be able to sort things out pretty quickly here.'

I liked New Zealand already, very much.

Jon and I had known each other for 18 months and he had fast become one of my core adventure buddies. We'd first come into contact when I was cycling around the States and he was busy driving a Land Cruiser 30,000 miles to China and back, as you do. We'd exchanged jibes via Twitter – him incredulous at my desire to engage in such a physically arduous adventure, and me bewildered by his dedication to sitting on his arse eating pasties and staring at a road for months at a time.

'Petrol head,' I quipped.

'Narcissist,' he retorted.

And so a friendship was formed. Having Jon there at the start of this run was a nice safety blanket. A modicum of continuity in a topsy-turvy place.

Jon is a project manager, and so his forte is giving people a kick up the arse. A phone conversation with Jon usually resulted in me feeling like a naughty school child who hadn't done their science homework. While I was planning the trip, he'd ask infuriatingly sensible questions, such as 'Have you set up your charity donation page yet?' 'What stove are you taking?' and 'Have you researched the weather?' The latter of which had led to me realising that things get mighty cold down in the Southern Alps of New Zealand during winter, and that running through there in May and June was potentially a terrible idea. Following failed attempts to protest that running in snow would make cooler pictures, I relented, switched the route of my run around and became a northbounder. I'd like to think that I might have made the decision without Jon's input, but I can't be sure.

Jon and I grabbed a takeaway and went and sat in the local park, which was beautiful. It was like an English country garden, full of fountains, lush patches of grass and flowerbeds bursting with colour. There even a wooden bandstand, but something felt odd. I stopped chewing on a morsel of dinner and looked at Jon, who was now sitting cross-legged opposite me on a patch of carpet-perfect grass.

'Jon,' I asked, 'where are all the people?'

I'd been struggling to get my head around New Zealand's population, or lack of, for some time now, but it just didn't compute. In a country with a land mass slightly larger than the UK there are just 4.5 million people. There are 8.6 million people living in London alone, and 64 million in the UK. Having looked at the Te Araroa Trail route, and noted that it didn't even go near most of the major cities, especially in the South Island, I realised that there was a strong chance I might end up quite isolated. I quickly cast the thought from my mind.

It was departure day, but nothing seemed to have quite sunk in. I picked up the first of what were to be five pairs of shoes I'd use along the way. One pair had gone ahead to Wellington, on the North Island, with my friend Emma, who had carried them with her out on a trip home last month. I'd handed two pairs to Jon who was going to post them to his uncle in Christchurch, and a friend of that uncle further down on the South Island. The final pair, I'd left in Auckland.

I'm a big fan of naming things. I name everything. I like to personify as many things as possible in life. It helps me understand the world better. If I name an object, I feel like I can reason with it. I feel like, maybe, we can be friends. Cars, bikes, boats… and therefore why should my trainers be any different? I'd resolved to name each pair of trainers after a famous duo. Left foot firmly nestled in Bonnie, I slid the toes of my right foot into Clyde and paused. Was I actually doing this? Holy heck. I took a deep breath and eased in my heel. The shoes were on, and I had a country to run.

3

Into the Woods

'Ah, we have a special guest joining us in the studio right now. Anna McNuff... Yes, Anna McNuff is starting her run this morning, running the length of New Zealand.'

It was 8.25 a.m. and I was sitting in the Southland FM's Invercargill studio marvelling at radio host James' incredibly Kiwi accent. I already loved the way that people in Southland said my name: 'Inna!'

Jon had loosely dropped into conversation that perhaps he might be able to get me into the studio. I confess I hadn't given it much thought, but now here I was in my pink and black T-shirt and a blue buff, holding my wayward locks out of my face, as I grinned from ear to ear behind a microphone the size of my head.

James continued: 'How you feelin,' Anna – actually, first of all... are you a little bit crazy?!'

'I am definitely a little bit crazy, but in a totally good way. I think we're all a bit crazy, aren't we? I'm just really excited.'

'Umm, there's crazy, and then there's running the entire length of the country kinda crazy,' Rach the co-host piped in.

We chatted back and forth for a few minutes about my reasons for the run. I filled James and Rach in on my amazing childhood with access to sport and the outdoors, and that I used my adventures as a tool to give a little bit back where I could. I explained that I'd be going in to visit schools along the way, and that I'd be raising money for The Superhero Foundation and The Outward Bound Trust.

'And did we hear you say that today is the day?' Rach asked.

'Today is the day! In T-minus forty-five minutes I'll be on the start line at the trailhead signpost, at Stirling Point, Bluff.'

Over the next few minutes we talked over all the details of the trip, with Rach particularly impressed at the fact that all my gear fitted into a seven and a half kilo backpack.

'Seven point five kg,' Rach gawped. 'I can't even keep it under the twenty-three kg limit at the airport when I'm going somewhere for a weekend!'

While talking to James and Rach, I could feel my spirits lift. This was it. It was actually happening. Having the chance to verbalise what I was doing, and seeing that they were somewhat impressed, it brought back a familiar feeling. I was that little girl on the football pitch again. I felt that respect. It was what I had watched my parents be showered with over their years of Olympic achievements, and now I had some of my very own. The self-doubt, criticism and concern over my right foot began to melt away with every word I uttered into that gigantic microphone. At last when James' final question came, I was ready. Ready to talk about the trip in the way I had always wanted to, but I had just become so consumed with fear until this point that I didn't have the chance.

'I can't believe you're doing it totally unsupported. Are you freaking out at all? I mean, are you nervous?' asked James.

'Oh, yeah. I mean, I've woken up at two in the morning, turning over horror stories in my mind, in which I end up alone and stranded up a mountain pass with a storm closing in. But I guess it just comes down to a choice about how you live your life. I would rather live it completely wetting myself with fear, but doing something worthwhile than staying safe and just bumbling along. That makes you prouder when you get to the end,' I grinned.

'Okay, well look out for Anna, folks, at Stirling Point in about forty-five minutes. This is One Republic, "I Lived". James and Rach on the hits ninety-eight point eight…'

We drove 30 kilometres south from the radio station HQ in Invercargill. Jon pulled into the parking bay at Stirling Point, joining three other cars and a camper van already there. Jon's friend, PJ, swung open the door of his gigantic Volvo and grinned. 'Coffee anyone?'

I was never one to say no to coffee, and besides anything that could delay the start just that little bit longer was most welcome. Slurping on the syrupy black liquid PJ had carefully concocted on the open boot of his car, I began chatting to the other two people who'd turned up. Husband and wife, Alex and Allison were friends of friends of a friend I'd met through Twitter. They had a wonderfully quiet nature and I adored them both immediately. Alex was white-haired, slim and wore large glasses. He spoke softly, asking questions about my average speed and preparation for the trip. I felt like a bit of a numpty when I told him that I'd been running 10 minute miles in training at home, so I hoped for a steady pace. He looked surprised.

'Ten minute miles? Wow, if you keep that pace up you'll be at Cape Reinga in no time.'

'Yeah, yeah, without the pack…' I mumbled.

Alex's surprise at my quoted speed threw me off guard somewhat. A 10-minute mile pace would equate to a 4-hour marathon, which wasn't the slowest marathon time, but it was by no means Paula Radcliffe's pace of 2 hours 15 minutes. Then again, my mile pace had come out of my mouth before I could stop myself.

I didn't have the balls to tell Alex that I had in fact only run with the backpack once. Ten days before leaving for New Zealand I'd thought that it was probably a good idea to go out and buy a backpack, and eight days before my flight, on our annual family Christmas Day 5 kilometre run, I'd decided that it was high time I practised running with it on. I slipped five 1-kilogram bags of flour into the backpack and headed off with my two brothers and mum for the traditional pre-turkey loop around the river. I struggled to chat and keep up as the bag bounced around on my back. Upon finishing and flopping onto the sofa at home I concluded that running with a backpack was hard, very hard indeed, and I wouldn't be doing it again until I started the run. The truth was that I had no idea what speed I would do and, had I known what I know now, there is no way I would have quoted a 10-minute mile pace at Alex. For a start, I wasn't accounting for the fact that New Zealand had mountains.

Alex had taken the time to write out a few trail tips on 'Sticky Notes' for me. He said this section of the trail was quite new, and had changed in parts recently since they had altered the old dump site into a beautiful estuary trail. He quizzed me on sections about the trail, to which most of my responses were: 'Umm, I'm not too sure on that *particular* bit,' and he responded by turning promptly back to his car to write me another note. It was really very sweet.

I was busily going over Alex's advice, which largely in-volved screwing up my face and losing interest very quickly. I'm a 'work it out when I get there' kind of gal, you see, which was precisely the reason that I had failed to read even 10% of the trail notes. I just couldn't take anything in until it was star-ing me in the face, or was absolutely necessary. Mid face-screw, I heard the distinct rumble of tyres on gravel. I looked up as a white camper van pulled across the back of the parking bays and ground to a halt. The passenger door swung open and a woman in her mid-fifties, with glasses balanced on top of her blonde hair, leaned out.

'Are you the runner? Anna, is it?' The questions came in an undeniably Aussie drawl.

I was a little perplexed. 'Umm… yes… that's me. Well, I mean, I don't think there's anyone else running from here today called Anna, so I guess that's me!'

'We heard you on the radio!' said the man in the driver's seat, in an even deeper Aussie tone. 'We just came down on the off chance we could find ya. You're crazy!'

'No way!' I said. 'I mean, yes way. I'm crazy, but that's awesome that you heard me on the show. Thank you for coming down. That's really lovely.'

We chatted for a few minutes about the journey ahead, and as usual, doing my best to deflect some attention and learn more about them, I bombarded them with questions about who they were, where they came from and what they were doing in New Zealand.

When the time came to leave, my little start-line troop and I stood in front of the iconic signpost at Stirling Point. Markers sprouted from the post in every direction: New York 15,008 km, London 18,958 km, Sydney 2,000 km… I was clutching my trip mascot, a little stuffed kiwi bird (called Kiwi Kev), and looked longingly at the one particular marker which read: Cape Reinga: 3,000 km, and took in a deep breath. I knew there was a lighthouse at the Cape that marked the end of the trail, and so I briefly shut my eyes and pictured it in my mind. A chill ran down my spine. Eyes open, I turned to Jon who was holding a camera and began the countdown: 'Ten… nine… eight…' Oh my gosh, was this about to happen? 'Seven… six… five… four…' Where do I go when I get around the next headland? 'Three… two…' Was there time for one more coffee? 'One… GO!' And I was off, streaking away from the mini start crowd, beaming with delight.

'Bye!' I yelled, raising my arms aloft and waving back at them as my trainers, Bonnie and Clyde, took their first few steps on the Te Araroa Trail. 'See you soon!'

Rounding the first bend, I was now alone. All I had was my breathing. The trail curved around the estuary and I now found myself running on an uneven lumpy surface through calf-high grass. It swayed wildly in the wind and, combined with the waves I could see crashing against the rocky shore, reminded me of Cornwall. How funny that the coastline of New Zealand should look like Cornwall, I thought. Clearly thinking *and* running was one multitask too far because I tripped and fell, outstretched arms slowing the speed of my face plant into the grass. I flopped onto my back and laughed. A deep manic kind of laugh that had any one witnessed they would have carted me off to the asylum pronto. 'Three thousand kilometres,' I muttered as I dragged myself to my feet. 'How in the world are you going to make three thousand kilometres, you doughnut?'

I managed to stay upright for the next mile as the trail wound in and out of light bush before merging onto Highway 1. This wasn't the most glamorous way to start a five-month run, but at least the going was steady. There wasn't a huge amount of road shoulder to run along and the dusty never-ending straightness of the single carriageway seemed to stretch on for an eternity, but the traffic was light and so I ran freely, absorbed in my own thoughts. I tried my best not to think about quite how far I had to go, and to just think about today instead. Today would do for now.

I settled into a rhythm, stopping every 8 kilometres or so to roll a tennis ball under my foot at the side of the road. Jon passed me in his car a few times, tooting and cheering and hanging out of the window while attempting to film all at once. He did make me laugh; I still couldn't quite believe that he'd flown down from his family home in Taranaki on the North Island to see me off. To have someone there on the first day really meant a huge amount. His antics distracted me from the task at hand, and for that I was grateful.

Day one passed without too much discomfort, and Jon and I celebrated completing the first 34 km with an assortment of food and a Fanta at a cafe in Invercargill. A message from my friend, Niall McCann, popped into view on my phone. 'Good luck Anna. I just told my partner what you're doing. She's an osteopath. She thinks you're crazy and says you're going to get osteoarthritis. There you have it! Happy running!'

Standing in the living room of a house in a tiny old mining village called Round Hill on the edge of Longwood Forest, I handed Kevin my maps. They were printed in black and white, in terrible quality ink, because… well, because I'd run out of time before I left the UK, having instead prioritised a last snack of my beloved beans on toast, and in the pre-flight bean haze I had forgotten to print them entirely, meaning I'd had to scramble to print them off in Auckland. My priorities were clearly well in order. Kevin was another friend of a friend whom it had been suggested I go to see, as he might be able to offer up some tips about the section of trail that led away from his house and into the forest.

The previous day had been tougher than expected. After stocking up on five days' worth of food at Riverton, I struggled to get my backpack off the ground and onto my back, but all had started well along Oreti beach. Bounding along, listening to Paloma Faith on my iPod, a mass of blonde curls being tossed around on the wind, I felt like me. I was so happy. The waves rose effortlessly into the air before crashing dramatically onto the shoreline to my left and sand made its way into my eyes, ears, nose and mouth. Largely because I was singing at the top of my lungs through all of it. I felt free. Like a child. I felt like I could run forever. But then I ended up getting lost on the beach (no, I'm not sure how you get lost running along a beach either). I had come further inland than expected and run 42 km instead of the planned 35 km. In another albeit shorter beach run today, my legs groaned and my back creaked. Still, here I was at Kevin's house at the end of day three.

'You've got a GPS though?' Kevin asked.

I grimaced. I didn't have a GPS and I was starting to feel like a right plonker. Why hadn't I brought a GPS? It was literally the most obvious thing I should've considered. I'd been so concerned with the physicality of the run that I'd slightly underestimated, nay, completely neglected to grasp the type of environment I'd be running in. From the 5 minutes I'd spent in the bush before arriving at Kevin's house, it had dawned on me that this trail might not be as easy to follow as I'd expected. Couple that with the fact that my backcountry skills were limited to say the least, and I could be in a little bit of trouble.

I did have a vague memory of considering buying a GPS at one point, but I had decided that it wasn't entirely in keeping with the 'adventurous spirit'. No, no – I was a paper maps and compass kind of girl. The explorers of old did things that way, and I would do the same. The fact that I hadn't used a compass in the past 18 months and had entirely forgotten how to use one was neither here nor there. This was a minor detail, and just added to that 'adventurous spirit.'

I had used a fancy GPS device once for a cycle tour but I didn't like the way the screen looked at me. It was so judgmental, so demanding, tyrannical even. In the same way I personified my trainers, I personified that GPS, and needless to say we did not get along. To me, the GPS was like one of those heavily loaded ego types in a business meeting who talks about everything in acronyms and scoffs before explaining his point very slowly in front of your colleagues, in a language he perceives your tiny normalised brain can understand. All in all, I'd decided that such an unfriendly fancy-pants electronic device didn't deserve an invite to the Te Araroa party. Evidently, my anti-GPS stance was going to make things harder than necessary.

'Hmm, I think I have something that can help you out,' Kevin said, as he moved across the room to a large filing cabinet in the corner. Kevin had helped develop this trail. He was part of the team that had marked it out, and maintained it. He was quite possibly the best person to advise me on how to get through to the other side without any dramas. I had lucked out.

Sitting on Kevin's sofa while he rummaged in the cabinet, I considered why I was so ill prepared. The reality was that I hadn't researched the trail in any kind of detail, because I didn't want to freak myself out more than I already had by telling everyone I was going to run it. I understood that much, at least. It was a well-tested, often used self-defence mechanism. For some reason, I despised dealing with or even thinking about a potentially serious situation until I actually had to face it. Then I knew that I had no choice but to deal with it. But guess what? Everything would always work out in the end, and so I never changed tack. Like with all so-called bad traits of our personalities, I decided that there had to be an advantage to this approach. I knew it would freak me out, so I didn't read about it, and lo and behold here I was, on the trail, on an adventure. So there had to be a merit in my madness.

Kevin and I hunched over a coffee table, now littered with maps he had pulled out of the cabinet, as he drew X's and dotted lines at various points to advise me on contours and route. I understood enough about maps to know what marked the edge of a tree line, and the confluence of a river, but I was also acutely aware that seeing something on a flat piece of A4 paper in Kev's living room was going to be very different to how it looked in reality.

'I'm really worried about you going up there, onto those tops without a GPS,' said Kevin, for the third time in as many minutes.

I'd learnt now that Kiwis like to refer to open sections of highlands as 'tops'. It was one of the many bits of terminology I would be getting to grips with over the coming months along with 'tussock' (some kind of grass) and 'saddle' (a low point between two peaks).

'If it's cloudy, don't even try it. You'll miss the marker poles and you can get yourself quite lost…' Kevin continued, a look of serious concern on his face.

Still, he seemed comforted by the fact I had a SPOT tracker, which sent out a message with my location every ten minutes. That tracker also had a series of buttons which would let my close friends and family know I was okay, or call in the search and rescue choppers and get me the hell out of there if really necessary.

We chatted for a little about the differences in trails in NZ to those in Europe or America. Kevin explained how so many of those he encountered doing the trail were entirely unprepared and it was really only luck that they made it through sections without disasters.

'People start the trail and they expect it to be a well-graded highway, like the Pacific Crest Trail. They take minimal maps, and not even a compass sometimes. Of course, most are coming south, so by the time they get down here they get it. But it's the ones starting off with nothing that I worry about.' He looked at me. I nodded and looked away quickly.

4

Picking up the Pieces

A new day was dawning in Southland, at the very bottom of New Zealand. It was now 10 a.m. and time to begin gathering up my stuff to leave. My lower back was sore and in spasm, which made any form of bending difficult. It possibly had something to do with the fact that I'd run 92 kilometres with a massive backpack over the past three days. I had stumbled my way along a mixture of sandy and pebbled beaches, around steep rocky headlands and along some portions of road – although I wasn't quite sure how 7.5 kg on my back could do quite so much damage. I wasn't entirely surprised, but at this early stage my back's moans were most unwelcome. Running was possibly the worst thing you could do for a sore back, I knew that much, and running with a backpack was probably even worse, but I didn't really have much choice. I felt rather silly complaining about back pain on day four of the journey, and so I kept schtum. I thought I'd done a pretty good job of masking the pain until I bent down to pick up a sock in front of Kevin.

'Back a bit crook, is it?' he asked.

'What? Oh, that… Oh, yeah, just a little. It's 'warming up'. It'll be alright,' I piped chirpily, hoping to God that it would.

It was now approaching midday and it was hot. That really sticky, humid kind of hot. We had returned to the point where I'd decided to stop running yesterday, and after hugging Kevin half to death, I'd run off into the forest alone. I thanked my lucky stars I'd taken the time to go and meet him. Everything Kevin had told me about the trail had pretty much doubled my knowledge from 'bugger all' to 'better than bugger all', and I had no doubt it would come in handy. But his concern for my safety had made me slightly anxious, and when things make me anxious I like to run away from them. In this instance, the running away was literal.

Over the past year I'd come to better understand my fears, and how they moved and presented themselves in my mind. For journeys like this, which had a number of fears related to it, I viewed each one as a thread. The kind of thick shiny thread that Mum used to do needlework with when I was a kid. For some reason, the 'fear threads' were bright red. Over time the fears huddled together: a complex tangle of apprehensive thoughts, bound by their own intensity and a lack of intention on my part to address them in any way, shape or form. Once in a tightly knotted ball, they could then roll joyfully out of sight, which was where I liked them to be. Neatly contained, manageable and out of sight.

Alas, around the edges of my fear ball will always be one or two loose ends. Dangling threads just begging to be tugged.

Pull one hard enough and the whole ball unravels. Before you know it, there is a mess of fears lying at your feet which you have no option but to deal with. And that in itself scares me. I have found that the people who care about you most, the ones that you let get close to the ball – they are the ones with the ability to unravel it. My mum, for example, is an expert tugger. As was Kevin, it would seem. Was I worried about getting lost in the bush? Yes. Was I worried that I was ill-equipped to take on this trail? Yes. Was I concerned that my back was buggered after just four days of running? Yes. Tug. Tug. Tug. I just had to run away before the whole damn ball unravelled.

My feet pounded on the soft earth of Longwood Forest. It felt good to be on the move again but the humidity levels meant that the heat from my body seemed to have no escape, and so as I ran, I began to encase myself in a mobile green-house. In the small space between where my backpack rested and my upper back, I was pretty sure it was hot enough to grow some tomatoes, or at least a tropical plant or two. Watering wouldn't be a problem as I was drenched in sweat. Beads of it formed in abundance on my brow and tumbled down my nose, before cascading off the end onto the forest floor. I sucked hard on the hose of my hydration pack, but evidently not often enough. I was dehydrated. I knew that much. I'd inspected my pee as I performed the ladylike 'danger squat' in the forest that morning, and observed that it was the colour of Calpol, and Calpol is never a good shade for one's pee to be.

I decided that I fancied running with music today, and so

dug out my phone and pressed play on Paloma Faith's *Fall to Grace* album. I always liked a strong female voice to get me through a run. Paloma had attitude, and I liked attitude. In between bellowing the lyrics from 'Picking up the Pieces' at the top of my lungs, I gulped in what oxygen I could from the sticky air around my mouth.

Pounding away and picking up the pieces with Paloma by my side, I was struck by how dense the forest was. I didn't think I'd ever been in a forest like this before. The ones in the UK tended to have a lot of space between the trees, but in this one there were very few gaps on the ground, or even in the canopy. The trail was easy enough to follow in the first mile or so of Longwood Forest. It was part of a well-trodden tourist pathway, laid out complete with faded signs explaining the old mining equipment or significance of a particular section. Every few minutes there was an orange triangle on a tree, letting me know I was still on track. As Kevin had explained, I was following an old mining sluice. A sluice is a narrow waterway cut into a hillside to help channel the water down from the top. In my mind this was going to be simple to navigate, but as the trail wore on I found that the sluice wasn't always visible on the ground, and that if I strayed even slightly from its path everything became very confused. In some places there were a number of other gaps in the forest floor, which looked like they could have been trails themselves, so I was frequently at risk of straying from the Te Araroa path.

After an hour of running uphill, I emerged at the side of

the mountain and realised I could see back down to Kevin's farm. I threw my pack on the floor and sat on it, shovelling wine gums into my mouth and sucking hard on the hydration hose again. I could see Kevin in the paddock. He was now just a tiny dot driving a 4x4 around in the top field. I wished I'd had some phone signal and could have called him. But instead I just watched in silence, the only noise the crinkle of my wine gums packet and Paloma's tiny voice coming from my head-phones on the forest floor. I breathed in again and listened. Nothing. There really was nothing up here. I wondered if I'd see anyone today on the trail. I thought the chances were slim. Most of the southbounders were still a month away from be-ing in this section, and many of those going north had started long before me. The concept of not seeing another living soul before dark was a little odd, and not one that I could entire-ly compute at this point. Taking one last look at Kevin going about his business in the field below, I thought about the fact that I might never see him again. How strange it was that I would drift in and out of people's lives like this for the next five months as I made my way up to Cape Reinga.

After the sanctioned wine gum break I decided that hav-ing music in my ears was actually becoming too much of a distraction. The forest floor was a complex maze of roots and slippery leaves. The combined attention required to make a good foot placement and trying to spot the markers was a little too much when put alongside recalling Paloma Faith lyrics, and so I turned the music off.

Besides, I'd begun to notice the birdsong from the trees above. I'd never really been a 'birdy' kind of person before, but the chorus was a pure joy, and surprisingly soothing.

I rounded a bend and stopped. That was odd. I squinted at the trail ahead, but it seemed to lead into dense bush. I padded towards it, slowly, gradually realising that it actually bent to the right, rather than into the bush. Looking right my jaw dropped.

'Holy crap!' I exclaimed. 'That is so bloody cool!'

In front of me was a scene fresh from an Indiana Jones movie. Rickety old wooden beams were arranged in two separate A-frames. In between them, single planks of equally rickety wood were laid out one after the other, forming a bridge beneath the A's and crossing a gap in the forest floor. All around were ferns and palms and native bush.

The trail dropped steeply down to the bridges. I couldn't quite see where it went after the second A-frame but I assumed it went up as steeply again on the other side. I wriggled down the hillside to the planked section, slipping and landing on my bum, giggling. I'd always loved dramatic settings. Disneyland was like heaven on earth to me. Anything make-believe and I was as high as a kite. But this movie set was real! And it was freakin' awesome. I ran back and forth over the planks several times, stopping at one point to set up my GoPro in the tree opposite to capture the full awesomeness of the situation.

Excitement pulsed through my veins for the next hour. I

felt like I was running on clouds. My head was also clearly in the clouds, when I came to and realised that I hadn't seen a trail marker for some time. Oh, God. When did you last see a marker, Anna? Think. I wracked my brain. It must have been 5 minutes ago. I looked ahead and couldn't see any orange triangles on the trees. Perhaps this was just a section without markers? But common sense (yes, I do have some) told me that was a little odd considering the markers had been regular up until now. I turned around and ran back the way I'd come, eyes fixed and scanning for the markers, but I couldn't see any. My heart began to pound. Where had I gone wrong? Had I even managed to come back the same way I'd been running for the past 5 minutes?!

Just then I caught a flash of orange out of the corner of my eye.

'You little bugger!' I exclaimed. The trail had taken a left turn and I'd run straight ahead instead. I breathed a huge sigh of relief. Those little orange triangles were my life raft. Only in losing them did I realise that. Without them I had suddenly felt very alone, and I had begun to descend into panic. Now out the other side, I laughed. The only every day sensation I can liken this to is when you lose your passport in the hour before you go to the airport for the trip you've been planning forever and you think, 'I'll just check my passport is in the bedside drawer, where it normally is,' only to find it's not there. The reality of the situation is a mild (and likely temporary) incon- venience. The mental picture you paint in the 3 minutes which

47

follows is, in contrast, a full life disaster.

'You bloody idiot, Anna. Pay attention, will you?' I chastised myself for the lack of concentration, took a drag of water from the hydration pack and set off again. Clearly I didn't chastise myself enough because within 30 minutes I was away with the fairies and had lost the markers again.

'Oh hell!' I sighed, and made my way back to where I had last seen a marker. Only this time I couldn't find a marker anywhere. I had reached a spaghetti junction of small ground trails on the contour of a hillside, separated by a few large trees. I stared at the junction and took a mental picture.

'That's fine,' I thought. 'I'll try this route up here to the left and if it doesn't work out in the next minute or so, I'll just come back to this point and try again.'

About a minute later I still couldn't find a marker, so I made my way back to the junction. But what I thought was the junction wasn't the junction at all. It looked entirely different. Now I had no way of knowing which direction I'd come from. I searched the floor frantically for trails, but every mark on the ground looked the same. Then I looked up at the bush around me. I span 360 degrees and felt my stomach drop. Everything looked the same. Every single direction looked the same. The same trees. The same roots. I moved my eyes over them as if in slow motion. Where was the sun? I couldn't even tell where that was as the canopy was so thick above my head. My mind started to spiral, and thoughts shot off in a million directions.

Every thought was magnified, and entirely irrational. The density of the bush around me was like a fog on my brain. My chest tightened and I started to get frightened, realising that the only person who could get me out of here was me, and I was an idiot. Upon that realisation I got angry. So very angry.

'Why the hell didn't you bring a GPS, Anna?!'

I got out my map and stared at it, before realising that was entirely useless as I had no idea where I was on it. I knew how long it was since I'd left Kevin's but I had no idea how quickly I was moving. I made a rough guess and resolved I was probably now 2 km away from a road to the north. The road ran across most of the bush, and so if I just headed north, eventually I would hit that road. I got out my compass, found north and began to bash through the bush. Through my bashing, nerves turned to anxiety, to manic laughter, back to nerves and into tears. It was official: I was mental.

An hour later I hit the road. I sat on it and sobbed. Four days into my trip and I was sobbing. Why was I crying? I considered what it was about that situation that had me so frightened. I resolved that it was simply that I hadn't been anywhere quite like this before. Getting lost had really hammered home how totally alone I was out here. The tears were partly borne of frustration too. I felt entirely out of my depth and completely foolish.

As I left the gravel road and entered the forest again, I had this odd feeling that people were with me, like I expected to see

49

someone on the trail in the next few minutes. That feeling carried on all day, and of course I saw no one, but I still felt they were there. A dog walker, a couple tramping in the opposite direction. They took a vague form in my imagination, but the reality of them being nearby seemed so concrete. I concluded it was a coping mechanism. I was juxtaposing my feelings of complete isolation with the notion of there being someone just nearby, should I need them.

At 4 p.m. Martin's Hut appeared in a small clearing. Thanks to a history lesson from our man Kev, I knew that Martin's was originally built in 1905 to house sluice maintenance workers. These men were employed by mining companies to maintain the sluice and ensure a steady supply of water for mining operations. They often lived by themselves in isolated environments and faced an ongoing battle to clear fallen trees and branches, and to repair flood damage. Martin's Hut is one of three gold-mining-era huts that remain on public conservation land in Southland. One of over 900 huts throughout New Zealand, these modest shelters are open to anyone who would like to use them, so long as you have a Department of Conservation 'hut pass', which I had tucked safely away in my pack. I wasn't entirely sure how much I was going to be using the huts along the Te Araroa – I had my tent with me after all – but it was nice to know that they were there, and always an option if I needed to bed down for the night.

I peered inside and found four bunks and an open fireplace. Hessian sacks lined the tin walls in some places, keeping out the wind that was blowing through the cracks in the construction. I could hear mice scuttling about on the floor and feel a draft from the fireplace. This was home for tonight, and it'd do just grand. My own little house in the middle of the bush.

I ran some cold water from the tap at the side of the hut into my camping bowl and did a 'bits n' pits' wash: an act which I stripped entirely naked to do. I did wonder what a fellow trail user might make of me, had they wandered from the forest at that very moment, but I resolved that the chances of someone coming along were slim to none. I emptied out the bowl and ran a bit extra in there to drink. I took a big gulp just as it started to rain.

Slipping into some dry clothes, I moved swiftly inside before inspecting the logbook. The logbooks were intended to act as a safety device. In the event that you went missing without a trace, the Department of Conservation (DoC) workers could check the hut books to see exactly when you passed through an area, giving them a better chance of finding you. Even if you weren't staying at a hut, it was etiquette to take the time to stop in and write in the book. As a consequence, they served a much more interesting purpose: in these books were the human history of each hut. I looked at a note that was laid on top of the book, which read:

'Water tasted a bit funky, so I dug out some leaves and a lot of sludge from the top of the tank. I'd say it'd been there a while. I'm not much

precious about my water, but I'd boil this one before drinking to be safe.

Happy trails!

Ron, from BC, Canada.'

I thought about the big gulp I'd taken from the tank just now, and considered its level of funkiness on a scale of one to ten. I put it at around six and concluded that my chances of a slow and painful death were minimal. Although Kev had also warned me about the chances of catching giardiasis (a nasty waterborne disease) in Southland – he'd had it himself, and based on his description of the effect it had on his stomach and rear end, I didn't much fancy catching it. Plus, giardiasis was like malaria: once you have it, it's in your body for life.

I stood there for a moment, wondering what to do now. It was only 4.30 p.m. and seemed too early to eat dinner. Then it occurred to me that I was rather tired. I was, in fact, incredibly tired. I'd run 27 km to make it to the hut and my hips and knees were aching. Emptying the contents of my backpack onto the floor of the hut, I picked up my sleeping bag from the pile. I unpacked it, laid it on one of the lower bunks and crawled in. For the next 3 hours, I drifted in and out of sleep, shifting position as waves of pain passed over my hips, thighs and under my feet. When I opened my eyes, it was just about dark and the rattle of rain on the tin roof was almost deafening. That was a good thing, I thought, as I needed a clear day tomorrow to get across the tops.

I remembered that Kevin had said that if it was foggy on

the tops I wasn't to even start out on them without a GPS. But I knew whatever the weather that I wasn't spending another day in this hut. I'd go mental. I set about making dinner and as I waited for the noodles to soften in the boiling water, I wrote an entry in my diary:

'Already feeling like I want to speed this section up and get back to seeing some people! Decided I like being on my own, but knowing others are nearby. This is a bit too remote for me. Running is the easy bit!'

In the quiet of the forest a strange set of emotions were swirling around in my head. Why, on day four of the journey, was I so rocked by the thought of being alone? I'd been alone before, and gladly. I'd ridden a bike for seven months, 20,000 kilometres, mostly on my own and never once felt lonely. I felt content, but I realised already that this adventure had a different feel compared to the American one. I decided in that moment that I'd probably be done with doing things alone after this. I chuckled at my own conclusion. Probably not the best thought to be having at the start of a five-month solo journey, but I couldn't help it. I craved being around people more and more each day. I'd seen no one today, but took comfort in the fact that Kevin was watching my tracker. I wondered what he'd have made of my tracker trail where I went slightly off-piste?

As dark fully set in I realised that there was an eerie feel to Martin's Hut. If I believed in ghouls and ghosts, I would have

ANNA MCNUFF

sworn there were a few hanging out in there. I picked up the
pen again and opened up my diary:

*'I'm not frightened right now, I'm not bored, I just don't feel especially
alive or connected to anything at this moment. It's very odd.'*

With a belly full of noodles, cheese, chocolate, coffee and
some God awful sugary yoghurt thing that I thought would be
a solid contribution of protein, but had in fact made me retch,
I lay back in my sleeping bag. I flicked open my kindle and began reading the first book in there. It was nice to have the time
to read, I thought: *Sane New World* by Ruby Wax. How very apt.

Clipping the buckles shut on my pack, I dragged it out outside and looked up at the sky. It was cloudy but far better than
it had been yesterday evening. It had been an odd night's sleep.
I'd woken to the noise of possums several times and at one
point the wind had swung the door wide open, which scared
the living crap out of me. Now, however, the open mountain
top was calling, and I was going for it. I took one last look at
what'd been my home for the night, and considered how many
others would stop here this season. It's a very strange feeling
to go to sleep in the middle of a forest with no one around,
and to wake up and set off in the same fashion. I found that I
had begun to talk to myself. Something that wasn't unusual for
me in daily life on the odd occasion, but was becoming more
pronounced with every hour I spent alone.

The lining of my stomach seemed to be constructed entirely from nerves as I made my way up the steep and slippery

climb and onto the tops. The weight of the backpack dragged me backwards and became heavier with every step. And my, how my back ached. The muscles in the lower section around my sacrum were sending dull waves of pain up my back and down my leg every 10 minutes, just to remind me they were still there. I became aware of how slow I was going. I was supposed to be running, but I really couldn't run this section at all, and it bothered me. I upped the pace, pushing off of each leg harder than the last, propelling myself upwards as hard and as fast as I could in sheer anger, and (in hindsight) wasting valuable energy.

Out of the forest and on to the tops at last, I breathed in the air. Oh, the space! The fact that I could see the horizon was a welcome change from being surrounded by tree trunks, roots and the dappled sunlight of the forest. A fog had just started to roll in, and I could see the reason for Kevin's cautious words. The markers had now changed from orange triangles to orange-capped poles. I could see one, possibly even two, at a time across what resembled a landscape of the Scottish Highlands, but I wasn't certain of how long that visibility would last.

I moved swiftly to the first pole. I placed my hand on it, and because it felt sort of, well, natural, I thanked it.

'Thank you,' I whispered, as if talking to the trail gods and offering gratitude at their showing me the way. This was madness. I knew it was madness, but the nervous shake in my hands and the genuine relief when I caught sight of the next pole in the vast plain seemed to justify it.

'Thank you,' I whispered softly to my new-found love, orange pole number two, even blowing it a kiss this time.

I'd been up on the tops for 30 minutes and from Kevin's description I knew there was one more open section to negotiate before descending into an old quarry to pick up a gravel road. I entered a section of head-high scrub and turned a sharp right. Suddenly, there was another body upon me. 'Waaaaaaa!'

I'd run straight into a man's chest. Embarrassed, I backed up.

'Hello!' I beamed at the first person I'd seen since leaving Kevin.

'Hi!' he smiled back, looking a little bemused. We were now a suitable distance from one another so that it was socially acceptable to converse.

'You don't see many people running this trail – not out here anyway!'

He looked at me inquisitively.

And so ensued a very pleasant conversation with my new BFF, Scott, about my Te Araroa mission. Scott was out training for the Coast to Coast – a legendary multi-stage adventure race that sees hardened Kiwis run, cycle and kayak across the South Island each February. Scott and I ran along together back towards the quarry pit where he'd left his bike. We chatted about his life as a dairy farmer, his wife, his kids and his travels around the world – of which, to my delight, there had been many. Scott had a gentle nature. He came across immediately as kind, curious and caring – like a brother – although I could see that beneath his soft exterior was a steely determination.

'Say, where are you stopping your run for the day?' he asked.

'Err, about fifteen kilometres from here. Wherever that is,' I replied.

'Sounds like you'll be near Scott's Gap. My family farm is only a few kilometres from there. How about you just call me when you're done and I'll come collect you from the trail? Take you back to ours for a feed and a nice soft bed?'

I was delighted that Scott had figured out I wasn't an axe murderer, and his was an offer I wasn't going to refuse. Perhaps in years gone by, I might have done, but now in my older and wiser days I was learning to accept help.

'That would be most awesome, Scott. Thank you,' I grinned.

Two hours later I was sitting on my backpack at the side of a hot and dusty Otautau–Tuatapere road. I pulled out my phone and dialled Scott's number. He'd be with me in 10 minutes. I used my new-found signal at the roadside to send my mum a direct message on Twitter. This is how we communicated when I was away on adventures. It was less expensive than text and I knew she watched my Twitter account like a hawk.

'Hi Mum! I met a man in the forest today. Going home to his for tea and bed! All well. Love and hugs. xxx'

Only on sending the message did I consider that perhaps its contents might be cause for alarm, but I shrugged and continued to wait on my backpack for my Longwood Forest knight in shining armour.

5

A Knight in Shining Armour

'Okay, okay, but this is your last go! You hear me? One… Two… Threeeeee!'

As the small child launched themselves from the brown leather sofa to my right, I braced myself to pluck two-year-old Iris from mid-air and then assist her in a continued flight across the room.

'Whee!' she yelled, as she flopped onto a matching sofa opposite. The brief post-impact silence was swiftly broken by the inevitable: 'Again! Again! Again!' amidst calls of 'My turn, Anna, my turn!' from her sister Ava, aged five. Eight-year-old Zach had decided that he was too mature for the proceedings, although he did drop in for a test flight every now and then.

'Uh. That's enough now, kids. Anna's been running all day – I think she'd like a rest,' came the voice of reason from the adjoining kitchen.

'Thank you,' I mouthed at Scott who was standing at the end of the room.

Scott had collected me from the roadside with his three little munchkins in tow. That awkward first few minutes of the car journey had quickly been broken by a barrage of questions from the back seat: 'Why are you running?' 'Where do you live?' 'Do you have a booooooyfriend?' The kids had taken it in turns to take up the role of questioner, and I had quickly realised that they were adorable. As a non-parent but one who loves children, my tolerance for the pint-sized people is usually high. Within one family, you normally get one or two good kid eggs in the bunch, but all three of these were characters. And I was smitten.

Though I ran 30 km the next day with all my gear on my back, Scott picked me up at the end of the trail and I got to stay another night with the Hindrup family, who had quickly become my Kiwi-life heroes. I admired Scott's wife, Chantal, in particular. She was one of those super mums: a trail-running, cake-baking, steak-and noodle-making, washing-hanging, kid-juggling machine. When the time came to leave the Hindrups, I was sad. It felt like I'd been there far longer than two nights; there was something about their family environment that felt so familiar. The happiness and calm I felt when sat at their dinner table nourished me. It weaved its way into the cracks in my mind that had started to appear in Longwood Forest. I wondered whether this was how people stayed on the road for years on end without seeing their families. Perhaps immersing themselves, if only briefly, in the family life of strangers was enough to keep home sickness at bay.

I craned my neck upwards. Where the heck was the next pole? I had managed to spot a line of poles from the riverbed, but now I was halfway up the hill, the incline itself obscured my view. I looked to my left and spotted a trail heading off into the forest. With no other clues as to where to go, I decided it was worth a try. Five minutes into the forest I was following a rough ground trail, which ended abruptly in a bush. I turned around and headed back out of the forest to find that it was starting to rain. The clouds had rumbled and groaned above my head for most of the day, threatening a downpour, and they were now beginning to make good on their promise.

The weather turned full-on biblical as I headed up onto the first ridge line of the Takitimu ranges. The previous days through Longwood had been tough, but the Takitimus were taking things to a whole new level. Green shrub covered slopes that led up to exposed sections of often loose granite rock. I'm sure that the view back down the valley towards the riverbed would have been spectacular, if the rain had allowed me to see further than the end of my nose. My knees were getting a pounding as everything seemed to go in an upwards direction, and steeply. Contouring was clearly not a 'thing' in New Zealand. Perhaps the concept just hadn't made it this far around the world yet.

Worse than the challenging terrain, far worse, were the voices in my head. My slow pace had been grating on me ever since leaving Invercargill. My pace on the flats was okay, but it was my speed up the hills that was really getting to me. 'An-naRuNZ,' I would repeat to myself in a sinister voice up a near vertical and slippery climb. It was a hashtag I'd developed for those following the trip. 'Well, you're not running much now, are you, Anna?' would come the nasty voice again and it continued. I was embarking on a journey to run the length of a country, and at every opportunity I would beat myself up. I hadn't been that hard on myself in a long time. In fact, since I'd given up rowing. I would row down a 2 km course, in GB colours, be in third place against countries from around the world and all the while the voices in my head would tell me it wasn't good enough. 'Well that was a rubbish stroke, Anna,' came the sarcastic voice. 'Here's an idea, Anna, how about you put your blades in the water at the catch?'

In the end I got so sick of the self-abuse that it played a large part in me retiring from the sport. It'd been a long absence, but the voices were back in this run, and they were driving me nuts. So nuts that I had even given them a collective name. Those voices – they were the soldiers of self-doubt and they marched frequently on my castle of confidence.

The start of the day from Birchwood Road had been accompanied by some hefty winds. After a long slog up and over Mount Linton, I'd taken on my first river crossing in the valley, and was feeling extremely proud of myself when I met a couple on the edge of Takitimu Forest.

'It's so windy up there,' the guy informed me.

'Ha! I can imagine!' I said. 'I've just been almost blown clean off my feet up on Mount Linton over there!'

They looked at me, the man's face now grave and serious.

'No, no, I don't think you understand. The wind up there is much, much worse. The worst you have EVER experienced.' He raised his hands in a few wild gestures for added severity.

I was all up for taking warnings from fellow trail users, but how was this guy to know what kinds of winds I've experienced in my life? I could have grown up on a Himalayan hillside for all he knew. Then the girl chimed in: 'And there's a guy up ahead who calls himself 'The Nomad'. I don't think he'll make it through the next section. Pretty unsteady on his feet.'

It was cold and still bucketing with rain up on the ridge line but there was no sign of the 'worst winds I'd ever seen' and for that I was grateful. Icy droplets pounded my face from every direction imaginable as I strained my eyes against a wall of moving water, desperately trying to identify where exactly the trail went. I pulled up the hood of my rain jacket and tightened the elastic toggle in a bid to keep the worst of it out, which seemed to improve visibility slightly. However, the granite rocks were slippery underfoot and my light trail shoes began to struggle.

The ridge line went on and on. Each time I crested a section, hoping it would descend, it just went up again. I stopped to take a video on my phone for the folks at home.

'Oh, my days,' I breathed. 'It's raining. I wish it was raining men, but it's not… it's raining… rain. And I'm now about seven kilometres from my shack for the night. Over there, somewhere in the back of the beyond. Come on yer shack!'

After an hour on the ridge, the poles finally led me into the forest and I started down a steep descent. Now under cover from the rain I realised that I was running low on energy. With all the hills and the rivers and the wind, I hadn't eaten much all day and was now starting to feel a bit shaky. I was only a few kilometres from the hut, but I decided to have a sit down in the forest to eat and take stock of the situation. Unfortunately, the rain continued to drip through the trees and I got cold very quickly. I decided to put some gloves on, as I was struggling to unclip my pack with numb, cold hands, and I moved off again quickly.

Setting off with my mouth crammed full of wine gums, I passed two more southbound trail hikers, Michael and Jack. Encountering four people on the trail in a single day was a real novelty. It was a far cry from the loneliness of Longwood Forest, and it calmed me to know that not all sections of the trail would be so isolated. From various resources – mostly the Te Araroa Trail Facebook page – I had gathered that there were around 200 people doing the entire trail this year. Around 170 of them were southbounders, and the remaining 30, of which I was one, were travelling northbound. Most of the southbounders had started back in October or November, and given that most took between four to six months to complete the trail, I knew it was likely I'd cross paths with these folk on the South Island section of the trail. The encounters, however brief, served to break up the day and filled my mind with fresh thoughts as I ran away again alone.

Michael and Jack were keen to stop for a chat, and early on in the conversation they delighted in telling me that they had got all the food they had needed by hiking off the trail. That is, they hadn't hitched rides to nearby towns as most trail users did, but had instead walked every step. I nodded at them and smiled.

'Great!' I said.

They looked at one another, and repeated: 'No rides at all. We've walked every single kilometre.'

'Er… great,' I offered again, this time a little softer.

I mean from what I could gather at this point in my own journey it was certainly impressive. Given that they were doing the whole trail, they'd probably added an extra few hundred kilometres to the trek, but I was baffled by their need for my admiration. Further on in the journey I would realise the importance that was placed on sticking to self-made 'trail rules' like this. Everyone had their own set of guidelines, of which they were intensely proud. It was ridiculous and entertaining all at once.

Michael and Jack were now only a few days from finishing the trail, having started at Cape Reinga back in October. I contemplated for a moment whether or not I envied them? I decided not, not yet at least. I was too excited about what lay ahead, although I would have loved to have had the time to sit them down and unearth all the stories they must have stashed away in their packs – the sights they must have seen and the experiences they'd had.

After leaving Michael and Jack at the entrance to the forest, the rain had eased up a little, and knowing that I was now only a few kilometres from tonight's shelter – Lower Wairaki Hut – I was in high spirits. Bounding along the trail, pushing off roots and rocks to propel me forwards, I spotted another hiker up ahead. He was a tall man, covered head to toe in black waterproof clothing and, assisted by two hiking poles, was moving steadily down the trail. On account of his hood and the noise of the rain, he didn't hear or see me until I was right upon him, which gave him a bit of a fright. The forest trail was only wide enough for one person at this point, and so the man kindly stepped aside to let me through. We had a brief and excitable exchange as I passed (well, I was excited at least), and I managed to ascertain that he was heading to the same hut as me for the night. I said that I'd see him there and moved off swiftly into the forest.

Upon arriving at the hut, I found another tramper inside called Clinton. 'Tramper' was a term I'd recently added to my Kiwi vocabulary – people don't hike in New Zealand, instead they tramp, and that made Clinton a tramper. He lived locally and had come for a weekend of hiking in the Takitimus. After a few minutes of polite chit-chat with Clinton, I turned my attention to peeling off my sodden clothes. I'd just about wriggled free of my rain jacket when the handle on the door went and the man I'd passed earlier came in.

'Say, going past me there, I thought who is this girl? She's like Sarah Outen! And then I thinks to myself, it can't be Sarah says I, for Sarah is somewhere on a bike in America right now.'

I'd quickly learn that Ron Sherk liked to speak as if he were regaling a tale from the gold-mining era; his Canadian accent and beaming grin adding to the authenticity of the storytelling experience. I was warming to his gentle and inquisitive nature.

'Sarah Outen?! I know her!' I exclaimed, sounding like a cross between Buddy the Elf and a stalker all at once. 'I mean, well, we're, umm, Twitter friends, if that's even a thing?'

I'd never met Sarah, but ever since entering the London adventure scene it had become quickly apparent that she was the crème de la crème of the adventure crop. I placed her on the upper echelons of the adventure pedestal, alongside many others I admired for not only their general badassry, but also their ability to share their stories with a wider audience as they travelled. It turned out that Ron was quite the fan of Sarah, and followed her adventures as closely as I did. It was nice to discover that Ron and I had a shared interest, and a niche one at that. It was something that served to create an immediate connection with this friendly Canadian, and I was intrigued.

Now out of his waterproof cloak, I could see what Ron actually looked like. I put him in his late fifties, with short grey and white flecked hair, kind brown eyes and one of those smiles that engulfed his whole face when it was cracked. He was 6 ft tall with an athletic frame and the kind of hands that looked like they were good at fixing things. It was the thought that he looked like a 'fixer' that jogged a memory.

'Ron?'

'Mmm, huh?' he mumbled, while peeling off his wet clothes. 'Did you leave a note at Martin's Hut, about the water in the tank…? Was that you?'

He paused, a soggy sock hanging limply from his left hand. 'Ooo! Yes, that was me! You didn't drink any of that stuff, did ya?'

'A bit…' I laughed, before thanking him for the warning.

I stopped for a moment to consider how comfortable I felt in a hut deep in the forest with two men I didn't know, and concluded that I didn't care at all. These two were clearly lovely. I did step outside and get butt naked around the back of the hut as opposed to within it though – I thought full-blown nakedness was a little too intimate for a first meeting.

Once warm and dry, Ron, Clinton and I spent the next few hours exchanging life stories. I lapped up every word of Ron's story. He was in fact 65 years old, far older than he looked, and from British Colombia in Canada. He'd decided two years ago that with his kids all grown-up and being separated from his wife, he'd sell up shop and spend his time travelling the world for the rest of his days.

'That's awesome!' I gawped.

'Well, what am I supposed to do?' he replied. 'Sit around cuttin' the grass at home, waitin' to die? No, siree, not I.'

He'd begun a mission to canoe across Canada. When he hit a river that was too narrow to be navigable, he took out the fold-up bicycle he had stashed in the canoe, attached the canoe on a trailer to the back of it, and pedalled to the next bit of suitable river. Ron's life had gone on this way for the past ten years. It was winter in Canada at the time, so he'd stashed his canoe in a bush and hopped on a flight down to New Zealand, where it was now summer, and set out hiking the Te Araroa Trail.

'So, you're going the whole hog?' I asked.

'Yes, ma'am. This season if I can, although I might run into the next one. I'm going to take it steady. I've got nowhere to be except here. I'm sort of a nomad. That's what some people call me. The Nomad.'

Ah, so Ron was 'The Nomad' whom Mr 'worst winds of your life' had told me about that morning. I was delighted that it had only taken me six days to run into another northbounder on the trail. Purely because we were travelling in the same direction, I felt a sense of kinship with Ron straight away.

What I loved more than anything else about Ron was that he hiked with a miniature carbon-fibre guitar in his backpack. 'Made just for me in San Francisco,' Ron said, as he lovingly stroked the body of the guitar.

When we all started getting ready for bed, he gave us a rendition of a few old-style country classics such as Johnny Cash's 'Folsom Prison Blues', some Patsy Cline and James Butterfield's classic folk love song 'When You and I Were Young, Maggie'. Then, slightly embarrassed, Ron went to put his guitar down.

'Well now, I don't want to be keepin' you all up with my moanin'…'

I looked up and smiled. 'Oh no, you carry on, please, Ron. I'm at about a ten-point-zero on my content-o-meter right now.'

He chuckled. 'Is that right? A ten-point-zero? That's very cute.' And he picked up the guitar and resumed.

I snuggled deeper into my sleeping bag. Through the day's scrambling and the 25 km covered since leaving Birchwood, I'd collected quite an assortment of cuts on my legs, all of which were beginning to sting in the stifling heat of the sleeping bag. The wind seemed to have given my legs and face a fair battering too. I ran my index finger over my top lip to confirm what I knew to be true. It was crispy. I wondered whether I'd wake up in the morning with one of those attractive windburn Charlie Chaplin-esque moustaches.

I cast my eyes over the jumble of sodden clothes, which we had strewn around the hut and suspended from anything that would take their weight. The roaring fire in the corner was kicking out a wonderful glow and enough heat to warm three weary bodies to the core. I watched as the steam rose from the wet clothing and mingled with smoke billowing from the fire-place. At that moment, I could think of nowhere I'd rather be than here. I was warm and dry, I had a belly full of food (more than I should have had, according to the day's ration) and best of all I was in good company. I decided that I liked this section of the trail. Having seen six people that day made it practically rush hour on the Te Araroa. Any more and it'd have made a local traffic jam report. That night, deep in the Wairaki Valley, smoke-infused Johnny Cash lyrics washed over a barely con-scious runner as she drifted off into a deep and peaceful sleep.

'River's up, Anna. I'm not happy with you going across that thing alone today.'

It was 10 a.m. and I was outside the hut rolling around on the floor doing my physio exercises when I spotted Clinton coming back up the slope towards me. I'd only done two river crossings up until this point, and both were entirely managea-ble – ankle-deep trickles to be precise.

The Wairaki River was a few hundred metres down a steep slope. Clinton offered to wait for me to finish my for-est-physio yoga session, and accompany me across the river – an offer that I felt was a tad over-chivalrous, but accepted. Even though Ron wasn't intending to leave for another hour he followed on behind, offering to take an 'action shot' on his smartphone as we crossed. I was a little bemused at Clinton's concern, but when I saw the river I was very grateful that he'd come back to get me.

'Holy schmokes,' I mouthed.

Twenty-four hours of heavy rain had turned what was presumably usually a babbling brook into a full-blown rager of a waterway. I had a nervous fizzy feeling in the pit of my stomach as Clinton and I linked up. Having read up a little bit on river crossings (mostly with one eye shut in fear whilst reading) I knew that keeping my trainers on for a crossing was a good idea – it offered me better grip than going barefoot. And seeing as I was in shorts, the only things that were going to get really wet were Bonnie and Clyde (my trainers). I was quickly learning that having constantly wet feet was part and parcel of taking on the Te Araroa Trail. Holding onto one another's packs, Clinton and I edged into the water. It was a less than graceful crossing to say the least.

Clinton, bless him, was on my upstream side, doing the best he could to break the force of the water before it made it to me. Right out in the middle, we were knee-deep and I almost lost my footing. I wobbled, and now attached to Clinton he wobbled too.

'Wooo whoo woooah!' I yelped, madly scrambling, arms flailing in a bid to regain my balance. 'Bloody hell, McNuff,' said the voice in my head. 'You almost just took out the bloke who's trying to help you. Keep it together, will you?!'

Clinton seemed a little shaken by my attempt to drown him, but as a native Kiwi, you could tell that this wasn't the first time a tourist had tried to take his life at a riverbed. I managed to keep reasonably cool and calm until we got within a stride of the far bank, at which point I became so overwhelmed with a sense of relief and delight that I leaned over and planted a smacker on Clinton's cheek.

'You are a gentleman!' I hollered, just as I lost my balance again and almost dragged both of us back into the river. 'Oops! Sorry,' I said, sheepishly.

Clinton followed me out of the water. I hugged him, thanked him again, waved at Ron on the far bank and off I ran into the forest. As he was only on a weekend hiking trip, I knew it was unlikely that I would cross paths with Clinton the gent again, but I had a feeling that wasn't the last time I'd see Nomad Ron Sherk.

Despite my refusal to read the trail notes and a lack of consideration about packing any navigational device, there were certain aspects of the run that I had gone to some effort to plan. However, it was fast becoming abundantly clear that my so-called plan for the daily mileage I'd be able to cover was worth less than the paper it was written on. In my naivety and lack of willingness to read anything about the terrain on the Te Araroa, I had grossly overestimated how far I'd be able to run every day. The aim was 32 km per day, running five days on with two days very light or off. I was seven days in now and I'd covered a total of 195 km, an average of 29 km per day. The five-days-on–two-days-off strategy wasn't really working as my miles were dictated largely by the distance between huts. I wasn't entirely sure where that plan had come from anyway. Why would I run in time with the working week? Every day was the weekend on the Te Araroa.

I had run for seven days in a row now without a break, and spent the morning questioning why on earth I felt so tired. Then I remembered that this was the furthest I had run over a week. Ever.

Queenstown was the first big mental milestone on the trail. It was over 300 km into the run and the first major town I would hit since the start of the trail at Bluff. A visit to Queenstown also held some personal significance. I'd wanted to make it there for over ten years now. When I was living in Sydney as a 19-year-old, I'd made a short trip to New Zealand, but was unable to afford the flight to Queenstown so it had remained on my to-do list for all those years. Although now older, I wondered whether Queenstown's reputation as a backpacker hotspot and an adrenaline junkie's paradise would suit me. Still, I was excited to find out at last.

It was wet underfoot on the trail to Aparima Hut. The recent rain meant that the multitude of side streams were more full than usual, and the icy water filled my trainers with every slosh through. I was in high spirits, if not a little tired, when I met two trampers just leaving the hut as I sat down for a bite to eat. They warned me to take the right turn-off to Princhester Hut, and said that they'd met a guy who'd got lost and been wandering around for two days trying to find his way back. I thought back to my experience in Longwood Forest, and for once I listened to their instructions. 'When you hit the flood plain – the big wide open part – the trail turns a sharp right. Don't miss it.'

I was on a steep learning curve with this trail, and so far I'd learnt that it could throw up several types of terrain. I'd had forest, slippery rocks, vertical scrub, rivers, and now it was time for the swampy wetland to make its mark. Tanking down the hillside to the flood plain of the river I became aware of a sharp pain in my right knee, on the inside of the kneecap. It was making me feel a little sick, so I poked it at intervals to do my best to relieve the discomfort. The good news was that it only seemed to hurt when running downhill or uphill. The bad news was that there was a lot of both over the course of the day. I put it down to all the climbing I'd done yesterday in the Takitimus. I'd barely taken a break and the added weight of dragging myself uphill with a backpack had made my knees creak some.

I was beginning to consider that perhaps I'd set myself quite a tall order for the day. Progress that morning had been relatively steady, and the miles through the forest had taken about as long as I expected. What I hadn't expected was how slow the progress would be that afternoon. If there were an award for the most uncomfortable, unnatural, frustrating terrain for a runner to move over, this section was it. The concept of a flood plain – wide, open, flat land running through the valley —sounded ideal. But this was a swampy, uneven marsh, coated in chest-high grass and punctuated with hundreds of tiny streams. The first challenge was to part the grass as I ran, doing my best to spot the next orange marker pole which was often obscured by said grass. The second challenge was that even if I could see the ground beneath my feet when I placed a foot on it, it was uneven and would likely throw my ankle in some unwelcome direction. Still, no matter how carefully I parted the grass or tried to keep balance of my step, I would get distracted for a moment and my foot could land not on solid uneven grass, but in a stream. I would then find myself with one leg hip-deep in the earth and the rest of my body still moving forwards. The result was a painful wrenching motion, a swear word or two and a very sore lower back. At one point I even accused the terrain of being a health hazard.

Every now and then the trail would leave the wetlands and duck into a forest, at which point I'd cheer loudly. I was begging for it to re-enter the forest at every opportunity, because in the forest I had a good sight of the ground and could run freely.

Just before the trail entered the forest for the tenth time, I stopped to collect some water from one of the larger streams. I remembered Ron's gift of mint chocolate biscuits and decided to have a little sit down and nibble on one or two of them. Naturally, nibbling turned into inhaling the whole pack, and on the other side of the pack, life looked a little rosier. I swivelled my body around so that I was facing back across the flood plain. In all my looking down at my feet, I hadn't clocked that I was running in the most incredible surroundings. Huge granite cliffs, some coated with a layer of lush green, burst from the ground on all sides, either leading to a plateau at the top or ending abruptly in jagged peaks. It looked more like a Venezuelan cloud forest than a New Zealand river plain. The abundance of colour was breathtaking. The bright blue sky and fluffy white clouds framed the straw-coloured sea of tall grass I'd been negotiating my way through with such difficulty. Watching now how the grass swayed collectively to and fro in the wind it looked remarkably gentle, apologetic even for all the strife it had caused me. I felt like I was on the set of *Jurassic Park*, as if I had travelled back in time to a point where nature ruled supreme. Apart from the clothes on my back and my backpack, there wasn't a man-made thing in sight. I wiped the remainder of the chocolate biscuits from my chops, and moved off into the forest.

The final section of the flood plain went on for what felt like forever. At one point, I ran clean out of energy. I was just so tired. I looked at my watch: 3.30 p.m. I reckoned I'd make Princhester Hut in another hour or so but with no GPS and no idea of exactly where I was on the map, there was no telling. My legs started to feel decidedly odd. It wasn't a feeling I was familiar with, even in my long runs. They were completely devoid of energy. I tried to ignore it and push on, but it was making running very tricky, especially over tree roots and down steep slopes, as my legs just kept giving way.

I was doing the whole day by 'feel'. It felt like I should be almost at the hut at 4.30 p.m., but by 6 p.m. I still hadn't made it. It couldn't be far now, I thought. I knew the hut was 500 metres beyond a stream, and so every time the trail dropped down to a stream, I got excited. Unfortunately, in the recent rain, streams had sprung up everywhere on the hillside, and not all of them were on the map.

I'd stopped three times to cry now, and although it helped relieve the immediate desire to throw a complete tantrum, really it wasn't helping the task at hand. My quad muscles were in agony. Every time I stopped, waves of pain would move across my thighs and knees, so I decided that I needed a new focus. I switched my thoughts to two words: 'keep moving, keep moving, keep moving…' I repeated them like a mantra and went into a weird trance-like state during which I focused on nothing beyond the next marker triangle. Although my body was tired, it was my thoughts that were the most destructive, and so I bound them to the trees and the triangles and continued with the mantra.

'Keep moving, keep moving, keep moving.'

I checked my watch again, it was 7.15 p.m. and I still had no idea how far I had left to run. I decided that I'd continue until 8.30 p.m., just before dark, and then reassess the situation. I considered just bedding down in the forest for the night, if I could find somewhere flat enough and dry enough to do it.

I was midway through chant number one hundred of

'keep moving, keep moving…' when I noticed that the trail had become more manicured beneath my feet. Was that…? Yes, someone had laid wooden sticks at the side of it as if to contain the soil. Like a pathway to a secret garden I followed it for another 3 minutes, my heart now beating fast at the possibility that the hut might be somewhere near. I crossed a small wooden bridge. A bridge! I'd waded through over 50 streams that day and not one had had a bridge. And then there it was… Princhester Hut! I could have cried. In fact, I tried to. I did that thing where I screwed up my face in a best effort to cry, but I had no tears left. I had nothing left. I was a broken woman.

It was 7.43 p.m. and, other than a short stop for lunch, I'd been running since 10.30 a.m. I wriggled out of my wet clothes and by 8 p.m. I began to feel incredibly sick. The pain in my thighs and hips, instead of getting better, was now getting worse. I picked up a dehydrated meal that someone had left on the shelf. It had a web address written on it in blue pen: 'WhioWhio.blogspot'. Whoever had left this meal was a saint. I boiled up some water, poured it into the packet, crawled into my sleeping bag and spooned the deluxe Mexican chicken and rice into my mouth. I lay down and began shaking. The pain in my legs was nausea-inducing. It was like someone was repeatedly scraping the inside of my thighs with a chisel. Every position was uncomfortable and all I kept thinking was 'please be okay tomorrow, please be okay…' I felt like an idiot. I had literally run my body to its limit, and I still had 2,760 kilometres to go.

I ran 100 kilometres in the two and a half days that followed the day from hell to Princhester. After an 11-hour sleep I left there feeling better than expected. The gods had shined on me, and allowed my body to recover overnight. The official Te Araroa route continued on bush trail to the north side of Lake Wakatipu, but I'd opted to take a slightly different path to Queenstown, via a ferry across the lake at Walter Peak. The sun was shining. I was making measurable and visible progress at a reasonable speed and the pain in my right knee had subsided to a dull ache. In stark contrast to the rush hour trail traffic that I'd encountered in the Takitimus, I was now well and truly back to being a solo traveller, only being passed by a couple of cars and two touring cyclists in those three days. On the first night, I had wild-camped in the tree line off the road, and enjoyed it immensely. I had also picked up a strange rash across my butt cheeks and the backs of my legs. I concluded it was from a stream I'd had to cross when I'd lost the trail and got on the wrong side of a fence. There must have been something nasty within that stream and it made me wonder whether the water I was drinking was entirely suitable. I didn't have to wonder for much longer as a nasty bout of diarrhoea confirmed my fears.

Still. I was happy. Especially when I saw a sign that said '70 km to Walter Peak'. Only 70 km until I could have a bed, a shower and a day off! It didn't even matter that I ate my last cereal bar for dinner the following night and subsequently ran out of food.

On the final day on the road to Queenstown, I literally leapt out of my tent and ran the 25 km to the ferry port at Walter Peak on nothing but fumes and smiles. With an empty tummy, I have no idea how I had the energy to run, but I put it down to sheer excitement that I was on the final approach to Queenstown at last. The winding gravel road joined the upper shores of Lake Wakatipu and I was in awe. Out here was the New Zealand I had seen in postcards. Huge snow-capped peaks on the horizon framed a turquoise blue oasis that seemed to go on forever. I had never seen anything quite that shade of blue before. The sun was shining brightly above and hitting the surface of the water in a way that made it spar-kle like a sea of diamonds. Golden fields lined the left-hand side of the lake and rolled gently off into the distance. I could see the odd cow and a few sheep dotted along the shoreline, but mostly the fields seemed entirely vacant. The landscape on the opposite shore was even more impressive. Great towers of jagged grey rock began in the clouds and plunged steeply into the waters below.

I rounded the final bend to the ferry station and across the lake; in the distance, I could see what my eyes had been craving for days – Queenstown! I was so elated. I'd passed the first test of endurance and had run 315 km to this point. Gaz-ing across the landscape at civilisation, I thought one thing: I whipped out my phone and took it off aeroplane mode. I hadn't had any signal since leaving Scott's house. Messages and notifications flooded in and I drunk in each and every one like a technology-crazed addict. I was back in touch with the world and by Jove was I glad about it.

Having not seen many people in the past few days, my thoughts mostly consisted of 'Oh my gosh, I'm, like, so out in the wilderness' and 'I'm a fully fledged survival expert'. This self-congratulatory bubble was swiftly burst by a sea of tourists who greeted me just a few minutes down the road at Walter Peak ferry station. Backpacks on fronts, sun hats and oversized cameras snap snap snapping away – it was like wandering from the set of *Castaway* and into a theme park. I found myself in the middle of hordes of day-trippers who had come across the lake from Queenstown. There was a gift shop, a restaurant, heck, I could even go on a farm tour if I wanted. Back in your box, survival expert, back in your box.

I hurried into the shop, threw an ice cream and a chocolate bar in the general direction of my face and requested a ferry ticket from the baffled young girl behind the counter. Having not eaten anything since the night before I was absolutely famished. I was well aware that it may seem rather impolite to begin eating the goods before I had paid for them, but my stomach had taken full control of my brain. The girl behind the counter looked me up and down, at my grubby legs and sun-sprinkled face, then she looked out of the window. 'Where's your bicycle?' she asked.

'No, no, no bike.' I said, a congealed mess of mint and

chocolate ice cream spilling from my chops and just missing the counter. I ran here.' I said, doing my best to be humble but on the inside bursting with pride.

'Ran here from where?'

'From Bluff.'

'From Bluff?! But that's, what, three hundred kilometres from here?'

'Yup. Three hundred and fifteen kilometres, according to my legs,' I grinned.

For someone who gets as high as a kite while keeping two feet firmly on the ground, I wasn't entirely convinced that Queenstown was going to be my 'thang'. How would I cope with such an explosion of activity? In my mind, I'd be dodging adrenaline junkies falling from the sky, ducking those swinging between bridges and side-stepping the ones at the bottom of their bungy, before they returned skyward from the ledge whence they came. In reality, I found it to be quieter than expected. I quickly adjusted to the backdrop of parasailers and shark-shaped jet boats in the harbour, and enjoyed the European-style waterfront – most agreeable for the lady with legs in need of a little downtime.

I spent five days resting in a small town, just across the lake from Queenstown, called Franklin. A friend of a friend had put me in touch with Barbara, who owned a house there and agreed to take in a waif and stray. She was a wonderful, kind woman, with a sharp mind and balls of steel. Barbara offered the perfect balance of space for me to do my own thing, and a caring ear and warm heart to mother me. I liked having a rent-a-mum on these trails.

I'd originally only intended to take a couple of days off around Queenstown, but with the state of my body and the realisation that this trail was going to be harder than expected, I decided a full mind and body reset were needed – something that Barbara thankfully encouraged. I spent my days, eating, sleeping, taking the odd trip into Queenstown centre to buy a few essential items, and even got an introduction to the game of Rummikub, which I played several times with two of Barbara's other house guests, Americans, Ann and Joe.

While in Franklin, I took full advantage of my new-found connectivity. I spoke to my parents, my brothers, a few friends, and Jamie from the Superhero Foundation charity. Jamie and I had had some general chit-chat about the trail to this point and the odd message here and there since I'd left Bluff, and I tried my best to play down just how exhausted I was. I hadn't raised that much for the charity pot so far, and I was feeling a little embarrassed. Plus, there was an added complication in talking to Jamie.

Jamie and I had first become aware of one another in June 2013 when I was about to start cycling through the 50 states of America, and he was at the start of running 5,000 miles across Canada, dressed as a superhero. I'd learned about his trip on Twitter and was rather impressed. It took quite a lot for me to be impressed, but there was something about this skinny chap from Gloucester running unsupported across the width of Canada that caught my eye. I read further and found out that he was running to raise money for children's hospitals. I flicked open JustGiving and threw £20 at his cause. A week later I received an email.

'Hi Anna,

Thank you for the donation to the foundations that support the hospitals 'GOSH' and 'The Pied Piper Appeal'. It really does make a difference.

Loved your message with the word 'redonkulous' in it, thought I only used that word.

Thank you again for the amazing support, Anna.

Sending you loads of running love!'

This kick-started a brief email conversation about launching a campaign to get the words 'redonkulous', 'amazeballs' and 'awesomesauce' added into the Oxford English Dictionary, complete with some friendly flirtation.

Fast forward two years and, unbeknown to me, a mutual friend had told Jamie about my plans for the New Zealand run. I hadn't had any contact with him since our dictionary discussion, but had loosely followed his trans-Canada run on Twitter. Jamie had now set up his own foundation and needed an ambassador who would fundraise for them to kick-start things. He and his cousin Kev had convinced me to put my run to good use and raise money for his charity to enable disadvantaged children to go on adventures of their own.

The complication when talking to Jamie now was that we may have had a little (big) smooch just before I left for my run. The smooch was, on my part at least, entirely unplanned. The only time I could meet all the trustees of Jamie's Superhero Foundation in one place was at the McDonald family Christmas party. On 27 December 2014, I hopped on a train from London and went down to meet Jamie and all the trustees. The party was a whole heap of fun, and at 5 a.m. I was performing an array of elaborate and risqué dance moves around the Christmas tree with Jamie's mum. Jamie and I had chatted on and off through the night, but I thought nothing of it, although I could swear I had a shot of the green-eyed monster when I looked across the room and saw him with his arm around another girl.

Out of nowhere at 6 a.m. I found a certain McDonald on the end of my lips. I'd started to protest, and then changed my mind when I realised that I actually quite liked him. He wasn't intimidated by me in the slightest, something I had found to be rare in the four and a half years I had spent being single until that point. I left his house later that morning after a slightly awkward breakfast cooked by his mum. What followed was Jamie calling me three times on New Year's Eve (I'd picked up on the third call), before him denying all knowledge of the calls the morning after. I always found this kind of late-night dialling, coupled with denial, to be an indication that someone fancies you. Four days later I boarded the plane to New Zealand.

Since I'd been in New Zealand, Jamie and I hadn't talked about the kiss at all. Our exchanges were mostly business-related with some strong flirting thrown in every now and then. Over Skype in Franklin we chatted about social media, donation links, and fundraising pages – on rare occasions I would venture some thoughts or feelings about the run, although I would always keep it light hearted and brush over the times when I'd struggled mentally or physically. As an adventurer himself, he seemed genuinely interested in everything I'd experienced on the trail so far, and it was always nice to share stories with someone who 'got it'. On paper, it was a confusing relationship, but I had put the kiss down to a heat of the moment thing between two people who got along well. It felt like we were friends, and with me on the other side of the world to him for the next six months, that seemed to be the best conclusion.

One thing was true, and it was that chatting to Jamie always made me smile. Our shared love of adventure and his jealousy at me being away and him being at home had reminded me why I had started this run in the first place. In the cold light of day and from the comfort of the cushion at the window on the shores of Lake Wakatipu, I used the chat with Jamie to force things back into perspective. I felt like a total wimp. Why had I found these first ten days quite so hard? I realised that everything, and I mean everything, had been a shock. The terrain, the navigation, the isolation – all of these things were far more than I'd bargained for. What had I bargained for? I couldn't even remember. More than that my body was quite literally in shock. I had destroyed it. I never thought this was going to be easy, but I also didn't think it would be this hard. I looked out over the lake and took a deep breath. I had been on a steep learning curve but I was ready for the next section. Now I felt like the journey was truly about to start.

6

The Soldiers of Self-doubt

Arrowtown was just 13 kilometres from Queenstown. After five days of rest it'd felt marvellous to hit the road again that morning. The dramas of the first ten days were now a distant memory, but the lessons were very much at the front of my mind. Take it easy. Enjoy. Go steady. Don't be so hard on yourself: these were my new set of intentions for the trail to Wanaka. As always seemed to be the way with Kiwi hospitality, Barbara, my host on the Queenstown outskirts, had sorted me out with a stay with one of the girls in her Mahjong group.

On my way into town I'd received a message from Ron's GPS device, which uses satellites to allow you to send messages from anywhere: 'Go to the Arrowtown cafe, tell the gal behind the counter who you are and you'll find yourself a free lunch there. I've got it covered.' Sure enough, I went into the cafe and found that Ron had put $15 behind the counter for me. I wolfed down a milkshake and a gigantic slice of lasagne gleefully. As I rested in Queenstown, Ron had caught me up, ploughing straight through Queenstown (he wasn't much of a fan of big towns), and was now ahead of me on the trail.

The old road to the now deserted hamlet of Mace-town rumbled on up the valley, dusty and wide, curving and winding above the grey gorges of the river far below. After a solid hour of listening to Guns N' Roses, which I had deemed an appropriate musical selection for such a dramatic backdrop, I stopped to check the next section of trail instructions. It read: 'Turn left and walk up the river' – only in New Zealand.

In a strange change of tactic, and perhaps because I had had more 'downtime' than usual, I had actually read the trail notes about this particular section. For some reason unbeknown to me, and despite having my scare in Longwood Forest, I still hadn't gone and bought a GPS. It was just an added layer of hassle and when I went in search of one in Queenstown, I couldn't find a store that stocked them. I'd buy one in Wanaka, I resolved. I knew that this was a tough section into the Motatapu mountains, which included using a river to navigate – something that would be simple to an accomplished outdoorsy person, but I was certainly not that.

Whilst enjoying my lunch in Arrowtown, I'd seen a Facebook update from Ron. We'd been keeping in contact ever since our meeting at Lower Wairaki Hut and he'd been adding extra notes to his tracker updates for me. Ron's latest message read: 'Best route from Macetown is up the river (Anna, exit the river at the extractor).' What the heck is an extractor? I wondered. It must have been a Canadian term for some kind of machinery, but I couldn't grasp exactly what. I meant to Google it before I left, but of course I'd got distracted, and as usual I assumed it would be obvious once I saw it.

The Motatapu mountains sprawled across the landscape like giant sleeping tarantulas. Green bodies and hairy tussock-covered legs forming sharp ridge lines and deep basins. Weaving its way between the arachnids, along the valley floor, was a nice, sensible, wide trail. But the 'trail chat' from other trampers had told me that this wide trail only opened once a year for a 4x4 race, and in fact the whole area was owned by Shania Twain's ex-husband. Apparently, Shania even visits the area from time to time. Oh, how I'd love to tumble through the doorway of a hut in the Motatapu mountains and find Shania cracking out a rendition of 'Honey, I'm Home'. (This will mean nothing to you if you're not a Shania fan. And in which case, shame on you.)

The Te Araroa's route through the Motatapu mountains is more undulating than the 4x4 version. At one point there was the option to take the river, as Ron and the trail notes had instructed. But still without a GPS and with nothing to tell me exactly when I should leave the river, I opted to cling to the safety of the pole markers which followed a flood trail.

I quickly learned that this route was a lady-ball-buster. Often no wider than a sheep track, it contoured round the side of mountains at an angle which, if moving at speed, required that I hang to tufts of long grass to prevent an ungrateful slide off the edge. I'd dip down to one of the dozens of narrow – yet deep – streams that punctuated the path, then run back up, finding myself above the cloud line gasping for breath. It was like a roller coaster.

Having spent so much of the first few weeks on the trail in dense forest, being at eye level with the clouds and surrounding peaks was liberating. From the river in Arrowtown, I'd now climbed up to over 1,200 metres high. I stopped for a moment; everything up here seemed so still. There was very little wind and the clouds were barely moving – instead they appeared as if suspended, mid-flow, in front of the green peaks opposite.

However, after each visit up to the lap of the gods, I'd find myself plunging steeply back down into a new section of lower ground. Down there, instead of being at eye level with the peaks, I was surrounded by them as four or five neighbouring mountains formed a deep basin. From each basin I'd look up and around and think, 'how the heck do I get out of here?' The contours of the land never had an obvious answer, but I could bet my sheep-rash-covered bottom dollar that it'd be straight up that tasty steep ridge line just in front of me. At times it felt like I was trying to climb out of a bowl of jelly. Challenging it might have been, but I was absolutely loving it. I ground myself into a sick rhythm on the narrow tracks and whooped with glee.

Way up there in the Motatapus, it started to get hot. I mean, really hot. It wasn't until I reached Wanaka that I found out the temperature had hit 37°C. Up in the mountains all I knew was that the cheese and chocolate in my pack had turned to smush. Deciding it was time for lunch, I scraped some cheese from the innards of my bag and smeared the now gooey curd onto a tortilla. I'd taken shade under a rock just by a natural dip in the land, Roses Saddle. I was enjoying the stillness of life above the clouds, when I heard footsteps on the trail below. I looked down and saw an elderly man making his way steadily around the mountain.

I was about to call out but then I thought better of it. The poor guy, I'd give him a fright. I tried a quiet 'Hello'. There was no break in his stride so I tried again, this time a little louder.

'Umm. Hi, there. Hello?'

He stopped for a moment, as if sniffing the wind but just as he was about to look up at where I was sitting he moved off again. 'Oh, sod this,' I thought.

'Oi! Up here! Hallllrooooooo!'

The poor fella nearly fell off his feet when he saw me. I moved down the mountain towards him, perching on a ledge just above his head.

'Ah!' he said. 'You must be Anna.'

What the…? And then it dawned on me. I smiled. 'So, you've met Ron then?'

Bill and I had a nice exchange in the sunshine, and he told me that Ron was only a day ahead of me now.

From Roses Saddle it was a short 30-minute jog to Roses Hut, where I intended to stop for a bit of a sit down before carrying on through to Highland Creek Hut for the night. It did start to occur to me that perhaps trying to run 34 kilometres that day, in this heat and over this terrain was a little ambitious, and my mind was made up when Roses Hut loomed into view on the valley floor.

It was stunning. Set in an open plain, it looked towards blue skies down the valley to the east. Several surrounding mountains, with sharp ridge lines towards their peaks, softened into rolling hills as they neared the hut. There were a hundred different shades of yellow and green in front of me. The straw-coloured knee-length grass on the valley floor was contrasted with the bright green grass on mountain slopes, both of them framing a river which wound its way down the valley out of sight. From way up on the hillside I could see that it was a modern hut with a huge veranda and there were two, no three people, like little ants, lying in the shade, enjoying the afternoon breeze. I just about bounded down there as fast as my legs could carry me.

'Hi, I'm Anthony,' said the man lying on the right edge of the veranda, as a woman emerged from inside and came to join him.

'Antony,' I repeated.

'No, Ant-thony,' he corrected me.

'Ant-thony,' I repeated back.

'Or you can just call me Finny?'

'Finny.' I liked Finny.

'And I'm Fiona,' said a woman with red hair and a brightly coloured pair of purple shorts.

'Hi, Fiona,' I grinned.

'And you must be Anna?' Finny asked.

'How did you…? Ah! You've met Ron too then?'

'We have indeed. Quite your number one fan is Ron.'

I beamed. I liked having a fan on the trail, and so soon on. It made me feel like this was less of a solo journey that way.

I was introduced to Carys and Jen, two young American girls who were also lying outside on the veranda. I threw my pack off onto the floor, taking a seat beside them on the cool wooden slats. Even though I was in the shade, the heat from the mountains was still wafting in over the deck. I turned back to Fiona, who had also just said I could call her Fi.

'Just so I've got this straight – you're Finny.'

Anthony nodded.

'And you're Fi.'

Fiona nodded.

'Finny and Fi.' I smiled. They smiled back.

'Yep! And we're even looking for whios.' The word sounded like 'fi-os'. Finny, Fi, fios.

'What are whios?'

'Whios. They're a rare blue duck that live on freshwater

rivers in New Zealand, but they're endangered.'

Finny spelt the word out to me. Whios, whios… I turned the word over in my mind… something about it was familiar. Where had I heard it before? Then I remembered.

'Did you two leave a packet of food in Princhester Hut? Mexican backcountry chicken?!' I screamed, barely able to contain my excitement.

'Yep, that was us! Did you find it?'

'Find it?! I wolfed down the whole god damn thing. And I'd had the day from hell!'

And so ensued a regaling of the day from hell. They too had found the swampy flood plain a challenge and, as most people did, had sensibly broken up the day with a stopover at Ahipara Hut. From our discussions I worked out that they'd left Bluff just a week before me.

After 30 minutes of chatting, Fiona asked, 'I suppose you'll be carrying on for the day now?'

I sat and thought for a moment as an internal battle raged in my mind. I'm a schedule kind of gal, you see. I like schedules, and so the thought of stopping here, earlier than intended, didn't sit well with me. Truth be told, it felt weak. But when I considered everything I had learned on the way to Queenstown, I was beginning to realise that the trail was bigger than me, and bigger than any plans I had. In reality I'd long since made the decision. This was a beautiful hut. These were wonderful people. I was entirely relaxed in their company, so why on earth, for the sake of making a few kilometres, would I push on to the next hut? It was already 5 p.m. so I resolved to stop at Roses Hut for the night. In informing Finny and Fi of my decision, I think I somewhat shattered their illusion of me as a hardened trail runner. I grinned at them: 'Ah, but I told you I wasn't a *real* runner now, didn't I? I just like to run.'

We wittered and nattered the evening away as Finny and Fi took great care and time to impart their knowledge of GPS devices. 'You can get a smartphone GPS app too, you know?' Fi asked.

Well, that was news to me, and so feeling rather foolish, I lapped up all the knowledge she continued to impart. As it turned out, Finny and Fi did this kind of thing rather regularly – tramping that is. Although they hadn't done a trail this long before, they were far more experienced in the ways of the New Zealand backcountry than I was. I learnt more about their cause, the whios and how they spent their weekends up in the Tararuas laying out traps to catch stoats.

Stoats, rats, rabbits and all other non-native ground vermin were a real problem in New Zealand. Once upon a time, the Land of the Long White Cloud had been a wildlife enthusiast's paradise. Full of beautiful flightless birds, some of them the size of ostriches, roaming free and happy (at least in my mind they were happy). And then the white man landed and brought over European vermin, it was game over for paradise.

The Māori had done their fair share of damage too, wiping out the moas – gigantic, slow and stupid birds that were an easy source of meat – but it was the white Europeans (or *Pakeha*, to give them the Māori term) who had caused most of the problems. The Department of Conservation now runs hundreds of rodent control programmes across the country, and volunteers like Finny and Fi were a huge source of much needed support. I learned much of this a few months later on in my trip, and I began to grasp that the killing of one species to save another was a double-edged sword. At this point, on my first meeting with Finny and Fi, I just saw them as some kind of duck warriors. I wanted to fashion them superhero suits – although they seemed to already be suitably dressed for superhero behaviour: Fiona in her bright purple shorts and Finny in a distinctive tartan hiking kilt. They had a cause they were passionate about, and for that I liked them immediately.

When the sun had dropped lower in the sky I decided it was time for a wash. While I wasn't precious about being clean, I had sweated out most of my body's salt content that day, 90% of which seemed to have been collected in my sports bra. Wondering whether or not I could reuse the salt as a seasoning for my noodles that night, I gathered up my molten bars of Whittaker's chocolate and headed for the stream.

'Where you off to?' Carys asked from the top bunk.

'I'm taking my chocolate for a bath,' I declared, as if it were obvious. I opened my palms to reveal three bars of milk chocolate that were slumped like a Dali *Persistence of Memory* clock in my palms.

One hundred metres away from the hut, I sat my bare behind down in waist-deep water and shivered a little. There was something oddly satisfying about being naked in a cold stream in the middle of a beautiful mountain valley, with my greatest possessions (chocolate bars) pinned under rocks in the water next to me and knowing that Shania Twain could stroll by at any moment. I sat there for 10 minutes before the cold got the better of me. I emerged with a clean body and fully solidified, if slightly deformed, chocolate bars. Everyone was a winner, I concluded, except perhaps the stream.

'Hey there Ron! What you up to? A spot of gardening?' I yelled, scrambling up a steep slope towards a lone figure in front of Highland Creek Hut. I'd run 13 km since leaving Roses Hut that morning and the heat was just about killing me. Ron threw his hand out and clasped mine, dragging me up to his level.

'You are incredible girl,' he said in his soft Canadian accent, before turning to explain the task at hand. 'Well, I'm thinking that people are almost at the hut here, but they've pretty much gotta kill themselves to make it up this slope. So I'm cutting in some steps.'

He said it so matter-of-factly, as if stopping your own transcountry walk in order to carve steps that would make the pathway easier for those that followed you was the most natural thing to do. I thought about one of my favourite Robert Baden-Powell quotes: 'No one can pass through life, any more than he can pass through a bit of country, without leaving tracks behind, and those tracks may often be helpful to those coming after him in finding their way,' and smiled.

'Looks like you've done a cracking job to me. Fancy a stop for lunch?' I asked.

After 10 minutes inside, I'd just about stopped sweating. 'Here, I got you this,' I said, handing Ron his favourite Whittaker's Hokey Pokey-flavoured chocolate bar as a thank you for his food donations at our last meeting – although, as I had failed to learn from my own chocolate disaster, what I actually handed him was a molten mess that once resembled a chocolate bar. 'You, umm, might need to keep it in the shade a while,' I added, a little embarrassed.

'And I got you this.' Ron smiled, handing over a bar of fudge. 'I thought I'd buy you something that wouldn't melt in the heat.'

How sensible, I thought. 'You're always looking after me, you are, Ron. I think I'm going to call you Coach Ron from here on in.' He mulled the new name over in his head a while, before deciding that he liked it, and so it was set in stone.

I was still aiming to run a further 23 kilometres to Wanaka that day, so we said our goodbyes again and I ran on. Although this time it didn't feel like a goodbye. I knew I'd see him somewhere again down the road. Friends on this trail were becoming like the friends I'd made on my travels over the years. A goodbye was never a goodbye. The good eggs, I knew I'd see them sometime, somewhere in the world down the line. It was 'until next time' that we parted ways.

'Why would you run it?' Brett asked. His face was dead pan but I detected an undertone to his voice. It was as if he were accusing me of trying to do something impressive. I had come across Brett and Michaela, a couple from England, and Peter and Andrew from San Francisco at the last hut in the Motatapus, which wasn't far from the edge of the forest and the shore of Lake Wanaka. This hut was beautiful too, and I began to wonder whether perhaps my beloved Martin's Hut, that first, dingy hut in Longwood Forest, was the only hut on the trail that had so many 'original' features.

Perhaps I was imagining his tone. I was tired after all. Was I being overly sensitive?

'Are you one of those sponsored athletes? Trip's been paid for, I suppose?' he continued.

Nope, there was definitely an undertone. I paused for a moment, remembering that this was his issue, not mine. I did what my dad always tells me to do when people try to tear you down. I took a deep breath and smiled.

'Because, I like running. I like how it feels. I'm not going for speed or records. I just, umm, like running. And I'm not sponsored.' I stared at him. He was winding up for a new round of questioning, but I decided that I'd had enough. 'Right! Better get going!' I added, leaping up from the floor and dashing off. I say dashed. I really do mean dash – I sprinted so hard down the next section that I began to hyperventilate. If the beautiful hut had been tempting me to give up on my plans to reach Wanaka at all, the interaction with Brett had quickly quashed that thought. I glimpsed Peter and Andrew, who had gone down to the stream for a wash, to my right. Although we'd only exchanged five minutes of small talk, Andrew's quips and Peter's cheeky grin hinted that they both had a healthy sense of humour, and so I ventured some of my own.

'I can see you getting NAKED!' I shouted at the top of my lungs.

They laughed and whooped in reply. 'Happy trails, Anna!'

Even though Brett's questioning about my motives for the run had made an attempt at dampening my spirits, I concluded that it had been a fantastic day so far – one that had started with waving goodbye to new friends at Roses Hut, and been fuelled by a lunch stop with one of my biggest fans. I relished in the beauty of the mountains that day.

It could have been a terrible day, on account of my slow progress and the sweltering heat, but today was a day I'd employed a new mental tactic. I called it 'cheerleaders only'. The book I'd been reading – Ruby Wax's *Sane New World* – was offering me a fascinating introduction to the world of mindfulness. I began to consider my own thoughts and the self-abuse that had accompanied my runs in the first ten days to

Queenstown. I decided that there was no way I could possibly put up with those thoughts for the next five months, and that the only person able to change that was me. On leaving Queenstown, I had started a new experiment. Every time I hit a tough section of trail and the voices of the soldiers of self-doubt appeared, I'd see it as an opportunity to let my cheerleaders out. And, boy, were my cheerleaders loud. I'd coo at myself: 'Well done, Anna!' 'That is freakin' awesome!' 'You are red hot!' (which perhaps wasn't an entirely helpful chant given the temperature in the Motatapus). Every now and then, the chief cheerleader would bounce into view and kick the captain of the soldiers square in the nuts, before winking at me and resuming her cheers. It might sound ridiculous, and perhaps simple, that positive thoughts make a challenging experience somewhat more enjoyable, but somewhere along the line I had forgotten that.

It's a good job the cheerleaders were with me, because on account of running on a camber around the side of a mountain and the heat, I'd developed three big, nasty blisters. At the top of the last mountain pass I'd pulled off my shoes to inspect the damage. Rather than wait for them to burst themselves mid-stride, I took control by raising my foot to my mouth and bursting each by sandwiching it between my two canines. A searing pain would ensue, but after years as a rower I was well used to coping with blister-bursting moments by now. There wasn't a blister that'd broken me yet, and these ones weren't about to try.

With 5 kilometres to go to my destination for the night, I ran clean out of gas. I had massively over-egged the climbs through the day and the now raw flaps of skin on my feet were really starting to sting. I slumped against a tree in the final section of forest, before the shores of Lake Wanaka, and shut my eyes, gasping.

'Only a few kilometres to go, come on, Anna,' cooed the cheerleaders. 'You got this.'

But I was done. I needed some kind of distraction, I needed a force stronger than any darkness out there. To get me through the final hour today, I needed the Dixie Chicks! Reaching into my pack I pulled out my phone and loaded up their album. I shoved the earphones into my earholes, dragged myself to my feet and began to sing. With the cheerleaders quieter now, my mind drifted to thoughts of the Glendhu Bay campground, hoping against hope there'd be a big campground shop. Maybe they'd have ready salted crisps? Please let them have ready salted crisps and a bottle of Fanta. Oh, how I'd like to have a bath in Fanta right now...

7

Northbounders, Assemble!

I didn't fancy setting an alarm – there was no need to, after all, and I woke up around nine naturally. 'I'll get going by ten,' I thought. Ten is okay. Three cups of tea, one cup of coffee and an awful lot of discussions about life, love and men later, I was still sat on Liana's couch. She was wonderful. I don't know what it is about a right good chinwag, but it really is food for the soul. Besides, it was pouring with rain. It was only a 12-km run to the hut on the Breast Hill track and as long as I made it there by dark all would be okay.

On arriving at Wanaka, a town I had fallen very much in love with, I'd taken a day off. In that day I had let my blisters heal, had the world's most painful sports massage, failed to locate and buy a GPS and been sent up on a free flight in a 1940s tiger moth plane, courtesy of Lake Wanaka Tourism and my hosts Duncan and Michelle. Well, mainly courtesy of Michelle, who was one of those 'make shit happen' kind of women. Her husband, Duncan, was the brother of a good friend from back home. I was always amazed when complete strangers took me in but his sister, Ailsa, had vouched for me and so I had found myself at the door of their family home. Michelle and Duncan, plus their adorable two-year-old Coll, were my kind of people. Michelle was a Kiwi, Duncan a Scot, and they'd originally settled in to a city life in Auckland, before deciding that they fancied embracing the outdoors a little more, and so had moved to Wanaka in the middle of the lesser populated South Island. Both could frequently be found on their mountain bikes out on the hills around the lake. According to them, time indoors was time wasted – something I was finding to be common among Kiwis. They were a family with a work–life balance that was actually balanced and it was a joy to be a part of for those 48 hours. The morning I left Wanaka, Duncan had cycled alongside me on the banks of the Hāwea River, and I was now hanging out with family-friend Liana on the shores of Lake Hāwea.

I needed to pick up a few extra bits to complete my supplies for the four days between Hāwea and Lake Ohau, and so I eventually said my goodbyes to Liana and ran the mile to the Lake Hāwea general store. As I ran away from the house I noticed that my left calf was sore. It appeared to be misfiring in some way, that is to say it was weak and wasn't helping support or propel me forward. I ran on, every now and then wincing as a jab of pain shot up the leg.

'General store' is a general term. I've learnt that general stores tend to have the most ridiculous assortment of both useful and useless items, with no apparent rhyme or reason to explain their presence on the usually half-empty dusty shelves. The Lake Hāwea general store, however, was rather pleasant. There was a very smiley lady behind the counter who greeted me as I entered, and I found two other hikers and a pair of Dutch cycle tourists sitting at the plastic tables in front of the counter. All of them had the same wistful look on their faces: 'Is it STILL raining?'

I promised myself I'd only stay for 30 minutes' maximum, and so naturally I ordered a ridiculous amount of food. A cheese sandwich. A brownie. A veggie stack. A flat white. Feeling rather full I then decided I really needed a date and orange scone too. This was of course because I wasn't going to see civilisation, or scones for that matter, for at least four days and that warranted eating another scone, just to 'stock up my scone levels' for the days that lay ahead. God forbid one's scone levels should dip below acceptable.

'I'll leave at 4 p.m.' I reasoned, looking out the window at the incessant rain. 'Maybe I'll leave at 4.30 p.m.,' I muttered, changing my mind, and went back to my Kindle.

When 5 p.m. came, it was still pouring outside, and I was still sitting inside. I'm not sure if it was the abundance of both date and orange in my bloodstream, but I came over all philosophical, and I began to think – what if the rain never stopped? What if someone announced that it would rain forever from this day forward? Would I sit inside? A life lesson dawned on me: you can't sit around waiting for the rain to stop. There may never be a 'good time' to go, but you just have to and hope the weather clears up. So at 5.30 p.m., I was resolute as I shoved the last crumb of scone into my mouth, waved goodbye to my new cafe friends and set off up the road. It was still raining and I felt terrible. My legs were sluggish and my stomach swollen from the unnecessary volume of food now lolling around somewhere between my oesophagus and my stomach. And, somehow, the pack felt heavier than yesterday.

I reached the start of the trailhead at 6 p.m. and looked aghast at the Department of Conservation sign: 'Pakituhi Hut: 4 hours.' Craning my neck upwards, I followed the line of the trail with my eyes, watching it snake and switchback up the sizeable chunk of land in front of me. It was steep. I'd accounted for a 10 kilometre run with a few bumps maybe, but not the full-on scaling of a mountain. I did some rapid on the spot maths and worked out that if it took me as long as the sign said, it would be dark long before I made the hut. I cursed myself. Why didn't I have a head torch? Note to self – must get a head torch.

I set off up the track, puffing and panting as I shifted my weight rhythmically from one foot to the other, the sporadically placed orange pole markers serving as a welcome distraction from my modest pace. After 45 minutes, I began to feel the first wave of anxiety building. Even though they were doing a good job of emptying their contents onto me, the rain clouds still looked menacing. As the skies grew darker still and the clouds more bulbous, they seemed to encase my lungs, suffocating me with each step. Try as I might, I couldn't go any faster. Making it to the highest point on the trail I found myself on a narrow section of land at 1,300 metres high. I began to get anxious every time I looked beyond my own feet. A steep drop to my left, a slippery rock to my right, and in all the cloud I was starting to lose the trail markers. Thoughts and tales of hikers slipping off trails began to swirl around in my mind. I was only an hour from a town, and yet I was scared. Truth be told, I felt like a wimp. And that made me feel even worse. I decided that I needed a distraction so I created a tongue twister, which I repeated over and over: 'The sheep shit is slippery beneath the souls of my shoes. The sheep shit is slippery beneath the souls of my shoes. The sheep...'

With my mind fully occupied with the tongue twister, I'd just about finished negotiating an especially tricky section of scrambling when, as if by magic, the rain stopped. The clouds parted just enough to offer a glimpse of where I'd come from and the sun emerged at last. And, oh my word, it was beautiful. The sun was breaking through the clouds at intervals, shooting beams of bright yellow light in every direction. The clouds parted a little more so that I could now see Lake Hāwea way down below. On route to the general store I'd been able to catch a glimpse of its crystal-clear waters, but from up here it looked vast, framed by granite-coloured mountains, which rose steeply from its shore all the way around. It felt truly special to be stood there at that moment. Like running through the rain had all been worth it for such a reveal of the lake in all her glory. A wave of joy began at my toes, made its way through my body, and high-fived every little nerve cell along the way, before finally exiting my mouth in the form of

'Holy crap! Would you look at that?!' I felt like I was on top of the world.

Post-world-topping, I was in a much better mood as I skipped off along the ridge. Thirty minutes later, the sun slid from view behind the mountain and the temperature dropped, but I knew I wasn't far from the hut now. It was then that I heard my name being called. What the? Who the? Where? I looked around and couldn't see anyone so I took a few more steps, and there it was again – louder this time, and more of a shout: 'Anna! Hey, Anna!' Then the dusky clouds parted and two figures appeared from the mist. Finny and Fi tumbled straight towards me and into my now open arms. I noted Finny was still wearing his trademark piece of hiking attire, which made me smile.

'Now there's a kilt I recognise!'

'We thought it was you,' Fi started. 'We saw a runner, and thought, surely there's no other runners out here?'

I spotted a third member of the welcome party just behind. 'Oh, and this is Joe by the way,' said Fi.

'Hi, Joe! I'm Anna. Nice to meet you,' I said going straight in for the hug. He was a little taken aback, but seemed to recover swiftly from the hug tornado placed upon him and managed to regain his balance. 'What are you all doing out here?' I asked.

'We came out to watch the sunset,' said Fi. I looked

around, she smiled and pulled a face. 'Yeah, not much of one going on in this cloud. Still, we found you! That'll do! Come on, this way.'

Finny, Fi and Joe led me the few final minutes to Pakituhi Hut. Inside, I found Peter and Andrew from San Francisco (thankfully fully clothed this time) and Julian, a quiet and brooding Australian who didn't say much. In fact, I'm not sure he said more than one word in the time he was there. Still, he smiled a fair bit, and he had a lovely smile. And he had an even better beard. I was a bit obsessed with beards. Seeing as I was female and couldn't grow one myself, I took great pleasure in admiring others. The bushier, the better. And Julian's was bushy.

That night I burrowed deep into my sleeping bag and read a few pages of *Into the Wild*, which I decided wasn't the best thing to be reading when you're actually in the wild yourself, before drifting off into calm and peaceful sleep. I'd only met Finny, Fi, Andrew and Peter a few days earlier, and for a relatively brief time, yet there was already something so familiar about their company. In a landscape that was forever changing, anything constant was a welcome addition.

After breakfast with Joe I packed up and watched as everyone in the hut hit the trail at staggered intervals. The sure but steady Fi and Finny left at 8 a.m., the slightly reckless high-octane-seeking Peter and Andrew departed at 9 a.m., taking a higher route along the Breast Hill ridge line and myself, sensible but always a little late, left at 10 a.m. to chase down the pack. I was struggling again with my left calf, which was still misfiring and took an hour or so to coax into a normal range of movement, but I was happy. Knowing the others were ahead of me on the trail made me happy. We might have been separate, but today we were a team.

By lunchtime I'd caught up with Peter and Andrew at Stodys Hut, 11 km further on. As an added bonus, Coach Ron was there.

'O, hey there!' he said, emerging from bushes to the right of the hut.

'Ron!' I ran over to him and gave him a hug. 'Err… where have you been? And what have you been up to?' I eyed the black marker pen in his hand.

'O, I've just been writing a sign to direct people to the toilet. It's hard to find you know…'

I loved this man. He was always considering those who were following behind him. And better than that, considering that they might need to take a dump. What a gent!

Peter, Andrew, Ron and I sat by the side of the ramshackle Stodys Hut, enjoying the sunshine.

'What time is it?' Ron yelped suddenly.

I checked my phone. 'Nearly 1 p.m.'

'I better get going!' were the words that left Ron's mouth,

although his body language said something entirely different.

This was another thing that I loved about Ron. He never rushed. He said he had no time for rushing. If there was any hint of stress in his life, I'd certainly never caught wind of it and I couldn't help but feel that this was a choice he'd made long ago. The path he'd chosen in life lent itself to fear and panic on certain occasions, but, as his tales of canoeing the Yukon would attest, not to stress. Cramming what remained of my cheesy tortilla wrap into my mouth, I threw my backpack on and headed off into the tree line.

'See you on the flip side, boyos!' I hollered at the trio of men, before dashing off.

'Laters!' came the North American chorus behind me.

There weren't many times on the run that I'd regretted the decision to wear trainers, as opposed to anything more technical or sturdy, but today was one of those days. Following the orange triangles, I dropped steeply down to the riverbed. The soft leaves underfoot were mixed with loose earth and hard bits of shale, making it nigh on impossible to remain upright. It was like a game of snakes and ladders – hard won progress up the slope could be undone in a matter of seconds with a slide right back down to the bottom. In several places, where the trail burst across an open slope, leading directly and sharply down to the river below, I was too frightened to look down. My slip rate was high and there was nothing to grab in these open sections if I lost my footing.

Despite the struggles, I was having a whale of a time. Spending a significant number of hours on my heels, sliding down forest slopes, was novel, and the lack of rhythm and order to the day was a welcome change. The ups were intense and tough-going with the backpack, but I enjoyed pushing off trees, using their sometimes unreliable roots to haul myself up climbs before skidding down the other side. I paused at the crest of one hill and took a good look at myself. I was covered in mud, the dirt under my nails was reaching near critical mass, and my legs were littered with scratches. I grinned a big childlike grin that comes from feeling like you've been let out to play, when the rest of the world is grounded.

At last the trail joined up with the Timaru River, which was the most beautiful turquoise blue against grey-and-white-flecked rocky sides. There was some kind of mineral in the water which gave it a milky appearance, and I'd never seen anything like it. I stopped to watch my feet move through the river, which seemed to behave more like cream than water. I picked my own pathway through the next section, crossing the river ten or so more times, before heading away from it and up onto a forested hillside. Just then, I heard voices up ahead.

Finny and Fi were on the pathway – they'd stopped and were chatting to a southbound hiker. Jory was walking the trail barefoot. He'd made his own pack frame from leaves and vine, and had been foraging and hunting for food along the way. As someone who gets flummoxed hunting for noodles in their backpack, I found this all rather impressive, although the little ex-vegetarian girl inside of me screamed when he spoke of spearing rabbits. He'd accessorised his Crusoe-chic look with a vine headband, which performed the dual task of keeping his locks from his face and filling me with style envy. We listened intently as Jory described his hopes for what the journey along the Te Araroa would bring. He wanted to feel more connected to his country, to his ancestors, to the land and to wildlife. I wasn't sure if killing the wildlife was the best way to be connected to it, but I liked his style. I admired the spiritual soul within him, and he had the cutest smile.

Leaving Jory, Finny and Fi chatting, I pushed on, continuing to follow the river but with more dramatic sidling now. It was pushing on for 3 p.m. and my energy tank had reached level zero. On account of all the climbing, my right knee was really starting to hurt too. I decided to poke it, because this is what one does whenever something hurts, and upon poking it I discovered that it felt crunchy. Yikes. That wasn't good. Crunchy was never good, unless it was crunchy nut cereal – and even that wasn't especially good for you.

It was 6 p.m. when I arrived at the six-bed Top Timaru Hut to find Kirstine Collins nestled quietly in one corner. Kirstine, a southbounder, was somewhat of a trail celebrity. Ex-military, and having recently returned from a stint in the Congo, she was renowned for keeping an incredibly detailed blog. She was the kind of lady who'd saw the handle off of her toothbrush and then drill holes in what remained of the stub, just to shave off a few extra grams, and her preparation for hiking the Te Araroa was meticulous. Her nutrition had its own four-page spreadsheet, plus she'd posted food boxes ahead for every single section. You could tell she didn't suffer fools, and took a no-frills approach to trail life. Her style wasn't my own, not mine at all, but I admired and respected her tenacity, and beneath the hardened exterior I detected a softer soul. The shame of it all was that she seemed to be enjoying her solitude, and so when I warned her that there was a moving trail party headed our way, she was visibly disappointed.

A few hours later Finny and Fi arrived, followed closely by the San Fran lads, and finally Coach Ron, who concluded his day's hike by doing a victory lap of the rock out the front, much to the delight of the party. That night, Ron picked up the guitar again for a round of country tunes and poetry. We were treated to another helping of Johnny Cash's 'Folsom Prison Blues', as well as an impressive rendition of 'The Cremation of Sam McGee'.

We listened intently from our bunks, chatting, eating, laughing and discussing tomorrow's impending weather. According to other trail users and those who had been using their GPS devices to get weather updates, there were rumours of snow and 50 mph winds up on Martha Saddle, the pass just along the river which separated us from the Ahuriri valley. Ron used his own GPS to contact his cousin Donna, who relayed the latest weather report for us from her home in Canada. 'Snow, wind and more wind. Best hunker down,' was her reply.

The following day was a write-off. We remained in our sleeping bags as sideways rain collided with the hut, and wind shook the walls. The only one who made a move to leave was, of course, Kirstine. Heading south, she didn't have a high pass to negotiate, but she did have an increasingly swollen river to cross several times. Thirty minutes after her alarm had gone off she was packed and ready to leave. She stood up, straightened her makeshift bin-liner rain protection, and announced in a suitably militant fashion that she was off.

A younger me would have been frustrated with such a weather hold-up, but older me had grown accustomed to enjoy how the adventure unfolded, and so I embraced a day of enforced rest.

'How do you fancy drinking that?!' said Finny, plonking a bottle of grey sludge down on the makeshift kitchen worktop.

'Oh, crap. We might need to start worrying about a water source,' sighed Fiona.

The torrential rain had turned our clear flowing river into a moving mud bath. Peter and Finny went out in search of a new water source, and returned triumphant an hour later. They'd found a side stream that still ran clear, and we had just enough to last us until tomorrow. I felt lazy, not getting out of my bunk to help, but it seemed that every time I made an intention to move, I'd just fall back to sleep. I must have taken at least three naps throughout the morning, and on one occasion I even fell asleep mid-conversation with Coach Ron. I was quite clearly knackered.

By 3 p.m. on day two in the hut, the rain had relented and the wind seemed to have dropped enough to make running a possibility, down here at least – I wasn't sure what it was doing up at Martha Saddle. Anxious about my schedule and about the days and miles that lay ahead, I decided to run a few hundred metres up the trail to see how it felt. It was one of those exercises that was entirely pointless, but I felt I needed something, anything, to help me make a decision. Funnily enough, I didn't learn or experience much in my 300 metre test run. The wind was strong, it was snowing lightly and my legs hurt, but really there was no reason not to leave. I could push on. Returning to the hut, I began packing up a bag to leave. I resolved to keep moving. Just because others were taking a day off, I shouldn't do that too. Coach Ron came in. 'Say Anna, you're not thinking about heading out there, are you? It's blowin' a gale, and that force sure is strong up on those tops. I wouldn't be going anywhere if I were you.'

Ron had sown a seed of doubt. I knew him to be a cautious fella, and protective of me at the best of times, but he was a seasoned outdoorsman.

'Oh, Ron, with your seeds of doubt,' I murmured, placing my bag at the end of my bunk and watching the group mill around.

Finny was deep in conversation with Andrew. Fiona was looking more relaxed than I'd seen her yet, lying in bed reading her book. Peter was outside, taking photos of the tumbling river, and Coach Ron was back practising his songs on the porch. There was something about Ron's presence that calmed me. When he was in the hut or on the trail you couldn't help but feel like everything was going to be okay.

What the hell was I doing? Why would I leave a hut full of people whose company made me stupidly happy, to go and sleep 12 kilometres down the trail on my own, in my tent? I came to my senses, unpacked my stuff and crawled back into my sleeping bag – much to the delight and cheers of the rest of the gang.

An hour later Ron came in. 'Well. That's me. I'm headed out.'

'Ron! You told me it was too dangerous out there.'

'For you maybe. You're running. Wind's gonna get ya when you're running. But not for a slow coach like me. I'm a tortoise, remember,' he winked. 'I'll be safe.'

I had to laugh, and the truth was it didn't matter. The real reason I'd unpacked my bag was because I'd realised that the friendships I'd solidify by staying were far more important than the kilometres I could make by going. And, in honesty, I needed the rest. My legs were just about the wrong side of screwed, and my left calf was starting to give me real cause for concern.

The trail up to Martha Saddle was well-graded, like a

bulldozer track as it wound its way in switchbacks up to the pass at 1,680 metres. I enjoyed the sick monotony of the climb and the sting in my lungs as I sucked in cold air. Reaching the top I could see the trail snake down the other side. It was snowing now, and soft flakes fell on my eyelashes and nose as they drifted haphazardly to the ground. I stopped to pull on an extra layer before beginning the descent. For some reason, I felt compelled to sing, and so as I ran wildly downwards I began working my way through The Commitments album – music I'd been raised up with. 'Mustang Sally' was followed closely by 'Chain, Chain, Chain' before I finished up at the bottom of the pass with 'Take Me to the River', which seemed rather fitting as I began to run alongside the Ahuriri River.

The Ahuriri river crossing had been on my mind for a few weeks. The trail advice was that this was a tricky crossing, and if the river levels were up it was best to wait it out, or find a way around.

During a consultation session with Coach Ron the day before, we'd found a plan B, which was to run an extra 12 km out of the way to the nearest bridge. Most didn't favour this option, as 12 km could add on a good few hours to a tramper's day, but as a runner those kilometres wouldn't cost me too much time.

I didn't feel the need to go and cross a swollen post-storm river by myself. Besides, I loved the extra miles – the grassy 4x4 track was easy-going underfoot and a nice change from the past few days. I could run freely, and let my thoughts run free too. Setting out on this run I thought it'd be the monotony that would be my undoing, but I now realised that it was the monotony I craved – for only then could I transcend and think about anything and everything. About my family, about my past, about books I wanted to write, and about places I wanted to live and to travel. About friends, about ex-boyfriends and every now and then about Jamie.

Approaching the river road where the bridge was, I spotted a silver car at the top of the hill. It seemed to be moving very slowly, and I had an odd feeling that it was looking at me. I mean, I couldn't see anyone in the car, but I just had this strange sensation that whoever its occupants were, they were watching me. The car disappeared down a dip in the road and I ran on.

I ran up the final rise, and there, where the trail met the road, were two people sat on the fence, and behind them was parked a silver car. They leapt to their feet and began shouting and waving.

'Anna! Woo! Yeah, Anna, go!'

I spotted some ginger hair on the guy and dark hair on the girl. Was it? It was! Duncan and Michelle from Wanaka! What were they doing here? I ran towards them, beaming, and they leapt off the fence and ran towards me. A smile overtook my face that my cheeks could barely contain. I couldn't believe they'd come all this way to find me. They threw their arms wide open and I gave each of them a long hug.

'We saw that your tracker had stopped moving,' Michelle panted between hugs. 'And we figured that you might be cold, and running low on food.'

They weren't wrong about the food. It was two days to Lake Ohau from here and the hold up in the hut meant that I only really had one day's worth of food left. I wasn't cold, but still I accepted their offer to clamber into their car. They climbed in too, and Duncan turned around from the driver's seat.

'Here. We brought you some coffee, and some chicken sandwiches,' he said.

'And there's some snacks in the bag. And some chocolate. We know how much you love chocolate,' Michelle added.

It turned out that they'd been watching the weather and my tracker, and were getting concerned about my supplies, but they'd also come down to tell me not to cross the river. They'd run out of signal to follow the tracker, but had bumped into Coach Ron an hour earlier near the river who'd told them I was planning to take the bridge around, so they'd come this way to find me.

A couple of hours later, after we'd exchanged all our gossip and had a good catch-up, Duncan and Michelle stuffed a final few packets of sweets into my hands, plus a big bar of chocolate and waved me back off on the trail. Running across the Ahuriri bridge, I knew I only had 6 kilometres to run to a camp spot for the night. Contrary to how I was feeling before they'd intersected me, my feet felt lighter than ever. I skipped the final few kilometres and found a perfect spot at 5 p.m. I pitched up in a patch of forest, on a bed of spongy pine needles, gathered some water from a nearby stream, cooked up some noodles, pulled on all my thermal layers and trusty beanie, and turned in for the night. The final thought that passed through my mind before I nodded off was one of contentment. That morning I'd left Pakituhi Hut certain that the day was going to be a bit crap. It just went to show, you never know what's waiting just around the corner.

I burst out of the tree line and whooped in delight. Straight ahead of me was an orange pole marker. I'd been concerned about finding the trail again after a night in the trees, but there it was, clear as day. I turned to the north and spotted Mount Ohau in the distance, coated with a layer of snow. I let out another whoop of delight at such a majestic sight. Following the poles with my eyes southwards, down the valley and onto the rolling hills from the day before, I was just thinking about how glad I was that I hadn't tried to cross the Ahuriri River, when I spotted two very familiar figures.

'Hey!' I yelled as I waved.

'Fancy seeing you here,' Finny quipped in his usual dry tone.

'Lovely weather, eh?' I retorted.

It turned out that my favourite Kiwi duo and I had camped just a few hundred metres apart that night without knowing it. I walked with them for 10 minutes chatting and laughing, before moving up to my usual running pace and bounding off.

It snowed lightly for the rest of the morning, transforming the scenery along the Ahuriri River to include several snow-capped peaks. I took comfort in knowing that the rest of the trail gang were never too far away, and passed them at intervals, each time stopping for a chat. First Peter and Andrew, and then Ron.

'Look at that, Coach Ron. Doesn't that mountain look like someone's come along with a big sieve and coated it with icing sugar? Sort of like a pointy Victoria sponge?'

Ron chuckled. 'Icing sugar, eh?'

Shortly after I left Ron, the terrain got tricky. Long grass combined with marshy and uneven ground made progress slow. The orange pole markers didn't seem to follow a linear path and so forced me to pay attention to spot the next one. I was actually relishing the challenge of finding the next pole but there was one thing that was really beginning to irk me, and it was a particular plant. The pokies, or Spaniard grass, really had it in for me. Their wide-leaf blades, with a thorn at the end of each one, took every opportunity going to jab me as I brushed past them. They frequently drew blood and, on one occasion, I slipped at the side of a stream and one drove itself a good 3 centimetres under my skin. I swore at them repeatedly, and shouted often. 'You, pokey thing, are completely unnecessary. You're not going to make any friends by going around poking people, are you?!'

I had just crested a saddle and was momentarily distracted from my ranting by a new addition to the horizon. There, right ahead and far below, was a bright blue lake set against a grey mountain. That was Lake Ohau and, boy, was it a sight for sore eyes!

8

The Bushwhacker Boys

I made my way across the car park and towards the front door of the Lake Ohau Lodge. Walking down a short corridor I found myself at the reception desk, where a young girl was busying herself at the computer.

'Hi, Hi there,' I said. 'I'm, umm, here to see Mike. My name's Anna.'

'Oh yes!' she said excitedly. 'We've been expecting you!'

I'd been put in touch with Mike via Jon Beardmore. Jon had taken one of my five pairs of trainers off my hands, and promised to find me somewhere to put them in the Lake Ohau region. I figured I'd need a change of shoes at the lake and it just so happened that his uncle knew Mike and Louise, who owned the Lake Ohau Lodge. I'd planned to take a day off at the lodge, and run out in a fresh pair of trainers.

The girl at reception radioed for Mike, and within 3 minutes he had appeared. He opened his arms and I went straight in for the hug. Mike was one of those people who immediately made you feel at ease. He was relaxed, straightforward and had a fatherly tone to his character. I'd managed to get some phone signal on the previous day, to let him know that I was running a day behind, and even over the phone he seemed lovely. His long silver hair was pulled back into a low ponytail, and his blue eyes shone and sparkled as he smiled.

There was a real charm about the Lake Ohau Lodge; it was simply beautiful. I don't mean the kind of immaculate, perfectly symmetrical kind of beautiful. No, this was truly beautiful. The lodge had real character; it felt more like a large family home than a hotel. After introducing me to his wife, Louise, Mike produced a package. 'This is for you, I believe.'

'Ah, awesome! Thank you.'

Inside the yellow and white postage bag were a new pair of trainers. I'd run 587.5 km in Bonnie and Clyde over the course of 22 days, along beaches and through forests. They'd done a grand job, but their soles were worn to a pulp, the rims were scuffed and there were small holes starting to appear over the toe section. The remaining 2,413 km would be done in one of four other pairs of shoes. I slid the new pair of red trainers out of the bag and marvelled at their freshness. This pair was to be named The Bushwhacker Boys in homage to the 90s WWE wrestling duo. The shiny new Bushwhacker Boys were in direct contrast to my body, which was distinctly old, battered and bruised.

Mike interrupted my train of thought. 'Righto, Anna. Dinner's at seven. You go and get scrubbed up and relax. I've put you on a table with some other guests. We'll see you then.'

Dinner was an old-school affair, where the general format

was to sit at tables with people you've never met before. During my two nights at the lodge, I had the pleasure of meeting a British couple with a holiday home in Martinborough – he was a retired ear, nose and throat surgeon and she was a mother who'd set up a business selling wood burners in later life and rediscovered her joie de vivre. Then there was the Australian lady, who was writing a book about the ten years she'd spent as an aerobics instructor in Hong Kong, and Karl and his young son, Kyan, who'd come to the lodge for a spot of business and to go fishing together. Everyone else seemed to be from the nearby east coast town of Timaru, although I'm yet to work out why.

That night over dinner, Mike and Louise took some time off from working to join our table. Mike came in with a bottle of wine, and it was gleefully passed around the table as he recounted tales of years gone by in this special spot. I learnt that the lodge had a rich and turbulent history. In the years' preceding Mike and Louise's ownership, the lodge and the attached ski field had been to the brink of closure and back again. Now it was booming. A hive of activity as mountain bikers, hikers and passing tourists stopped in. Lunch, a beer, an overnight rest – the story was always the same: 'Oh, we love it here. We've been coming for years.'

In the morning I woke enveloped in crisp linen sheets and marshmallowy soft pillows, looking out through floor-to-ceiling sliding doors at Mount Cook in the distance. On the second morning, I woke up feeling one million times better than I had on arriving. My left calf was still giving me some jip, but, as a whole, I was a new woman. I propped myself upright and stared at the vista. Was this my life? Yes, this was definitely my life. I was here, in my marshmallows, looking out on Mount Cook. Holy moly. I lay there for a good 30 minutes, just staring. If only all mornings could begin this way.

I sauntered down to breakfast, popped my head round the door to say hello to Mike and Louise, located the familiar faces of Kyan and Karl, and proceeded to fill my face with an assortment of cereal-based goods.

After breakfast I called my parents and gave them a visual tour of the lodge's surroundings. They oohed and aahed at the mountain landscape and the turquoise volcanic lake just below the lodge. I always delighted in my parents' faces squished on a screen – Mum usually doing things like accidentally muting me and putting me on hold. Seeing them brought on a small wave of homesickness, but this was the most confident conversation I'd had with them yet. And by that, I mean that I felt the most confident about what I was doing, that embarking on this run was a good idea. I could now talk to my folks about huts and river crossings and mountains – something I'd never been able to do before, and that made me just a little bit proud.

I spent the rest of the morning faffing and delaying my departure as long as possible. I had 34 km to run to the small town of Twizel that day, but I knew it was along a cycle trail so the going would be more straightforward than many of the previous sections.

I was sad to be leaving the lodge, and a little tearful as I hugged Mike and Louise goodbye. At midday, I finally left. The first 5 kilometres were the most horrendous struggle and took me almost 45 minutes, as I shuffled along in the now un-bearable heat. I realised that taking just one day off meant that my ankles had swelled up in some kind of stress response, but they hadn't yet had time to reduce back down as they had done during my break in Queenstown. My left shin was in ag-ony as it misfired every time I tried to move it forward.

An hour or so later I passed a small clearing on the shores of Lake Ohau, and decided it was too tempting a spot to pass up. It was now mid-afternoon, but I resolved that it would stay light long into the evening and I would rather do as much as I could to enjoy the day than rush things.

Besides, there really wasn't much difference between snail's pace and sloth pace anyway. I flopped, lifeless, under the shade of a willow tree, and pulled out the packed lunch that Mike and Louise had made me. I then stripped off to my under-wear and took a dunk in the glacial waters. It was windy, and freezing, and in the shadow of the adjacent mountain, looked simply divine. Extracting myself from the water, I checked the map. 'I can't have too far now,' I thought, closely followed by: 'yikes! Still 18 km to go and it was getting hotter.'

The temperature out on the plains between Lake Ohau and Lake Ruataniwha showed no mercy as it continued to rise.

Completely out of water and with a mouth that tasted like a dead budgie had taken up residence in it, I slumped in the shade of a tree and took a short video for my Facebook followers. Only in watching it back did I see how delirious and clearly dehydrated I was. I lay there for 40 minutes in what I later found out to be 38°C heat.

The wide, open sand-coloured Canterbury plains stretched on for an eternity. Aside from the deep turquoise of Lake Ruataniwha, everything seemed to take on a yellowish tinge. I could see the heat rising from the ground, making the gravel shimmer in the distance. I worked out that I was now 3 kilometres from Twizel – today's finish line destination – and by my reckoning that was about 3 km too far at this point. My mouth was dry, my head throbbed on account of my own self-inflicted dehydration and all I could think about was ten steps at a time. Three boys appeared on the road up ahead. They had all the tell-tale signs about them of Te Araroa Thru-hikers (those completing the full trail) – large backpacks, hiking poles, shaggy beards, and unkempt and unruly hair. They must be southbounders and how nice that they had one another for company, I thought as they approached.

Before long I was chatting away with Randy, Jack and Simon – three American friends who'd decided to spend the US winter hiking the trail. After we'd exchanged niceties, I looked down at their hands, laden with plastic bags brimming with food – presumably purchased on the way out of Twizel. I couldn't take my eyes off the vegetables. Even though I'd had my fill of fresh food at the lodge, days without so much as a whiff of my five-a-day meant that I constantly craved more. 'You've got lettuce…' I said, wistfully eyeing one particular bag in Randy's hand, and without any real awareness as to what was coming out of my mouth. Lettuce was hardly a conversation topic after all.

'Ah, yeah. Do you want it?' Randy asked, moving to take the lettuce out of its plastic and deliver it to me. Was this guy for real?

'You're offering me your lettuce?' I gawped. 'You're on your way for days in the bush, and I'm going into town, and you're… offering me your lettuce?!'

I swallowed a lump in my throat and began to choke up. Tears welled in the corners of my eyes. I just couldn't believe the kindness of these boys. Fresh food in the bush was a premium. Of course it wasn't that big a deal, but I was rather exhausted and even more emotional, and so the offering of lettuce was like being offered an organ. I declined but thanked them profusely, and hugged them all to within an inch of their lives. With just one kilometre to go to the centre of town, I stopped at a small restaurant, where I proceeded to spend half of my day's budget on a very posh-looking version of fizzy orange, a plate of gourmet ice cream, sprinkled with rose petals, and a bottle of water so expensive I was sure it would be laced with diamonds, but I just didn't care. I found the campground and, though it was only 7 p.m. and the food had revived me somewhat, I fell straight into my tent and a blissful sleep.

Twizel was quite possibly one of the oddest towns I had ever passed through. It is one of New Zealand's hydro towns, and was built in the 1960s to offer housing to workers involved in the Upper Waitaki Power Scheme. The population of the town trebles in the summer months as Kiwis flock to their holiday homes there. Despite the summer rush, it has an eerie kind of feel. A large sports field separates the town in the centre, and there's a silence about the central marketplace which gives off a horror-film vibe.

In the morning I found myself having breakfast at a quaint little Twizel cafe with Ron. He'd also rolled into town the night before, and it was lovely to see him again. We chatted and laughed about previous events, as well as our experiences of navigating through the Spaniard grass on the way to Lake Ohau Lodge. It turns out that Ron had taken as much exception to the aggressive nature of the plants as I had.

'You know Anna, every time I'm going down those tricky steep sections, I can't help but feel that it's a wonder that you haven't tripped n' hurt yourself yet.'

'Ron! Don't jinx things, please!' I protested.

'No, well, you know… I mean, just go careful now, won't you? I'll always be worryin' about you havin' taken a fall somewhere.'

Ron and I chatted back and forth for an hour or so longer

than I planned. I had 30 km to run that day, and a late start wasn't the best idea. But there was something very familiar about Ron, and it's always hard to leave an old friend.

At midday Ron strolled with me to the edge of town and waved me off as I trotted back to the trail. I ran away feeling refreshed, something which always seemed to be an after-effect of chatting with him. It didn't even cross my mind that I might never see him again – we had bumped into each other regularly enough up until this point, so it didn't occur to me to be sad about parting ways again. But as it turned out, that was the last time I would see Coach Ron on the Te Araroa.

I opened my eyes and peeked out of the tent, nestled on the shores of Lake Pukaki. I had taken shelter in a lightly covered area of bush and it had been an odd night. At 3 a.m. I'd been woken by a possum. It had somehow made it under the outside tarp of my tent, and was now pawing at the bag of sweets, which I'd left next to my head. Thankfully between us was the inner mesh from my tent, plus of course a very stoic Kiwi Kev, who was clearly keeping watch. I informed the possum (whom I had named Patrick by this point) that he was a cheeky bugger and shooed him on his way. I'd stopped a little earlier than intended the previous day, so had 43 km to run to make it to Lake Tekapo. I left at 11 a.m. and absolutely flew for the first 30 km of the day. It was a scorcher but the gravel road made for swift progress – I was on fire. On fire and assisted by the entire Avicii album, which I blasted through my headphones all day.

I stopped a few times to marvel at the sheer beauty of Lake Pukaki on my left. At the top of the Braemar Road turn-off, I sat on its shore, eating an energy bar and revelling in the sweet sound of silence. It was then and there I decided that this would enter into the list of one of my favourite places in the world. The bright turquoise waters lapped at my feet and led directly to the mountain range to the north-west, where a snow-capped Mount Cook kept watch. It was so very silent, and that made me feel like it belonged to me. For those 10 minutes, this was my lake.

9

A Hut Full of Hunters

Tekapo was a unique place. The natural beauty of the turquoise lake, the quaint patches of manicured grass and the tiny lakeside church all added to its charm. In fact, the only thing I didn't like about Tekapo were the tourists. Swarms of tour-operated buses would pull in each morning and flood the town centre, which I found to be quite ill-at-odds with the area's natural calm and beauty.

Tekapo had an exciting history too. In between glugs of strong coffee and mouthfuls of steaming omelette at a local cafe, I read that in 1855 Scottish shepherd-turned-sheep-stealer James Mackenzie had happened upon the basin along with his faithful dog, Friday. Together they stole a flock of sheep from the local land, herding them inland to avoid being caught. Eventually the law caught up with Mackenzie and captured him, but his faithful canine sidekick remained at large.

Friday was a clever pooch and allegedly continued the work of his master alone, driving the flock of sheep inland – something which prevented the authorities from recapturing the sheep. It may seem odd that you would honour a dog who would aid a sheep-stealer, but local farmers later commissioned a bronze memorial to Friday, and in fact to all working collie dogs, which now stands on the shores of Lake Tekapo near the ironically named Church of the Good Shepherd. The setting for the church is beautiful. Perched on the shore of the lake it stands alone, modest, simple and unassuming in design. Having got my fix of history from Friday's tale, I finished my omelette, gulped back the last of the coffee and stood up, ready to get back on the trail.

The following day, I was inching ever closer to the highest point of the entire Te Araroa Trail. I climbed upwards towards Stag Saddle at 1,925 metres high, which, according to my guidebook, 'offers spectacular views over Lake Tekapo and beyond'. In front of me, there was nothing but a thick blanket of fog. I couldn't see further than the end of my nose. Worse than that, I couldn't even see the lay of the land to work out which direction I was supposed to be headed in. I pulled out my phone and loaded up the GPS app. It was temperamental at the best of times, but I prayed it'd work on this occasion. I stared at the screen for 5 seconds during which it remained blank. I closed the app and loaded it back up. Still nothing. I then tried turning my phone off and back on again, which didn't work either. 'Great,' I sighed. Looking around once again at the fog, I wondered which direction I should take a stab at, in the hope that I might stumble across a marker pole.

At the top of Stag Saddle, at this highest and reportedly (although I couldn't see it) most 'stunning' point of the trail, my phone started to buzz. I'd wandered into a small pocket of phone signal. There was message from Coach Ron. 'Poles aren't very frequent, or non-existent to the saddle. Just keep upping and you'll find the right spot.' I turned the phone on to aeroplane mode again to save battery, and began to feel a little frightened. Every move I made forward in search of a marker pole, my backwards path was encased in cloud, so I couldn't retrace my steps even if I wanted to. The fog suffocated me. It sat on my lungs and my brain, clouding any clear train of thought, other than: 'Where the heck do I go from here?' I felt ridiculous. Well, actually, in hindsight I felt ridiculous. In reality, at the time, my fear was real and justified. I was disorientated. I gained a small understanding of how people got lost in blizzards. When everything is a wall of grey and cloud, any direction could be the right direction.

My phone beeped to indicate that the GPS app had kicked back into life. A little pink triangle appeared on the screen, blinking.

'YES!' I whooped.

As it happened, I'd been stumbling off at 90 degrees in the wrong direction – thank goodness for the GPS. I corrected my path as I continued to climb, negotiating over small boulders and loose rocks. After 5 minutes a bright orange pole came into view.

'There you are, you little bugger!' I shouted at it. I always seemed to attach emotions to these poles. Some days they were for me, and others they were against me. I often thought of them as naughty school children who like to play hide and seek, just to wind us trail users up.

Scrambling over the top of the saddle, I at last dropped below the cloud and could see again. The sense of relief was palpable and I breathed a huge sigh. I could now well understand how people might panic in fogs, and how sheer panic wasn't conducive to getting yourself to safety.

I flopped onto the floor outside Stone Hut and looked up at Finny and Fi, who were already there, chilling outside. I had seen them briefly in Lake Tekapo a few days earlier. They had pushed on when I took a rest day and, as ever, I was pleased to see them. Fi got all motherly and placed a jacket around my legs. It felt nice to be mothered.

On the day I'd been climbing the Breast Hill track from Lake Hāwea, I'd made a new rule. If the Department of Conservation (DoC) time on the sign said that I couldn't make it before darkness set in, I wouldn't go on. I was finding the trail increasingly unpredictable. Sometimes I could halve the DoC time, and other times I was just inside it. It depended on a whole heap of things, and so I decided to play it safe from there on in.

'You going on?' asked Fi, pulling her jacket a little tighter around my legs.

'I'm not sure,' I replied, now snuggled next to her and feeling all rather safe and calm.

'Did you hear about Coach Ron?' Finny asked.

'No, what about him?'

'You know Stag Saddle?'

'Yes! I remember it well, I couldn't see a bloody thing up there!'

'Well, clearly Ron couldn't either. He took a wrong turn, went over the wrong saddle and ended up in a completely different valley!'

'No way!' I laughed, thinking about his message of advice, which had clearly been sent before he realised his mistake. 'Is he okay?'

'Yeah, fine, stumbled into this hut at 9 p.m. rather flustered and apparently recounted the tale to everyone!'

'Oh, Coach!' I muttered. 'You couldn't make it up!'

By now five hunters had gathered outside the stone-clad Royal Hut, with one more up the hill. The older pair looked rather exhausted. They'd tried to drive in a 4x4 all the way up to the hut, but the trail had become too narrow so they had to abandon the 4x4 and bring everything in on foot. Royal Hut was only an eight-bunk hut and that meant that if I stayed here tonight, someone was going without a bed. Etiquette dictated that it's first come first served in these huts, but I wasn't entirely sure if my sprint past the two oldest hunters in the last 100 metres was enough to warrant me a bunk for the night.

'Say – what's the trail like between here and Crooked Spur Hut?' Finny asked the hunters.

They looked at one other. They didn't seem to have done the trail for a while. 'Ask Ethan – he works at Mesopotamia station. This is his backyard, he'll know. Hey! Ethan! Come here!'

Down the hill came a tall boy bounding at breakneck speed. 'Yup?' said Ethan, skidding to a halt just out the front of the hut.

'This lady wants to know what the trail is like from here to Crooked Spur.'

'Ah, piece-a-cake,' he replied.

'She's running it,' the hunter elaborated.

'You're running? Even more piece-a-cake. You'll be there in 90 minutes, max.'

I looked at Ethan again, more carefully this time. He looked like something fresh out of *Castaway*. His hair turned a golden-sandy colour from the sun, his veins ran close to the surface of his arms and his legs were like a racehorse's. There wasn't a scrap of muscle wasted, nor an inch of fat on him. Ethan clearly belonged in the hills.

I looked at the floor and bit my lip. If I was going, I needed to go now.

The oldest hunter broke the silence. 'Well… Anna. If you do stay, I mean, we've got a load of extra food. And we ain't carrying it back out again! No bloody chance!'

That was it. I had an offer of food and the chance to hang

out with Finny and Fi again. Plus, I was sure that Peter and Andrew would turn up soon. We were overbooked for the night at Royal Hut, and so a discussion ensued as to how we might fit everyone in. It seemed to be the general consensus that the two young boys would bunk in together, or sleep on the floor. 'It'll be good for them,' their dad said. 'Character building stuff, y' know.'

I settled into my sleeping bag and began to read, as the boys discussed the afternoon's hunting of tahr – goat-like creatures that lived in these mountains.

'I shot one right through the throat!' exclaimed one of the young lads in glee.

I felt a bit sick.

'Yeah, it was only a tiny little thing, but it exploded everywhere. The ones around it got covered in blood.'

I gulped hard. I think my noodles may have just come back up. Most of the boys went outside to drink the beer they'd lugged in, so as not to disturb us. Ethan didn't drink, and so climbed into his sleeping bag in the bunk below mine, and chatted with me, Finny and Fi.

Being entirely honest, I fancied Ethan. He couldn't have been more than 22, and yet I, a 30-year-old woman, fancied the pants off him. Did this make me a sick individual? He had an innocent and genuinely curious nature, which you couldn't help but trust. He'd been on an Outward Bound course as a kid, and talked openly about the struggles and how it'd changed his life. I loved his lack of regard for airs and graces, and the fact that he knew nothing about a life which revolved around desks, computers and offices. All he knew was the land. He knew about animals and farming and history. He was a breath of fresh air, and I couldn't help but be intrigued by him, by his sandy hair and his racehorse legs. The chatter between the four of us slowly died down and I was vaguely aware of the laughter and cheers coming from the lads outside as I drifted off into a deep sleep. Again, choosing the company of friends new and old over making progress on the trail had been a choice well made.

It was 9 a.m. and I was running late. Having been woken up by a loud hunter's fart, and the inevitable whiff that followed, I'd said my goodbyes a few hours earlier to the gang at Royal Hut. I had climbed out of the river valley and was now in the one adjacent to it. I was sad to leave Finny and Fi, as I knew that they were due to take some time off the trail soon for a family funeral, but I also knew that I'd run into them again before the trip was out. I just had that feeling. We had bonded and they had become my family on the trail.

I'd arranged to meet Kev and his mate Syd at Crooked Spur Hut, just at the edge of the Two Thumb range. I'd never met Kev before. But he was a friend of a friend (of a friend) and had emailed the previous week to offer me a ride around a rather big, scary river called the Rangitata. Having implemented the new DoC-time-before-dark-time rule, and found the lure of a night with a hut full of hunters too much to resist, I was half a day overdue in my arrival. With no means of communicating with Kev, I'd decided to leave as early as possible that morning to make the rendezvous point. I wasn't too worried. Having spoken to Kev briefly before leaving Tekapo, he seemed like the most laid-back bloke in the southern hemisphere, and I figured he'd know I'd appear sooner or later.

It had been a tough morning's run and my left calf was getting really painful now. I'd been running for 2 hours and was now caught up at the bottom of a steep slope, having a WWE-style wrestling showdown with some waist-high tussock. The Bushwhacker Boys (my trainers) weren't helping me out as much as they should, given their wrestling credentials, and the tussock had just about pinned me to the ground. I was on the third count when I heard a whistle. I broke free from the tussle and looked upwards at the scree slope ahead of me.

There, silhouetted against a bright blue sky and ever so slightly obscured by wisps of encroaching cloud, were the outlines of two humans, one of whom was waving.

'Hi Kev!' I shouted at the top of my lungs, '…I'll, err, be there in a minute,' which seemed like an obvious continuation, but something I should mention, just to be polite.

In fact, I lied. It was a good 5 minutes before I'd scrambled my way to the top. Conscious that I didn't want to be perceived as slow, I attacked the climb. Between gasps for air and an effort to relocate my lost lungs, I made the top and reached out a hand.

'Hi... I'm... Anna,' I gasped.

When referring to either the Rangitata (a big river) or the Rakaia (an even bigger river) I often got them mixed up. I'll assert that I wasn't alone in this, and many other trail users also did the same. Sometimes I even went for a hybrid river name: the Rakigitata (sounds like an Indian side dish) or the Rangania (sounds like an STI). The fact is there are so many places, obstacles and logistical things to be dealing with that my brain can only really function a week or two ahead, which is why when southbounders began helpfully telling me about places in the North Island, I could see their lips moving, but all I heard was lift music.

Anyway, I digress. These rivers. They are big and braided and gnarly. And when I say 'braided' I mean that they sprawl into a multitude of channels, of different depths and speeds, so really you're crossing seven rivers. According to reports on-line and hearsay on the trail, the Rangitata, for example, will take you around 2 hours to cross, and sometimes you might get halfway and realise that you can't continue on, leaving no choice but to turn back.

Introductions made, along with a loose plan of action for the day, I bounded down to the Crooked Spur Hut on the other side of the scree slope, with Kev and Syd following close behind. Despite my efforts to run as fast as possible down the slope, I was a little embarrassed when the lads arrived at the hut, just a few minutes behind me.

'I can see why you don't need poles!' chirped Kev, commenting on and doing an impression of my running style. 'Running with your arms out like that – you're like an aeroplane that's about to take off!'

Over the course of the past month I seemed to have adapted my running style. Bounding was no longer an option, so instead I had transitioned to a low shuffle, placing my arms wide in anticipation of the many falls and tumbles I was bound to have each day. Any upwards movement was movement wasted with a pack on, and, as such, I now ran like an ape. What was worse was that down steep slopes, on slippery terrain, I was only a few minutes faster than walkers. I had a word with my slightly bruised ego, and consoled myself with the thought that these boys looked like they had been in the mountains since they were nippers. They were seasoned trampers. It was going to take a fair amount for a girl from south-west London to impress them.

'You fancy something to eat?' asked Syd.

I always fancied something to eat, and the fact that Kev and Syd had brought in supplies was a major bonus. I'd felt rude eating too much of the hunters' food, and so hadn't eaten any of it for dinner, but had stuffed a piece of white bread with cold venison stew into my mouth as I ran out the door that morning. It was now 3 hours on and I was starving. All I had left were a few crackers and some wine gums, so I gleefully munched on the apples, apricots, scroggin (the Kiwi name for a bag of nuts, chocolate and fruit) and oysters from a can. I never knew until that point that you could get oysters in a can. They weren't nearly as revolting as I'd expected, and, in some kind of sick, slimy, salty way, they were rather enjoyable.

As it turns out, both Kev and Syd were rather accomplished outdoorsmen. Syd casually regaled the time he'd climbed Denali in North America, and it became quickly apparent that he was somewhat of a backcountry dude. Kev was similarly dude-esque, although admittedly he wasn't quite in Syd's league when it came to alpine climbing.

'What's the most memorable climb you've done?' I asked Syd.

Turns out it was a night he'd spent stranded on the Mount Cook Grand Traverse – an icy ridge line that connects the low, middle and high peaks of the mountain. Syd told me that one of the group had broken a crampon and so the going was slower than they'd expected. They'd had to spend a night on the ridge and continue the traverse at first light.

'Yeah, I guess it was pretty hard to sleep with a sheer drop to either side, but I slept a bit. At least I brought my sleeping bag with me, just in case. The others had nothing,' he told me.

As we followed the trail down to the river, the landscape opened out to offer a 180-degree view of the basin and its surrounds. The scenery was incredible. The riverbed was enormous, I could see that much, and it was by far the biggest river

I'd ever seen. Snow-capped mountains were dotted across the horizon and one set of mountains to the left was almost blue in colour.

'So, what do you want to do about this river?' Kev asked. 'I can just run you into town for supplies and drop you off on the trail the other side, or you can come back and spend the night with me and my wife at our home in Geraldine, and I can run you back in the morning? It's your call.'

I was due in Christchurch in three days' time to begin giving a week of school talks about the run. The original plan had been to run the extra 400 km round trip into Christchurch and back to the trail, but I was behind schedule, way behind schedule. Having spoken to those who lived on the Canterbury plains, they told me that running via the roads to Christchurch was a terrible idea due to the heat and lack of civilisation.

As we rumbled off down the long gravel road in Kev's car, I bit my lip and considered the options. My aim was to run an unbroken line through the country, and so I resolved that I would take a week off the trail. I'd go to Christchurch to do the school talks I had booked in, and have a few days of rest there too. Then I would find a way to get back to the Rangitata River and carry on. Truth be told, my body was a bit of a wreck. The pain in my left calf was becoming unbearable and I really needed to do something to get it back on track.

I thought for a moment about what people would think of my decision to leave the trail for a week. I decided that I didn't care. This was my journey after all. I could spend my whole life chasing the approval of others and I know that I'd not make it to my grave happier than if I simply sought my own approval in how I spent my days. Christchurch it was then.

10

Earthquakes and Booty Shakes

Four years on and the wounds of a city ravaged by multiple earthquakes were still open for all to see. I hadn't been sure how I'd find Christchurch, but I found my trip there to be a true blessing. To get a first-hand look at the lives of individuals being rebuilt from the rubble was possibly one of the most humbling experiences I'd had.

When the September 2010 quake hit, it was 4 a.m. From those I spoke to, most reported that they didn't even make it out of bed. Paul and Sheila, my hosts for most of the week, told me that they'd just turned to one another, held on tight and braced for the end. To hear them describe that scene put a significant lump in my throat. I cannot begin to imagine what that feels like. It made me want to call all of my loved ones then and there.

The more devastating February 2011 quake created the biggest peak ground acceleration recorded anywhere in history – a vertical movement with a force of up to 2.2 times more than gravity. It was this acceleration and the close vicinity to the city that led to 185 people losing their lives, over 100,000 homes being damaged and a further 10,000 being completely destroyed.

Everyone in Christchurch has a story to tell. One woman was 2 minutes away from entering a shop, where everyone inside was killed. Another man wasn't sitting in his chair by the window as usual that day – a window that broke into large jagged shards and spread across the living room. I heard the tale of another young lady who'd run across town, as far and as fast as she could, in sheer panic and a bid to escape the worst of the aftershocks in the central business district.

But from great tragedy, hope springs eternal, and the tales from Christchurch are no different. Art, music and funky pop-up malls now dominate the city. I visited the cardboard cathedral, a life-size church made in part quite literally out of cardboard (albeit reinforced in many places) – erected as a temporary replacement for the city's original gothic stone building. Each year on the anniversary of the quake, residents place a traffic cone outside in the street, with an agapanthus in the top. These cones aren't just a memorial to those who lost their lives, they are a nod to the future. A reminder that amongst them live a community of people with the strength and spirit to prosper, when all the physical elements of their world have fallen into disrepair.

One week later, I found myself bouncing around on the front seat of Hamish Woodhouse's truck, along the gravel road to Mount Potts. I was feeling like a new woman after my time off in Christchurch – mentally refreshed from all of the school talks delivered, and physically rested, thanks to Paul and Sheila's hospitality.

When it was time to leave Christchurch, my friend Hollie drove me out to her family home, back near the Rangitata River where I had left the trail the previous week. I'd met native Kiwi Hollie during a stint she'd spent living in London. She was an ultrarunner and adventure sports nut who was in training for the world's toughest footrace, the Marathon des Sables, and was, by all accounts, as mad as I was. When I told Hollie that my backpack buckle had broken – a defect I had thought wasn't that big a deal, until I realised that a tight hip belt was crucial to stopping the bag from jumping all over my back as I ran – her dad, Hamish, had instantly offered to help. He got out his workbench, ransacked his garage for old backpacks and, using nothing but a rivet gun, a hammer and a can-do attitude, he transplanted the straps from another bag onto my own. I woke in the morning at the Woodhouse household feeling refreshed, especially after Hollie's mum, Boo, whipped me up a breakfast fit for an Adventure Queen.

I hugged Hamish goodbye as he left me at the riverside, on the opposite bank to where I had left the trail with Kev and Syd. I trotted joyfully away from him, enjoying my reunion with the wide open dramatic landscapes of the Rangitata river basin.

I knew the first day back on the trail was going to be a little, well, weird. I expected that much. In the week off I had gone through a range of emotions. I'd felt a deep sense of guilt at taking the time off, a guilt which I had at last reasoned with before becoming consumed with new, most unwelcome thoughts. I wound myself in knots, questioning what the hell I was doing. Was this run making any difference, to me, to the kids I spoke to, to the lives of others or was it just a selfish indulgence of a dream? Later that day my thoughts turned to the future. What would I do when this was all done? How would I earn money? Would I go straight back to office work? Could I do that? Did I want to do that?

Although the time off had turned out to be a wonderful idea physically, it took some time for my mind to readjust. On the trail, the days were simple, the challenges immediate, the problems few. Off the trail, I had time. Time to let my mind wander, and with no outlet or distraction for my thoughts, they ran amok, like a bull in a china shop crashing and thrashing from one ridiculous topic to the next.

It had taken a few days for my mind bull to calm down. And at last, in Christchurch, I had begun to revel in the feeling of being 'normal'. It was nice to do normal things like go for walks and drink coffee and meet people for dinner. So, at last, when the time came to return to the trail and face the 2,200 km still left to run, I was itching to get back out there. As an added bonus, the pain in my calf had now disappeared.

The trail was easy going and the first 10 kilometres of the day passed in a flash. Dark clouds were looming all around, chasing me down the valley, but I continued to push on along a 4WD track in the hope that I could outrun the weather. Alas, the smooth start wasn't to be an indication of how the rest of the day would pan out, and over the next hour I began to feel incredibly lethargic and bored. How was I bored in my first day back on the trail? I couldn't seem to let my mind drift as it normally did when running, and so every step, every kilometre, became hard work. It was like swimming through treacle. Getting lost and taking a wrong turn at Lake Clearwater added a little spice to the journey and broke up the monotony at least, but once back on track all I wanted was to lie down and sleep. And then I realised something – if that's what I wanted to do, then I could do it.

I picked a small patch of long grass just off the trail and pulled on some clothes and my duffel coat. I felt like Mark Beaumont, like a real adventurer. I had read so many books about adventurers being too tired to carry on and falling asleep in the shade of a tree by the roadside, but I had never done it myself. I pulled on my hat and rested my head on my backpack, enjoying the warmth of the sun as I drifted off to sleep.

An hour later I opened my eyes and sat up, a little disoriented. The lethargy had gone, the nap had done the trick and I was on my way again. My body felt better, but my thoughts still took some effort to control. I practised positive thinking, and I practised it often. Each time a bizarre thought entered my brain, such as 'You know you're not running this much faster than you could walk it, don't you, Anna?' I would stop. I would talk to that thought aloud like an insane person, and effectively tell it to bugger off. Or, better still, I would reason with it, I would acknowledge it, and offer another explanation.

It was the battle between the cheerleaders and the soldiers of self-doubt once again, and it raged on like a civil war in my mind for the whole afternoon.

Feeling buoyed by a mind now full of cheerleaders, I pushed on to Manuka Hut, which had been recommended as the nicest hut in this section. Inside the hut I found two young boys from Israel and an even younger German boy called Johannes, who was 19 years old. I already had the impression that the Germans were an adventurous sort, and Johannes did nothing to dispel that myth. For a young lad he had all the confidence of a middle-aged man. He was sprightly and spoke without a hint of shyness.

My little bout of lethargy and the subsequent nap seemed to have done me the world of good, and despite the battle with my thoughts, I had travelled further than intended that day. I'd made it 32 kilometres since Hamish had left me that morning, and I reckoned that wasn't too shabby for a first day back on the trail. I allowed myself a gigantic smile and a moment of self-congratulation before settling down to cook dinner at Manuka Hut.

The trail from Manuka Hut the following day was varied and challenging. It was rough and unformed in many places, meaning that each hiker had taken their own route between the marker poles. That left very little ground trail and so slowed me up. I had to concentrate hard not to roll my ankle on the uneven grassy mounds, and take care when crossing scree slopes. While a loss in footing and a slide all the way to the bottom of the valley would no doubt have been fun, it would probably have removed much of my bum. And I liked my bum – all of it. Yet, I revelled in the challenge of this section. I enjoyed using my now slightly improved navigational skills and the challenge of spotting each pole, which were sometimes obscured behind a mound or dip in the trail. The adrenaline rush of finding the next orange marker was akin to a treasure hunt. I was entirely in the moment in this game of runner's hide and seek.

The backdrop to the days of challenging running was a playlist of classic 90s and early 00s anthems. On one particular afternoon, OutKast's 'Hey Ya!' had come on my MP3 player. I sang along in time with the rhythm of my feet, and then I became overwhelmed. Overwhelmed with the urge to stop and to make this patch of grassy ridge line my very own dance floor. The power of the 2001 number one held me in a vice-like grip and forced me into action. I planted the Bushwhacker Boys firmly on the hillside and shook my arse like it was a god-damn polaroid picture. I danced like nobody was watching, because they weren't. I stayed on that ridge line dancing alone amidst the clouds for three full songs – the 80s classic 'Footloose' followed OutKast, and I concluded the mountain dance-a-thon with a number from the Black Eyed Peas. I may have been concerned about losing time by slipping down a scree slope, but time lost to dance was time well spent.

I realised that the days when I sang and danced on the

trail were good days. It had been a while since I had indulged in both, let alone with such virtuosity that OutKast's anthem had offered me. Running on, I resolved to sing and dance as often as possible to cure all my ills.

After the unique experience of spending a few hours running in the rocky riverbed of the Ashburton River, I had made my way over Clent Hills Saddle at 1,480 metres high. I was still getting used to the novelty of running in riverbeds – it was something I'd never experienced before and certainly wouldn't be able to do in the Thames back home. After a night's stay in a very cold and tin-clad Comyns Hut, I found myself bounding down to Rakaia River, full of beans and in love with life. Music and song again played a large part in my joy that day, as I bounded down the slope to the river, singing at the top of my lungs.

The wide 4WD track snaked back and forth like an alpine pass all the way down to a river basin that was wider and even more impressive than the Rangitata. There was no denying it, I was as high as a kite – not only was it the grade of the trail, and the ease with which I could pick up speed, nor the fact that from here on the rest of the day was mostly downhill, it was that Rakaia River was another milestone. Another section done. Joy was too small a word for the emotion I was experiencing. I was elated. The mornings in the Ashburton river valley had been crisp and cold, but the days were warm and, better still, I was still ahead of schedule. After that sluggish start at Mount Potts a few days back, today had well and truly marked the day that I rediscovered my mojo.

Unlike the Rangitata, which could be crossed with care, the DoC and Te Araroa authorities advised that under no circumstances should trail users try to cross the Rakaia River. So it didn't take me too much thought to decide that, just as with the Rangitata, crossing this river wasn't something I needed to do. Instead, I opted for an extra 80 km run around the Rakaia to the nearest bridge, along a hot and dusty road towards the small town of Methven. It was a choice that was really easy to make, because a rumour on the trail was that they had great burgers in Methven and I couldn't leave Canterbury without finding out.

That night, I sat entirely secluded in a roadside pine forest, on a soft bed of needles. I ran my hand over the top of my head. My hair felt disgusting. From one pass of its surface, I now had enough grease on my hand to lube up a car engine. Although I could wet wipe my body each evening and give the bits n' pits a good going over, the hair was one thing I had to leave to its own devices. My hair, curly by nature, had a mind of its own at the best of times, but that night it really took on a personality. I pulled a few strands from my ponytail and raised them into the air. To my delight, they stuck there, entirely upright and at 90 degrees from my head. I took a snapshot of the moment on my phone. Snuggling into my sleeping bag for the night, I opened up the recently taken photo and had a good giggle. I had well and truly made unicorn status. A dirty, greasy haired unicorn – the finest and rarest kind of them all.

11

Harsh Words

Upon arrival in Methven I immediately began taking care of 'business'. I set about seeking out and inhaling a long-awaited burger, before de-unicorning my hair at the home of Olivia and Gareth. Olivia was a beautiful blonde-haired Welsh woman and the best friend of a friend from home. She and her husband – tall, red-haired, farmer-extraordinaire Gareth – were Instafriend types. They embraced my madcap adventure plans with gusto and within 30 minutes of crossing the threshold of their home they had nicknamed me 'puppy McNuff' (on account of my ability to get excited about just about anything apparently), and we were already plotting when and how I would return for a visit once the run was over.

I was sitting in Olivia and Gareth's spare room, sorting through kit when my phone began to buzz. It was a video call from Jamie McDonald.

Jamie and the team at the Superhero Foundation had been a great support in the first few months, but Jamie especially. Despite the mild awkwardness that our romantic liaison had the potential to create, he'd already become my go-to person on the run. Truth be told, he inspired me. He wanted to change the world, made me snort with laughter and my soul seemed to quieten down just a little when I spoke with him.

A phone call with Jamie was like he had taken all my worries, wrapped them up neatly and held on to them. Leaving me feeling lighter, somehow. Like it was all going to be okay. I didn't have to deal with the weight of my anxious thoughts anymore and, against the backdrop of an already weary body and a confused mind, that felt simply wonderful.

'McNuff! How's it going?' he started, flopping onto his bed in Gloucester, topless.

'What time is it there?! What are you doing up?' I replied, trying not to check out his chest.

'Ah, yeah, it's five a.m. or something. I don't know, I'm just getting in. Anyway, answer the question, how are you?'

I paused briefly. 'Yeah, good, good. Really good.' I blurted quickly and smiled, before pausing again. 'I mean, it's hard. Really hard...' my speech slowed... 'but that's okay. I'm getting used to every day being hard. And it's good,' I smiled.

'Bullshit, McNuff.'

'I'm sorry?'

'Bullshit. I said bullshit. You're bullshitting yourself. You're running across a country and you're making it look like you're on a stroll to the shops. I know it's way, way harder than you're letting on. I've been there. I know you're lonely, I know you're tired and I definitely know you're crying.'

I was shocked. He'd never spoken to me like that before. Jamie was a relaxed, informal and carefree kind of guy. This was so direct and serious. Where did that come from? And, furthermore, bloody arsehole. How did he know?

'But… I, I mean… I…'

He cut me off: 'How do you want to be remembered?'

'What?'

'How do you want to be remembered?'

'What kind of question is that?!' I asked. My reply snappy, as he was now starting to irritate me with his demanding tone.

'Err… I don't know.' I looked at the floor and thought. How did I want to be remembered? I looked up. 'As someone who made a difference?' I said, going up at the end of my sentence more than was acceptable for a non-Antipodean.

'That's a rubbish answer,' he solemnly informed me. He was right. I was embarrassed. It was weak. If that's all that went on my gravestone I'd be sorely disappointed.

'You're in danger of being remembered as a caricature.'

'A what?!'

'A car-i-cat-ure. As someone who always appears 100% okay. Someone who can do things without any struggle…'

My voice started to wobble. The corners of my mouth did that thing where it feels like someone's put a fish hook in each side, and is dragging them down. I tried to smile, but the muscles in my upper lip just wouldn't relent. That really hurt. It stung like a bitch. I couldn't smile my way through this.

'Why don't you drop your sodding guard and just show people how hard it actually is?!' His voice now had a pleading tone to it. He wasn't angry. In fact, he was remarkably calm, and that made it even more difficult to take – because his words carried a hint of reason. He ploughed on, turning the knife in an already deep wound his words had left. I had a feeling he knew that he would be upsetting me, but it seemed he'd reached a point where he couldn't hold it in any longer. I was learning that Jamie was nothing if not honest.

'Because people don't want to read about doom and gloom – that's why,' I replied.

'Look, I had the same thing on my run, and I had this very same call from a friend. I know it's hard but I'm just trying to help you see what you can't, because you're in it.'

'But it's just not *me* to put that kind of stuff out there.' I continued, trying to get him to understand why sharing the tough parts of the journey felt so ill at odds with my personality, or rather the person I thought myself to be. 'I don't want any pity. I want to be the reason people smile of a morning. I don't want to drag them down with all my chat about what hurts and why it's hard.'

'But it's not the truth, Anna,' he continued, his tone much softer now.

I opened my mouth to speak but nothing came out. There was silence.

We said nothing for 30 seconds. I'd look at him every now and then, and he was looking directly back at me. I said nothing.

Just as I opened my mouth to speak, his battery cut out and the line went dead. Neither of us called the other back.

I strode into the kitchen where Gareth and Liv were making me dinner and I began my rant.

'How dare he?! He doesn't know me. Who does he think he is?!' I raved.

Liv came and sat next to me on the sofa, and in her wonderfully calm Welsh tone offered up some wisdom: 'I'm sure it's just his way of trying to help?'

I sighed. 'I know, and I think he's right, which pisses me off even more.'

I was angry and on the full defensive. Jamie had hit a real nerve and I was fuming about it. Here was this guy I'd only known a few months telling me what I'm doing wasn't good enough. All I wanted to do on this run was have an adventure and help some people in the process. I was tired, so very tired. Arranging school talks, blogging and doing as much as I could to help raise the level of donations and here he was telling me I was behaving as if I were some kind of fraud.

The truth was I didn't like being sad. As an emotion, I'd

never really known what to do with sadness. It just didn't sit well with me. I'd avoided all funerals growing up, opting instead to stay behind at my parents' house and make the tea when my four grandparents and both great grandparents died. The only funeral I'd gone to in 30 years of life was when my mum's best friend died, and that was to support Mum. As I didn't like dealing with sadness, I didn't really fancy sharing it with other people. I was always other people's pick-me-up, after all. I was the sunshine that brought light to an otherwise dreary day. That was me; that was who I was.

I didn't want to leave it there and I felt I needed to make the point, however subtly, that I knew myself better than Jamie did, so I wrote him a message.

'I don't have a problem with letting people know how tough it is, you know. It's just that… I only choose to share it with my close friends.'

I then proceeded to sulk for a few days and ignore the subsequent message, which contained a mild apology for the way his opinion had been delivered, and a reassurance that what I was doing was 'FLIPPING AMAZING'.

I wandered the one mile from the campground to the top of Lake Coleridge and, perched on a large boulder at the end of the lake, I sat for almost an hour. The conversation with Jamie had been on my mind for the past few days, and I was softening towards his words and their intention. With each step along the trail our disagreement seemed to matter less and less. Now here, in this beautiful spot, it didn't matter at all. No one could touch me on these boulders. This was what adventure was about, I resolved. It was about opening my eyes and appreciating the now. I looked and I listened. With every 30 seconds that passed, I heard more and I saw more.

A green slope punctuated with eerie granite formations lay directly to the east. Lake Coleridge to the west was far bluer than I expected – perhaps it was something to do with it being so still up here. The last droplets of milky blue water clawed and trickled their way across the flats to join the Harper River. I could hear the cyclical rush and subside of the wind through the jagged mountains beyond. The roar was deafening, like a jet engine. Clouds shrouded the ridge line to the north, slowly drifting south-east. The sun was now low in the sky, covering everything in a subdued and faint orange glow.

Two birds, with white bodies and black wings, danced and played in front of me before moving off, gliding effortlessly just centimetres above the lake. I followed them with my eyes as they moved down the lake and realised I was looking back on where I'd run from this morning. It was only 22 km away, but I was effectively looking at the past. Just as tomorrow, this would be the past. As with all moments in life, I remembered that I will never be here again. Each day, whether I move physically or not, I place a part of the journey behind me. Sitting there, on that rock, I felt I was seeing the world at its most peaceful. I felt at my most peaceful.

Something about the surroundings and their silence turned me sentimental. I began to think on how beautiful the world was. And to consider what beauty was, exactly. I resolved that it is intricacy. And diversity. It's the way the verdurous slope to the west sat in deep contrast to the grey crags of rock that framed its descent to the riverbed. It is change, constant change, my own and the landscapes that I pass through. It's that the clouds shifting from smudges into lifelike forms. How they nestle in the valley without need for direction nor instruction. Above all, beauty is natural. It is that man played no part in the creation of these intricacies. That's what I found most beautiful of all.

The following morning, I was raring to go. I'm not sure whether I felt rejuvenated by the company of the boys who'd arrived at the campground by the lake later that night, by the beauty of the lake itself, or it was that I'd decided to stop running early at 2 p.m. the previous day, but this morning I felt so freakin' alive and so unbelievably refreshed. For the first time since starting the trip my legs didn't hurt, a change I welcomed with open arms. Rather than me dragging them limply through the grass, my knees were sprinting ahead of me, and it was all I could do to keep up. I'm not entirely sure that the four trampers I met en route to the next hut knew what to think of me as I bounded enthusiastically up to them, quizzing them about their names and lives before scampering off again. I was happy and as high as a kite.

The trail through this section of Craigieburn Forest Park

was stunning. It zigzagged across a wide riverbed in the Harper Valley, and passed a rock formation known as The Pinnacles. The rivers here were more like streams, gently babbling, and even where they were knee-deep, they were completely manageable. This was something of a relief after the stomach-knotting dreams of the previous night, which involved finding myself repeatedly submerged in rivers I couldn't climb out of. Drifting away from and back to the river's edge, the trail finally settled parallel to the Harper River, taking me right along its path. The grass was soft underfoot and there was enough of a trail cut to make the running easy. I padded along, bounding from one section to the next. The sun was shining. Candy floss white clouds moved effortlessly through a pale blue sky, aided by the gentle breeze. I stopped and looked around, up the valley and back to where I'd come from. All I could hear was the babble of the river, the birds and a breeze. I sighed a deep happy sigh, before pushing past another batch of tall Pampas grass. Their regal feathers swaying to and fro in the breeze, as if in agreement with my own contented state.

Hamilton Hut was the biggest hut I'd encountered on the trail so far. The wood on the outside was painted in a dark mahogany. A huge veranda covered three sides, looking out on a wide shingle riverbed with a creek running haphazardly through the centre. On the opposite side of the river were strange rock formations carved out over thousands of years by waterfalls. The grass surrounding the hut was yellow, and glowed even more golden in the afternoon sun. Birds twittered and frittered around the hut, every now and then stopping to rest on the veranda.

Inside I found a stone fireplace, a wood burner, two large wooden tables, a drying rack and… running water from a tap! What luxury was this?! There was even a bedroom, an actual bedroom. Eighteen beds in total, stacked three bunks high – leading up to exposed timber beams in the rafters. This hut's reputation had preceded it – this was the renowned 'Hamilton Hilton'.

Also inside the hut was a hunter named Paul. I liked Paul instantly. In a previous life I might have freaked out at the concept of entering a strange wooden building in the middle of the forest and passing men's boots and a gun propped up at the door outside. But these were not sights to fear, in fact, they excited me. I'd grown used to meeting hunters by now and I loved it.

As an ex-vegetarian, one who had stuck it out for 22 years, I'd spent more of my life not eating meat than eating it. A liking for meeting hunters might seem a little strange, but to me it was a different world – there seemed to be such an art to it. The tracking, the equipment, the stories, and best of all the camaraderie. I admired the hunters for their desire to get out into the bush with a close friend or two, maybe a son or a daughter and to spend that time together. Vegetarian or not, a day outside amongst nature with people you love had to be better than sticking your kid in front of a TV screen any day.

Paul told me that he'd been coming to this hut for the past 40 years, and he seemed confused by its recent surge in popularity. I told him all about the Te Araroa, and explained that there were almost 200 people travelling along it this year, in both directions.

'Well, now that makes much more sense,' he said. 'Normally there's just a few of us here. Last night the hut was full! All eighteen beds. With people from all over the world! I knew they said something about a trail, but I was beginning to wonder what was going on.'

The fact was that the hut was not only on the Te Araroa route, but it was also within a day's hike from Arthur's Pass Village and Bealey – two very popular and accessible tourist towns.

Paul was a chatterbox, and that's saying something coming from me. We got on famously – talking about his family, the need for the simple things in life, and… love. He became obsessed with the fact that I was single, and seemed to have taken it on as a personal crusade.

'Oh, no, no, no. We can't have that – beautiful girl like you, why haven't you been snapped up?! Right. Let me think. Let's find you a fella.'

There was a silence, during which I presumed he was scrolling through his mental Rolodex of suitors. Where would the mental wheel stop? On a banker, a lawyer, a rogue musician? Footsteps on the porch interrupted my thoughts and put a stop to Paul's mental search for my Mr Right. Through the door came Paul's best mate, Alex, a 78-year-old Austrian-born Kiwi who'd been out in the bush hunting for 6 hours. Grandads of the world, take note. According to Alex, age is no reason to shy away from a gruelling day in the mountains.

I took a break from chats with Paul and Alex to make a trip to the Norski – the Nordic toilet system that has been a saviour of trampers New Zealand-wide (think of it as a fancy version of a long drop). As I sat down inside the small wooden Norski outhouse, the note on the back of the door made me giggle: 'However much you hate the world, please do not throw rubbish in these tanks. Occasionally toilet paper will form a raft, upon which may float a pyramid of poo. There is usually a poo stirrer rake under the hut to sink the raft and reduce the smell. Please feel free to use this tool, if this problem is encountered on your visit. We DoC rangers can't be everywhere at once.'

I grew immediately excited. A pyramid of POO?! I removed myself from the Nordic throne and swivelled around to look down the long drop. Alas, I was disappointed to discover that there was no pyramid of poo for me to sink on this occasion. What a shame, and such a missed opportunity for a ruddy good game of Battleships.

Later in the evening we were joined by Katsumi, the most stereotypical Japanese man you could ever imagine. Bowing and shuffling his way through the door, and slurping noodles noisily through dinner, his comments were limited mostly to the answer 'yus' and often accompanied by a swift nod of the head. I admired him. The man could barely speak a word of English and yet he'd come to spend six months travelling a backcountry trail. I wondered if I'd be brave enough to do the same in Japan. There was also Swetlana, a 19-year-old German girl who'd made her way over the pass on a day trip. She had no map, no GPS and had fallen in the river along the way. I was swiftly learning that the Germans on this trail were an adventurous breed all of their own.

We chatted our way through dinner – Paul offering and cooking me up some fresh venison from his kill that week, and sharing the extra bottle of wine he'd 'accidentally' packed. I threw my stash of chocolate out on the table, which began a sharing fest as everyone else emptied the contents of their food bags and sat back with a hearty: 'Help yourself!'

That night I shut my eyes and was content again. To be surrounded by people, and in the middle of a beautiful land-scape. The running had played a secondary part to the journey today. Today was about the scenery that I had had the pleasure to move through, and the people I'd encountered. It was the perfect mix of every adventure ingredient, and I decided that I liked days like these.

In the hut the following morning, having waved everyone off and on my own once again, I took a rare opportunity to study my reflection in the rusty head-height mirror on the wall. I lifted up my shirt and slid it off. I slipped out of my shorts and stared at the person in the mirror. She looked like me, only different.

The freckles on my nose had come out, the blonde highlights had grown out of my hair, the bones in my hips were protruding more than normal. I ran my hand over my lower stomach. It was flat. It hadn't been flat since I was 23. The veins leading down to my crotch were blue and running close to the surface; I'd never noticed that before. My calves had grown by at least a centimetre, and where my thighs once tumbled haplessly into my knee joints, they now instead slimmed down and went there purposefully. I think this is what they called definition, and I had some.

I looked at my arms. My upper arms didn't really look too different, but for a sharp line cut by the exposure to the sun each day. The hairs on my forearms were blonde, forming a pale carpet of fuzz over my now darker skin, and the veins on my arms appeared to pulse closer to the surface, as if ready to report for duty at a moment's notice. I guessed I'd probably lost 6 kilograms since starting the run six weeks earlier.

Getting dressed again, I felt compelled to thank someone, anyone, for this little pocket of heaven I'd spent the past 12 hours enjoying. I pulled out one of the thank-you cards from my pack (I always travel with thank-you cards, because you never know when you might need to sincerely thank someone) and began to write. I decided to write to the Department of Conservation, seeing as they were the ones who looked after the hut.

'To whichever lovely DoC person collects this,

I just wanted to say thank you!! This hut is an oasis! I'm sure that hunters and trampers drive you nuts from time to time, so I just wanted to say how wonderful it is every time I make a hut. The work you do is invaluable and allows so many of us to live out our adventures in this rockin' country!!

Thanks again,

Anna from London, running the Te Araroa Trail :) xxx'

Running through Craigieburn Forest, I was enjoying the gentle rustle of wind through the trees. I bounded around the corner and found myself careering headlong towards five fully grown men. Well, now this was exciting. I hadn't seen anyone since I'd left the hut that morning and to see five people, what a treat! They were moving at a substantially greater pace than I was (read: any pace at all) and so I stepped up onto the bank of the trail to let them pass.

'That's a big pack you've got there,' said the man who I assumed to be the leader of the pack.

I was a bit embarrassed. These guys looked like 'real' trail runners, and I was far from a 'real' trail runner. 'I'm, err, running the Te Araroa Trail,' I replied softly, starting to move off and pass them, so that they could get on their way.

The leader stopped. 'Are you?!' he exclaimed. 'Bloody hell.'

I stopped and looked at them again – they were all wearing the same red T-shirts. Red T-shirts, red T-shirts, I thought… now where have I seen red T-sh… And then it hit me.

'Which one of you is Mal?' I demanded in an excited squeal. The man in the middle pointed to the leader.

'Are you Mal?! As in, Mal Law?!'

The leader looked a little taken aback, but slowly said, 'That's me…' but before he could finish I'd engulfed him in a hug so tight a boa constrictor would be impressed.

'You. Are. A. Legend!' I shouted, my face now firmly nestled on his shoulder.

'Err… thanks, and who am I hugging?!' he laughed.

'My name's Anna! I've heard all about you, and what you're doing. I think it's just bloody wonderful. You're a total legend!' I repeated. Of all the people, in all the places, I'd run into Malcom Law.

Needless to say, I was a big fan of Mal and his work. Despite not being entirely sure what he looked like, and having not heard about him until I'd arrived in New Zealand, I was a fan. Mal was a big deal and a Kiwi institution. His 'about me' profile describes him as 'a passionate trail runner, adventurer and fundraiser for good causes'. He'd run NZ's Seven Great Walks (before there were nine) in seven days, and raised hundreds of thousands of dollars for charity. He is especially passionate about the benefits of adventuring and running for mental health. Two years earlier Mal's brother-in-law had hanged himself and Mal was the one who discovered him. To raise funds and awareness for mental health charities, Mal's latest challenge was to run 50 marathons in 50 days, taking in 50 of NZ's peaks. On day 54 of my run, and day 27 of his High-Five-O challenge for mental health, our paths had collided.

I had a brief chat with Mal and the gang. I think he thought I was slightly mental, but this is usual for people who meet me for the first time. I chatted to the others about the fact that I knew there was a pub somewhere at the bottom of this section of the trail, and I was really looking forward to a beer. I should have double-checked whether there was actually a pub somewhere at the bottom of the trail, but I didn't want to be a bother. These guys were on a mission of their own. We hugged (again), although this time I hugged all of them – I hated to deprive anyone of a hug, after all, and we parted ways. Running away I now had one thing on my mind – beer.

I'm not really a drinker. I mean, I have the odd pint here and there, and a glass of wine, but I've never really needed alcohol for anything. Dance floors, speaking, the courage to ask out boys: I'd just do it anyway. But on this particular day, I couldn't locate the pub in which I was to enjoy my long-awaited beer, and I'll level with you all, I lost my shit.

Of course, it wasn't about the beer, it's never just about the beer. It was a wider tantrum resulting from a dangerous dabble with the notion of expected rewards. It would start with the words of a passing southbound tramper, e.g. 'there's a pub in that town with great food, amazing chips!' At first, the information would glance off me, of little consequence. But later, as the day got harder and the going got slower, the beer and chips were all I could think about. They were my reason to keep running; heck by this point they were my reason to keep living. What kind of chips would they be, I'd wonder? Double fried, triple fried, or perhaps they'd be rustic wedges? I certainly hoped that they weren't those fries-impersonating-chips. They were the pits. And the beer. How cold would it be? In its gigantic Bavarian style tankard, how smooth the amber liquid would feel as it slid down my oesophagus.

As the day got hotter and the going underfoot turned to thick clay sludge, all I could taste was that beer. The bubbles of the thin layer of foam dispersing across my lips as I wrapped them around the glass. The slight pause having gulped down three or four mouthfuls of ale, to take a hot triple-cooked, crispy, fluffy chip in my hand, and cram it into my mouth. The steam hitting the roof of my mouth, and in stark contrast to the cool film left by the beer.

Having run through the miniature metropolis of Bealey and only found a fancy lodge that would make me a packed lunch (but no beer), then having come off the main trail and run 1 km up a windy road into a residential area, hoping to find a pub at the top, I had returned to the valley floor. 'Where is this sodding pub?'

I began to trudge onwards, certain this so-called pub was a myth, passed on by trail users to torment me.

But then, a little further on, lo and behold, I saw it: 'The Bealey Hotel 500 m.' Wahoo! I literally couldn't contain my excitement. I sprinted my heart out all the way into The Bealey, where I necked two pints of Speight's Ale in the space of 30 minutes and a whole tray of slightly soggy but equally satisfying chips. I was decidedly tipsy as I left. The final 11 kilometres to Arthur's Pass Village flew by, and there was only one explanation – beer power.

12

Rock Bottom

I was stuck at the YHA in Arthur's Pass Village, having experienced what Kiwis called 'real west coast weather'. It had pounded and poured for the past 48 hours, creating new rivers in the street and causing the existing rivers to swell.

Rain wasn't really a problem in itself. I was fine running in the rain. In fact, I quite enjoyed a shower from time to time to break up the monotony, but the next section required that I cross the Bealey River, and the rain had made the Bealey River angry. Its swirling, bubbling, white-watered appearance let me know that I wouldn't be crossing it just yet.

I'd run 5 km off-route up to the YHA to pick up a food parcel which I posted ahead from Christchurch, and a new set of trainers which I had christened Frodo and Sam. I realised that the last time I'd been in a hostel, I was nineteen. I strutted around the kitchen, considering the differences between my 19-year-old and 30-year-old self. I remember being more nervous back then, awkward, self-conscious even. Now I definitely couldn't care less. If I wanted to use the only remaining ring on the hob in a crowded kitchen, I would damn well use it. I decided I liked being 30, and carried on making my noodles.

I woke at 8.30 a.m. and clambered into the shower.

Watching the soapy water swirl down the plughole, I contemplated the day ahead. I was ready to get going, but at the same time I'd become quite accustomed to staying still. I'd enjoyed the constant stream of people and families moving in and out of the hostel. The doors held open, the dancing to and fro around the kitchen as I waited patiently to wash up my plate, whilst keeping an eye on the kettle I'd boiled and hoping no one else got in there first and stole my water. My ears had habituated to the noise of air brakes – tourist buses that rolled through the village twice a day, and the subsequent throng of disappointed-looking holidaymakers. Holidaymakers who would then pile into the cafe to fill up on muffins and coffee before slumping into chairs as they realised that the west coast weather had well and truly ruined their plans to enjoy two days in one of the South Island's best hiking areas.

'Hello, petal,' came my mum's voice out of the iPad. 'How's that weather?'

I'd been keeping 'basecamp' updated on the hold-up via email over the past couple of days, and it was nice to have some time to speak to them properly. I was actually amazed at how my relationship with my parents seemed to go from strength to strength via Skype. I resolved that it was because we found ourselves in a rare situation where both parties were making a concerted effort to communicate, and were genuinely interested in what the other was up to. I enjoyed speaking to my parents because with each conversation out here I reverted to being a true child. A child who wanted them to know as much as possible about what I was doing, and to be proud of me. Every now and then I contemplated who would be proud of me when they were gone, but that thought seemed so dark and far off that I quickly cast it from my mind. I recognised that they were, and are, without doubt two of the most important influences in my life. If I wasn't making my parents proud, then what was the point? I considered that perhaps I also did things to make myself proud and this really was what this trip was about – to be able to stand at the lighthouse at the end of my journey and feel proud, but I wasn't entirely convinced of that just yet.

'What's the river doing?' Mum asked, a serious tone to her voice. I'd always tried to strike a balance between telling Mum enough information about my present situation so as to convince her that I was adequately prepared (which was mostly a lie), and not sharing too much so as to stoke any worry-fires in her brain. It was a fine line, and I often revealed too much in admitting that I was apprehensive about the section ahead. As soon as words to that effect had left my mouth, I'd have to backtrack, playing down the worry or convince her that it was a good thing I was worried. The conversation usually went as follows:

'Anna, I'm a bit worried that you're so worried about these river crossings…'

'But I am worried, Mum.'

'Yes, I know. And that worries me.'

'Isn't it better that I'm worried than carefree and reckless, Mum?'

'I suppose so.'

'If I'm worried it means I'm taking it seriously. I'm treating it with respect.'

'Okay, petal, but I'm still worried.'

I was still working out exactly who I should tell when I was worried about things on this trail. I'd elected not to be so open with my fears in videos and blog posts, but even among those that I passed on the trail, there seemed to be an assumption that because I was out here running this thing, that I was bulletproof, which couldn't be further from the truth. It was exactly what Jamie had called me out on in our last conservation. The fact that he was right didn't make things any easier to deal with. I was perpetually anxious. Despite the odd confession to Mum, I didn't want to tell my parents – I knew it would give them sleepless nights and only exacerbate my guilt. There was really no sense in trying to communicate my fears to my friends back home – wonderful as they were they had no concept of where I was or the irrational fears that played out in my mind. I couldn't really confide in the other trail users I met either. They had concerns of their own, and I found that they were often unable to hear my concerns, or they would simply add to my fear by making me concerned about sections I hadn't even considered yet.

Instead, I internalised most of my worry. It manifested

itself in lucid dreams or sleepless nights, in undercurrents of anxious thoughts that ran beneath my everyday existence like sewers in a city. Above ground everything functioned as it should, but down there was a complex maze of rivers, swollen with poisonous self-doubt.

I walked outside to check the levels of the Bealey River one last time. It was at last down to a manageable, gentle flow. Leaving Arthur's Pass Village and resuming the plod-shuffle hybrid I'd developed over the past two months, I felt sluggish. Sluggish was no way to be with 2,000 km still left to run. As usual, I'd eaten far too much on the days off in town and my pack, now bursting at the seams with five days' worth of food, was decidedly heavy. After an hour of self-talk and a spot of singing in a bid to aid my distraction, the dull ache in my legs began to relent. I hit the trail turn-off to Goat Pass, manoeuvred myself to the banks of the Bealey River and inspected it carefully. It didn't look like the friendliest river in the world and was still flowing fast, but it was definitely passable. Unclipping the pack, I eased my way into the water and began a tentative crossing. At its deepest point, the water was thigh-high, but it was just about on the right side of manageable. I made the other side, leapt clear from the river and let out a triumphant whoop. I was on my way! I was on to the next section at long last!

Dancing merrily along the wide, rocky bed of the Mingha River, I followed the trail upwards, scrambling and sliding on mud and roots as it sidled the banks of the valley.

Reaching Dudley Knob I took the time to look back on where I'd come from. It was stunning: a rich carpet of green scattered with slim waterfalls. I was stoked to be out there. I felt alive and free as I set off again, only this time I had added some lung-busting singing.

It was then that I spotted a strange plant underfoot. It was black and flat and seemed to cover everything in sight. What kind of moss grows like that? I wondered, crouching down to get a closer look. It was carpet. I worked out that the renowned coast-to-coast race had happened on this section of trail just three weeks earlier. An annual race that sees hard as nails Kiwis run, bike and kayak across the country. The race is run south to north on this section, so I was going against the grain but using the same route. I found it bizarre to be in what felt like such a lush and unspoilt wilderness and running on patches of carpet, but I decided that being on a race course had its benefits, because where the trail became boggy and too slippery to navigate at any respectable speed, the carpet had been laid, or, better still, wooden slats put in position. Further on towards Goat Pass there were even complete sections of boardwalk. I couldn't believe my luck.

'Well, would you look at that?!' I said aloud, bounding gleefully up the evenly spaced and perfectly level steps towards the pass.

At 5.45 p.m. I arrived at Goat Pass Hut. I wrapped my fingers around the cold metal of the door handle and braced myself. I'd been warned about this hut. It was one of the more popular ones on the trail and I'd been advised not to go up there at weekends. Reports of 'hoards' descending upon it each night, and hikers forced to sleep on the porch because all the bunks were full, were rife. I crossed my fingers that there might be at least one bed going spare and pushed the handle firmly downward.

'Hello!' I called, poking my head through the small crack in the door and preparing my very best welcome grin. I was greeted with a wall of silence and an empty room. There were no people. There was no… anything.

'Hello?' I called again, stepping inside and assuming that someone was in one of the two bedrooms I could see to the left. Nothing. I was alone. How strange. I settled into what now felt like a very large and cold living space. I began to make dinner and studied the visitors' book. It looked like a large group of French hikers had left that morning. Reading their notes, I could see that they'd been stuck up here for the past two days, unable to get across the Bealey River and into town. It seemed that they'd run low on food and got a little bored. I was sad to have missed them, but glad that they too had made it out and onto the next section of trail.

That night, my sleep was disturbed by vivid and bizarre dreams. I dreamt about being chased by a big black dog and trying to climb a tree in the wind, which I kept falling out of. I had no idea what this all meant, but it left knots in my stomach and I awoke frequently in a sweat.

When morning came, I woke up cold and shivering. Stepping outside the hut I found that I was shrouded in cloud and it was raining lightly. Whether it was a result of the peculiar dreams or the cold night's sleep, I felt uneasy and was, for want of a better term, entirely creeped out. I wrote in my diary: 'Get me out of here and off this mountain. Where is everyone?! Let's hope there is some southbounder heading my way. The next few days could get pretty lonely otherwise. I think I'll prepare for the worst – not to see anyone.'

Despite having only left town that morning, I'd decided in the hut the previous night that I didn't like being alone. It might not sound newsworthy, but it was the first time that I had actually admitted it to myself, rather than trying to pretend I was okay with it. Being alone just became less and less fun every time it happened, and it was happening a lot. I resolved that I'd push out some big mileage and try to make the next town, Boyle Village, within four days. Alas, I then made the mistake of reading about the next section, which revealed that there were 'frequent and repeated river crossings', and that these were 'impassable in heavy rain'. I read on to find out that the Deception River can be dangerous after heavy rainfall and navigating it will require up to 30 compulsory river crossings. I let out a little whimper.

I started the descent of the Deception River in an odd mood. The boulders and pools at the source were slippery and hampered progress significantly. As the stream widened, I could run a little alongside it, although the downside was that I now had to begin to cross it repeatedly. And goodness knows, I hated river crossings.

Everything felt weird. The eerie clouds in the valley, fragmented memories of the dreams from the night before, the lack of people where there should be an abundance of them: all of these things put me on edge.

The intention had been to make it through this section quickly and with minimal fuss. The reality was that I was travelling slowly and constantly nervous. It took me 3 hours to cover the first 4 kilometres of the day. Three bloody hours. Some of the crossings were uneventful, others involved a careful negotiation of some large boulders, and miniature plunge pools. Most crossings were only knee or thigh-deep, but on one occasion I was up to my chest, and although the flow was more manageable at that kind of depth, I didn't like it one bit. Even worse was that the cairns (small piles of rocks that are left to mark the way) that were supposed to be offering guidance on the best places to cross, were about as useful as a chocolate teapot. On one crossing I got halfway out into the river and felt a force on my legs that was far too strong. I had to backtrack and run 10 minutes upstream again to find a more suitable spot.

Every now and then, dark thoughts would escape my subconscious (where I liked to keep them locked up) and seep, most unwelcomely, into my conscious brain: 'What happens if you slip, Anna? How about if you get your foot stuck under that big boulder over there? What about if you go face first into that rock, Anna? You know no one's going to find you for a few days, don't you? What happens if your GPS tracker doesn't work?'

It was ridiculous. Although there was a small basis of rationality in my thinking, as with all fears, things had been exaggerated in my mind and blown out of all likely proportion. I wanted to turn around and scream at my own mind. 'Shut up! Shut up! Shut up!' I was tired, frightened and frustrated. And when I get frustrated, I cry. So I cried and swore and shouted at the trail, informing it of how sodding ridiculous it was. Then I cried some more.

Post-cry, life seemed a little rosier and I began to make steadier progress down the track, getting used to the crossings and accepting that this was only one day, and that this day would soon be over. I was even beginning to relish the challenge and the painstaking calculation that went into each river-crossing attempt. Things were looking like they were on the up when, ever so slightly distracted, I stepped off a rock and some undergrowth gave way. I felt something in my foot shift. My ankle buckled sideways and the full force of my bodyweight piled onto it. There was a loud crack, as a shard of pain shot through the outside of my foot and up my calf. I dropped to the floor.

I sat there for 5 minutes, too afraid to move for fear of

what I might find. This was it, I thought. I've broken my ankle. I shut my eyes and willed it to be okay, making bargains with whoever I thought was listening, and promising that I would be more grateful, and pay more attention next time. I felt the waves of pain move across the ankle bone and, over the next few minutes, emotions pounded at the shores of my mind like waves. Now I was angry. So very angry.

'What the heck have I done to deserve this?!' I blurted through pain-soaked tears. After 5 minutes of anger, despair rolled in, before self-pity and a return to anger. I decided then that it was time to move. Leaving my pack where it lay, I hoisted myself from the floor and tentatively placed my ankle on the ground. It moved. That was a good start. I tried a little weight and that seemed to hold too. It wasn't broken at least. I took three test steps forwards. One, two, thr… It gave way again. Pain sliced its way through my ankle − I hit the metaphorical roof, and then the literal floor.

I realised it was sprained, and I resolved that I could cope with a sprain at least for long enough to get me to a camping spot to assess the damage. But anyone who's ever rolled an ankle knows that your body takes it as some kind of permission to repeatedly let it collapse.

Three hours later I'd lost count of how many times I'd now gone over on my ankle. I was in a firm state of self-pity, in an obscene amount of pain, and verging on delirium. I followed a flood track above the river which, on account of all the recent rain, was a certifiable mess. Flood tracks are put in place on sections of trail where the riverbed route becomes impassable in heavy rain. Thinking about the recent few days of downpour, I had to assume that the flood track was a better option on this section. Alas, the trail markings were nigh on impossible to find and after clambering over fallen trees and hauling myself up muddy slopes for 30 minutes I changed tack and decided that the best plan of attack was to slide on my butt down to the riverbed. Once down there I tried to cross the river, before realising that the flow was too strong and there were no viable crossing points. This was an even worse option than the barely navigable flood track, and so I sighed and hauled myself back up the muddy slope, where I continued to clamber, bush-bash and scramble until I emerged from the forest and into a grassy valley.

Dazed, but relieved to have found a spot to stop at last, I hobbled to fetch some water from the river and pitched my tent. Crawling inside, I eased off my trainers and stared at my right ankle. It was angry. What was once a slight curve around my ankle bone was now a gigantic bulge. My ankle was the size of a planet. Venus, perhaps even Jupiter. I prodded it. Then yelped. Legs outstretched, I placed it directly next to my left one, which looked positively emaciated in comparison.

Gaze firmly fixed on the ankle-planet, I pondered whether I was being a complete wimp. Why had I found today so difficult? Perhaps it was that the river crossings were more of a challenge than usual? Or was I just a stupid girl from London who had bitten off more than she could chew? I wondered whether I'd even tell local Kiwis how frightened I'd been today. Quite frankly, I was embarrassed, and they'd probably just laugh.

I knew by now that days on the trail weren't ever about one thing in particular. They were a combination of elements – tiredness, terrain, weather, emotional state. For some reason, today the elements had collided in such a fashion that I felt completely out of whack. The jagged edges of fear, loneliness and frustration had made welts in my mind deep enough to allow self-doubt to creep in. And once self-doubt gets let in, it runs riot. The voices that had been so vocal at the start in Auckland returned, and this time with good reason.

My stomach growled. It had been 5 hours since I'd eaten a cereal bar for lunch and it was now 8 hours since breakfast. I was too tired to even fire up the stove and so instead mixed some cold water into a sachet of porridge. I threw in some dark chocolate for morale purposes and, spooning the cold sludge concoction into my mouth, considered my options.

I resolved that there were two. The first was to accept that I needed to get my ankle seen to. There was a swing bridge a few kilometres back which would take me across the main Otira River and onto a road. I could hitch a ride from there back to Arthur's Pass Village and sit it out for a few days. I didn't like that idea at all. The thought of sitting immediately made me feel suffocated. I had already been climbing the walls in that village waiting for the rain to subside. I didn't think I could go back and not go certifiably mental. Plus, there was more rain due and who knows when I'd be able to get across the river again?

Option two was to attempt to push on. The only problem with that was that I was going deeper and deeper into the backcountry and it was four days until the next town. If I got myself into trouble, getting out would be difficult. I could see the newspaper headlines now: 'Stupid British girl goes on into the bush with a busted ankle – what was she thinking?' I didn't even know if I'd be able to put enough weight on my ankle to move in the morning. It was getting bigger by the second, and it had now developed its own pulse. Even if I could use it, I couldn't afford to move much slower through the next section – today's escapades had already lost me half a day's progress, and I wasn't carrying much in the way of emergency food rations. Then there was the fact that tomorrow's section contained more river crossings. If they were anything like today, negotiating them and keeping myself safe with an injury was going to be a challenge, and one that I wasn't sure I had the energy to face.

I wanted to call someone, anyone. Not being able to verbalise my options to anyone made me realise how often I sought out the opportunity to talk things through in everyday life. They say a problem shared is a problem halved, and in my case I always found that a problem shared was a problem solved. I gained clarity when I could let my thoughts out for a little runaround. They were far easier to understand once out in the open, roaming free, as opposed to bumping into one another within my already cramped brain. However, I had no phone signal and no way of speaking to anyone. I was entirely alone.

This was rock bottom, it had to be. Mentally I couldn't feel any worse, and physically I was screwed. I let that realisation sink in for a moment and then considered throwing a tantrum. I began to screw up my face in an attempt to cry, poised like a child about to throw their toys out the pram. Then something very strange happened. A veil lifted and I was overwhelmed by a deep sense of calm. The dark cloud, casting a shadow over my thoughts, took its cue and moved away. I had food, I had shelter, I had water and, above all, I was still here. Things weren't that bad. In fact, they could be an awful lot worse.

'Get a grip, McNuff,' I muttered. 'You're okay. It's okay.'

I wrote in my diary: 'I so badly want a hug from someone I know right now. Just someone to just tell me it's all going to be okay. This is not fun today. Today was not fun at all. Tomorrow is a new day.'

I lay down and picked up my phone. I decided to sanction a percentage of the remaining battery to cheer myself up. I scrolled into my texts and spent 10 minutes reading back through old conversations with friends. Snorting and laughing, and in some instances marvelling at my own wit, I immediately felt calmer and more connected. I snuggled into my sleeping bag, letting my now heavy eyelids rest. The last thought that passed through my mind was a vow: tomorrow would not get to me like today had. Tomorrow I would be stronger than I had been today.

13

The Pants of Perspective

Setting my empty coffee cup down beside me, I rummaged around in my bag until my fingers found what I was looking for. Pulling out the mess of brightly coloured Lycra material, I laid it flat so that I could see the entire pattern. Moments earlier, over another morning's serving of cold porridge, I had remembered something. I'd thought in spending over five months on the trail that perhaps, just perhaps, I was going to have one or two days when I didn't want to get out of my tent and run, and instead I might just want to curl up in a ball and cry. For this situation, I had packed myself a secret weapon – a pair of magic Lycra pants.

One leg was adorned with a unicorn, the other with a robot. Both were engaged in a fierce battle and above them was a star-spangled night sky. Naturally, across that sky was a bright rainbow. I eased the leggings tentatively over my bulbous ankle and wriggled my butt into them. I smiled at the sight of my legs, which now looked ridiculous, especially as the placement of the unicorn horn meant that it pointed directly at an intimate part of my female anatomy. 'Now that's more like it,' I thought.

Everything around me, the facts, so to speak, would

indicate that I should be miserable, but it was scientifically impossible to be miserable whilst wearing these pants. They were a sheer act of defiance, flying the flag of ridicule in the face of what should be a serious and grave situation. I laughed, and immediately felt more like me. The me that had become buried the previous day under despair, exhaustion and self-pity. I felt a little flame inside me reignite, and I remembered that I was a lucky girl. I thought about the fact that I was on this trail by choice, and that I have the freedom and opportunity to travel to places that others may only dream of. After mulling over these thoughts, I decided to name my secret weapon: these were to be my pants of perspective. Putting them on had certainly done the trick. Mentally, I was strong again and I was ready for whatever the world had to throw at me that day. I set about making my ankle strong again too.

Ten minutes later I finished strapping up my ankle and sat back to admire the handiwork. My foot looked like a Christmas present that had had a fight with a disgruntled elf. I'd employed the basic principle of trying to remember where my tendons and ligaments might run (were they tendons and ligaments?) and the job that each might perform. The tactic seemed to work, and I paused to congratulate myself on having actually had some strapping tape in my bag in the first place. For once, I was prepared for an eventuality. Girl Guides eat your hearts out!

I'd decided that going back to town and resting just wasn't an option. Being stationary again would drive me nuts. It just wasn't something I was willing to do. Instead, I resolved that I would hobble on, and see how far I could make it. If it was really that bad I could hobble back on myself the next day. That way, even if I wound up moving backwards, at least I had tried to move forwards first. That seemed about as good a philosophy as any for life, let alone ankle injuries.

I tested out the newly supported ankle-like structure and found it to be pretty solid. Possibly a little too solid and I couldn't be entirely sure that my toes were getting any blood at all. Still, that ankle was going nowhere, and what was a little loss in circulation if I could save any further damage? For the first time in two months I set off with an intention to walk for a few hours. It was an intention that made me sick to my stomach, but running really wasn't an option and I figured that walking was better than not moving at all.

The first 2 hours were slow going, although the trail was kind to me at least, offering up a grassy 4WD track where the only things likely to throw my ankle over were unexpected clumps of grass. The level of concentration I was having to maintain was exhausting. I had to think about the placement of my right foot with every single step. The moment I let my thoughts stray, I'd wobble, trip and go over on the ankle. To my surprise, I was actually enjoying the walking. Although I still felt guilty about my new pace, I'd taken the pressure off, reasoning that I might run a little in the afternoon if the ankle felt okay.

The next section was trickier. The stones of the Taramakau riverbed and the river crossings posed a new challenge. I did my best to stay calm as I moved through the usual ritual of crossing and re-crossing the river. Every now and then I'd be able to make out a footprint in the grey sand, nestled between the stones of the bed. These comforted me. Knowing that someone else had come this way relatively recently somehow made me feel less alone. I metaphorically scooped up each print I came across and placed it in my pocket, saving for a time when I was alone in my tent. Were any of these prints Andrew's or Peter's, I wondered? Finny's or Fi's? Neither pair could be too far ahead.

Knowing where to cross the river relied on being able to accurately assess the flow, force and depth in each section. Sometimes I chose wisely. Other times, not so well, and as the morning progressed I grew increasingly lazy. At one point I tried to cross the river next to a fallen tree. I knew full well that anything such as trees or boulders were dangerous to be around when the flow was strong. A small slip and you could find yourself trapped beneath it, so it was wise to avoid them. On this particular occasion, I'd hesitated for 10 minutes, trying to backtrack over to another tributary, but it seemed like finding a 'safe' place was a near impossibility. 'Oh, stuff it!' I thought, growing impatient and moving into the river at a spot near a tree that looked vaguely passable. I made it halfway across without too much trouble, and found myself calf-deep in a shallower section. I paused briefly to catch my breath and to congratulate myself on such a good choice of crossing spot, but it was only then that I saw how fast the water was moving on the other side of the shoal. This didn't seem like a good idea, but the bank wasn't too far now and I was damned if I was going back on myself. I could feel myself getting angry.

'Why the hell do I have to cross so many sodding rivers?' I said out loud. This is bloody ridiculous,' I continued, addressing my imaginary audience, who nodded in sympathy.

I took a deep breath and shuffled tentatively out into the river. I was knee-deep now. A few more shuffles and I was up to my waist. The water swirled past my hips and bore down on my thighs. 'Just a few more…' I ground forward and put my left foot on a rock, which moved. My weight transferred unexpectedly onto the injured right ankle, I yelped and lost my footing. The water wasted no time in finding a gap between my feet and the riverbed and swept me clean off them. In a last-ditch effort to maintain any kind of balance, I flung myself forwards, arms flailing and scrambling for the bank, which was now only a few metres away. Three flails later, my feet found the riverbed once again. I scrambled up onto the solid ground, cursing my impatience, and laughing at my stupidity. In the scramble, I'd dunked my entire backpack in the river. I only hoped that the dry bags inside were doing their job.

Back on the trail a little later, and now somewhat less soggy having dried out in the late-summer sun, a figure appeared up ahead. I smiled as he approached and he smiled right back. He was tall, dark haired, with intense blue eyes, and as it turned out very, very British. It was clear that we were happy to see one another. I offered up a hug, which he accepted as I explained my odd gait.

'I'm normally running, honest. It's just… I busted my ankle yesterday.'

'I believe you, I believe you,' said Edward, looking downward at my thighs.

'Just look at your legs! They look like runner's legs. I mean, you look like you've been running with legs like those,' he added, awkwardly.

Edward, a southbounder doing the whole trail in the opposite direction, was quite possibly the best person I could have come across at that time. He was my medicine, a little touch of home: for Edward was a man who seemed to have been having a worse time of it than I was.

We were both itching to indulge in a favoured British pastime: moaning. Edward's beef was largely to do with trail markers, or lack thereof, and sections of the track which were impassable due to heavy rain. I nodded, enjoying the passion in his voice. I don't think I'd ever heard anyone moan quite so intensely. If moaning were an Olympic sport, he'd have topped the medals table there and then.

He paused before reaching the final item on the heavily overloaded moaning agenda. 'And another thing. What is it with all these river crossings?!'

This was my cue. I snatched the moan-baton from his hands, and ran with it, explaining the events of the day before, and my morning's swim. We jibed back and forth, as Edward continued sarcastically: 'It's like someone designed the trail to take in as many crossings as possible. Oh look, there's a river. Let's loop it right over here, just so we can take people through this raging torrent that may or may not kill them'

Once our mouths ran dry and we could moan no more, we bid one another a very British ta-ta and parted ways. I hobbled on down the valley, determined to enjoy what remained of the day. The sun was shining and the surrounding landscape was beautiful after all. Edward's moaning had lifted my mood immeasurably and had been just what I needed. It was like watching a soap opera. As soon as you learn that there are people in the world worse off than you, suddenly everything is rosy once again.

It was 3 p.m. when I made Locke Stream Hut. Shunting open the wooden door, I shrugged off the pack and checked the logbook. What I read scrawled in the line above my own made me dance a little jig. 'Great to be back on the trail after 8 days off catching up with family! The Whio Warriors, Finny and Fi.'

Yes! They were back on the trail and now just 3 hours ahead of me. I stared at the open door. Surely they'd stop at a hut not too far away, but which one? Could I track them down tonight? I looked at my ankle. It was the size of a house but I hadn't felt much pain in it for the past 2 hours. In fact, the ankle pain had been replaced by a searing sensation in my neck and back from staring at the floor beneath my feet. The strange new motion of walking seemed to have given me tendonitis on the top of my left foot. Both of these new ailments had done a sensational job of removing my focus from the ankle pain, and so I was grateful.

Captain Sensible reared his head, and I decided to call it a day there. I'd made a promise to myself that I'd only push on if the hut were a dump, and although I could see that some mice had taken many dumps within it, this was a nice hut. Capable of sleeping 16, it was nestled on the banks of the Taramakau River. Its original timber beams were still intact, and the only new addition since it'd been built in 1963 was a huge veranda. It was a good place to spend the night. I'd made 20 km since 8 a.m., which would do for the day. I was delighted to have made it any distance at all.

Sauntering the 50 metres down to the river, I set about scrubbing my two sets of running gear, before stripping off for an icy bath. I'd lost all sense of modesty, and was becoming incredibly at one with butt-nakedness. The water was freezing. Following a splash-and-dash-style scrub, I pulled most of my body out over the river, and sat on the edge for a further 5 minutes to ice my ankle. The sand flies seemed to enjoy having something to munch on, and much as their bites were an irritation, they were a welcome distraction from the cold water. I pulled a beanie on over my wet hair and looked up to my right. I could see the river tumbling over boulders as it forked off in two directions. Despite the pain, the unexpected river swim and the struggles of the day, I felt very content. I had moved forwards, and that's all that mattered. Knowing that Finny and Fi now weren't far away had carved just enough space in my mind to be able to appreciate where I was too, and for that I was grateful.

I returned to the hut, dusted the mouse droppings off from the kitchen work surface and set about making dinner. Spooning noodles into my mouth, I remembered that today was 10 March – my dad's birthday. It was a thought that dampened my otherwise chipper evening mood. I stared at the floor and felt a sadness bubbling in my belly. I'd loved to have called him to wish him a happy birthday, but I couldn't. I pulled out my phone and wrote him an email instead, even though I wouldn't be able to send it until I made a town. My thoughts started to rumble off their contented track and I began to wonder what on earth I was doing. Out here, on my own, not being able to wish my own dad a happy birthday – a choice that I, and I alone, had made. Was I completely selfish? I decided that it wasn't something I wanted to think on too much tonight. I had had a great day after all, so I refocused on the task that lay ahead.

All being well, it would take me a further three days to reach the State Highway 7. From there I could resupply with food at Hanmer Springs, and even take a day's rest before coming back to the trail. I decided that I was looking forward to having some phone signal, and being able to call someone and have a good solid cry. Maybe my mum, or possibly even my friend, Emma. I didn't think I wanted to worry my mum too much with the aftermath of the ankle incident. I resolved that I just needed to get through the next few days. I pulled on my pants of perspective again and wrote in my diary: 'Push on, Anna.'

Moving into the bunk room, I thought about the fact that I'd quite like to call Jamie when I made town. He'd get a kick out of this story, for sure. He liked a good story – best of all when there was some personal suffering involved. I tried to figure out exactly what it was 'we' were doing. Were we speaking to one another because we had to, or because we wanted to? I certainly wanted to, but what was his motive? Did he even have a motive? Did he actually like me in a romantic way? Come to think of it – did I actually like him in that way or was he just another person I craved to plug a growing sense of isolation? I shrugged off the thoughts, left them in a pile on the floor and clambered into my sleeping bag. As I shut my eyes, my final thought was of the following day's challenge – Harper's Pass.

Sweat poured from my brow and dripped onto the mass of leaves and mud beneath my feet. Droplets formed on the end of my nose as I paused briefly to look back down the valley. I was now nearing the top of Harper's Pass, and somewhere on the way up I had officially rediscovered my mojo.

I'd begun the day using a walk-run hybrid, concentrating hard as usual on the ground beneath my feet. The fact that I had a substantial ascent up Harper's Pass made things easier. It allowed me to wriggle free from the ton of self-imposed pressure, which I found myself pinned beneath so frequently. I physically couldn't go much faster up this hill – walking or running made little difference. The steep gradient of the pass, combined with negotiating slippery muddy sections due to the recent rain, forced me to a steady pace. I struck an internal bargain and allowed myself to run the flat sections on the way up. As long as I kept the ankle in line, it didn't cause me too much pain. I had also tried to run the downhills, figuring that this was a good place to pick up the pace. That turned out to be a disaster, and after going over on the angry ankle three times, I thought better of it. Something about the speed and lack of control when running downhill just kept throwing me over on the ankle. I would yelp, wince, swear, tell myself off and slow down again to a fast walk.

Still, I was in high spirits as I crested the pass. I enjoyed the sick sensation of my lungs gasping for oxygen, and my back being soaked in sweat. Once again I saw the world around me in full colour. I whooped in delight and took a video to upload to Facebook when I made town.

'Bloody hell – it's been a tough forty-eight hours…' I started. 'But I am officially back in the game!'

The valley below was awash with a dense green. As far as

the eye could see was native bush, separated by the Taramakau River, brown and filled with mud after the previous
night's deluge.

Out of the bush ahead of me came a young wiry-look-
ing lad with dark hair and a purposeful gait. I was soon deep
in conversation with Vitali from Belarus. An adventurous and
friendly soul, I liked him immediately and even more when he
began to talk about adventure racing.

'Every year in Belarus we do Red Fox Adventure Race,' he
told me. 'We climb round... how do you say... big rocks...?'

'Boulders?' I offered.

'Yes, yeees, big boulders! Boulders by the sea. And you
must throw yourself into the... umm, into the...'

'The water?'

'Yeeees – the water! You must throw yourself into the water! It is very dangerous.' He threw his head back theatrically
and laughed heartily. Snapping it forward again, he added,
'Sometimes you might die. My friend, he almost died...' He
paused again. 'You should come! Do Red Fox Adventure Race
with us! We need girl in team.'

'Err, Vitali, but you just said I might die?'

'Yeees, yeees, you might, but it will be fun! No?!'

We chatted for a while and then parted ways as I agreed to
stay in touch, in case he needed a girl to volunteer for potential

death in the Red Fox Adventure Race sometime in the future.

'It was real pleasure to meet you, Anna. One day, you come adventure with us. I will show you my home.'

During our exchange, Vitali had reminded me about a natural hot spring in the next section. I had considered steaming straight past it, but I knew it'd be one of those things that other trail users would talk about. 'Did you go to the Hurunui hot spring?' they would coo. 'No, I couldn't be arsed' didn't seem like quite as good a response as: 'Oh, yes, wasn't it splendid?!'

Besides, I enjoyed stories about places such as the Hurunui hot springs. They felt like myths of old. Information passed from person to person through hearsay alone. There was very little written about the hot springs and their exact location so finding them would be a challenge. I brought up my screen grab of the notes for this section of the trail, and read: 'When you come across a wall of rock that has the tell-tale signs of sulphur, look up to your right, follow the track for 2 minutes, and you'll come to the pool.'

I thought I'd missed it, and accepted defeat at the hands of the revered springs. But just then the intense smell of sulphide began to fill my nostrils. I saw a pile of sulphur-covered rocks, and wedged within them was a big stick pointing up the hill. This had to be it. This had to be the elusive and mystical Hurunui hot springs! I climbed up to the natural pool of geothermic energy. The wonder of nature, the glorious and timeless oasis of purity, which was, as it turns out, a stinking mass of green slime. Layers of sludge covered the pool's surface and cascaded over the edge. To the right of this natural hidden wonder, was a faded Department of Conservation sign which read 'Do not place your head under the water. We accept no responsibility for damage or injury to your body.' Atop this sign were a pair of equally faded men's red underpants. 'Well,' I thought, 'I'm here now, I might as well get in. Maybe it has some kind of healing powers. Let's keep this dream alive.'

I peeled off my sweaty clothes and stripped down to my birthday suit. Lowering into the water, I faced out from the side of hill, and looked upon the open forest. I watched speckles of sunlight dance on the ground between the trees and breathed in deeply. A waft of unwelcome sulphuric air rushed up my nostrils, but on the whole I decided that the pool and its accompanying odour wasn't actually too bad. The scum surrounding my shoulders seemed to have some kind of moisturising property to it, and the view was splendid. But just as I began to feel the pool might redeem itself, I felt a nick on my left shoulder. And another on my back. And then another on my cheek. 'Sand flies!' Little buggers. They were everywhere. I pushed my body lower into the pool, determined not to be put off by the invading swarm.

After grinning and bearing my way through 3 minutes in Hurunui hot-spring hell, I was being eaten alive. I couldn't handle it any more. I let out a war cry, jumping from the water and sprinting to where I'd left my clothes. Alas, the sand flies gave chase, and I was now surrounded by them. With more of my body exposed, I was a gigantic hunk of fresh meat and they were lining up, forks in hand, for a three-course dinner. I slapped, squelched and swatted them as best I could, but it was no use. I had to move. I grabbed my backpack, threw it over my shoulder, scooped up my clothes and started down the hill, away from the blood bath as fast as I could. What a treat it would have been, had another hiker come along at that very moment. The sight of me, naked as a baby, clothes in arms, hobbling through the forest with arms flailing wildly.

Fully clothed once more and now sporting an impressive assortment of sand fly bites, I passed Cameron Hut, and then Hurunui No. 3 Hut. In each I checked the logbook, and saw that Finny and Fi were only 2 hours ahead of me. I checked my watch. It was 3 p.m. I had another 2 hours of sunlight to make the final 10 kilometres to the next hut. They had to be at that one.

I padded alongside the Hurunui River, my gait now a full-blown run as I grew accustomed to dull waves of pain and concentrated intensely on the placement of my right foot. Approaching the hut from the forest, I caught sight of a shadow moving inside. The silhouette was that of a woman, and it looked like she had short hair. Fi had short hair. I couldn't contain my excitement as I crept silently around to the front of the hut, where I spotted something that made my heart swell. There, propped against the door were two carved wooden sticks. Beneath them were two pairs of boots that were unmistakably Finny's and Fi's. I placed a foot firmly on the step and shouted, 'Yay! I found you!' swinging open the door with gusto.

Finny was sat at the table to my left. His bemused expression dropped and gave way to a gigantic grin: 'No way!' he exclaimed.

Fiona was to my right, perched on the edge of the sleeping platform and leapt to her feet, arms open wide for a hug. I moved into them swiftly, almost suffocating myself in the process. My body relaxed and a huge tension lifted. It was the hug I'd been waiting for.

These were two people who knew me so well. Despite having only met them three months ago and not seen them in the past six weeks, they were old friends. There was no need for airs and graces here, no need for pleasantries. I could be myself. And best of all I could relay the events of the past three days without fear that they thought I was exaggerating, or being soft.

Finny and Fi had had quite the adventure in their time off the trail. They'd been to Christchurch, Methven, Geraldine, back to Twizel and to Fiona's childhood home of Otemata-ta. They'd had a full eight days off and stocked up on love, family, food and friends. Finny had enjoyed the reaction of his daughter Alley to his slimmer and more adventure-esque appearance. Since I'd seen them last Finny's hair had grown substantially, as had his beard. He estimated that he'd now lost around 8 kg since starting the trail.

What I loved about these two was that after 30 years together it was clear that they were still very much in love. They thanked one another for even the smallest tasks – passing the coffee, moving their shoes over to the fire, pulling out the toilet roll from the backpack – and they complemented one another's personalities perfectly. Finny was a laid-back, sarcastic, shy dreamer. Fiona was a realist, a planner and the more outgoing of the two. Above all, they were having fun, and having fun together. I looked at these two and hoped one day I'd find my own best friend to adventure with. I'd like that very much.

The mother of all catch-ups continued over dinner, coffee and chocolate. Finny commented on the change in the dynamic of their relationship off the trail, about how they'd begun to get scratchy with one another once back in the realms of 'real life'. It'd been a nice break, but they were keen to get back to the simplicity of life of the Te Araroa. As the evening wore on I realised that the simple act of offering and sharing food was a joy and a novelty I'd been missing. To top it off, this backcountry hut was one of the best I'd been in so far. A gigantic living space led into two shin-height Japanese-style sleeping platforms, separated by a wood burner. Our storytelling was frequently interrupted by noises from behind the burner, where it appeared that the Hurunui colony of mice had selected the corrugated sheet of metal as their home. We discussed what might be going on back there, watching mouse after mouse disappear into it.

'I reckon they've got a whole apartment block,' I proffered. 'Spiral staircase, penthouse suite, cheese shop – a real little village?'

These mice weren't shy and we watched, fascinated, as a duo caused havoc in the kitchen area. I'd never seen a mouse jump double its body height before, but these two were going for it, dancing their way effortlessly between pots, pans and the piping. It was a perfect after-dinner show.

That night I lay wrapped up in my sleeping bag, listening to the familiar sound of Fiona's snoring. I fell asleep with the largest, most immovable grin plastered across my face. I was in the company of friends once again. I wasn't alone anymore and I was happy.

I marched into the Rustic Cafe in Hanmer Springs and picked up the menu. Mouth dribbling, I ordered French toast, a date and orange scone, a square of rocky road, a berry smoothie, an omelette and a flat white. The waitress looked at me, aghast.

'I'm sorry, I haven't eaten since yesterday lunchtime,' I announced.

I'd run 10 km that morning before drawing a line in the sand at the side of the road, and hitching the 30 km to town to resupply. It was now 11 a.m. and I was ravenous. I returned to the table out the front of the cafe and sat down next to Finny and Fi. We'd managed to arrive in town just 10 minutes apart. I hadn't seen them in the two days since leaving them after our reunion at Hurunui Hut. I'd run an extra 10 km up the road to Boyle Village to make sure I maintained an unbroken line for the continued journey and they'd hitched a ride as soon as they'd made the main road. Finny thanked me for the sweets I'd left for them along various sections of trail (mostly on signposts or tree stumps), and explained how he'd developed an unhealthy obsession with dead animals on the trail. He was a photographer by trade, and was fascinated by how neatly (or not) the dead animals seemed to be preserved.

We three chatted about Coach Ron. According to the logbook in Hope Hut, Ron had now left the trail. His three-month Canadian visa had run out, and he would return in the summer of 2016 to continue where he left off. I felt sad that I'd not managed to catch him up, but all at once I knew I'd see him again one day. His final note had read: 'Well, my time's up. I'll leave the trail at Lake Sumner and return home to Canada to care for my parents. Finny, Fi, Andrew and Peter, it's been a real pleasure. Anna, I wish you'd listen to more of my advice, and here's some more. Take it steady and remember to not let speed 'de-feet' me. Go well. So long!'

Sitting out the front of Rustic Cafe we suddenly became a magnet for all Te Araroa trampers within a 100-km radius. This cafe was the bee's knees, and the trampers swarmed like flies. Other trampers would walk past, do a double take at our large packs and smelly appearance and stop to ask, 'Are you guys doing the TA?' If this were the Appalachian Trail, or the Pacific Crest Trail, this probably wouldn't have been such an event, but for the relatively small number of people who were on the trail to have eight of them in one place was a special treat. We were like Power Rangers. Avengers. Assembled from all walks of life, heading in different directions, united by a common cause.

Come 11.30 a.m. there were eight of us crammed around a small picnic table outside the cafe: Gabriel and Mel, whom I'd first met in a campground in Twizel a month back; Geoff, an Aucklander who was walking the trail in sections, supported by wife, Judy; Finny and Fi; and then there was the quiet guy sat to my right. Now, he really looked like a tramper. He was sporting a straw hat, and his gaunt cheeks led down to a small tuft of beard. His eyes were sunken, but kind, and framed by dark circles. He looked weary but there was a wistfulness about him. He reminded me a little of Robin Hood, and I was intrigued.

'Hi there,' I said, turning to him and introducing myself. 'I'm Anna.'

'I'm Ugo.'

'Oh, nice to meet you, Hugo.'

'No, no – U-go.'

'Oh, sorry – nice to meet you, U-go'

What kind of name was Ugo, I wondered? Had his

parents got drunk and forgotten to add the 'H' to the birth certificate? Or was this some strange Eastern European variant of the often-favoured middle class name.

'Where are you from, Ugo?'

'New Caledonia.'

'You're what?! Are you frickin' serious?!'

He nodded. That was it, I was off, running sentences together and unleashing my verbal diarrhoea all over his tufty beard: 'Oh-my-gosh. New Caledonia?! This. Is. Amazing! I've never met anyone from New Caledonia before. I mean, it's just so far away. Tell me about it. What's it like? I mean, what's it like to live there? To be a Caledonian? In fact, are you a Caledonian? A Caledonese? No, that sounds like a dog breed. What do you call yourself?'

Hailing as I do from the land of the Queen and tea, New Caledonia in the Pacific Islands is one of those places I'd only ever read about. Like Bora Bora and Vanuatu, I'd dribbled over the images of golden sands and huts built on stilts out into the ocean. It was like another world, and somewhere I fully accepted I may never actually visit.

Ugo paused. He opened his mouth to speak and I sat poised, ready for the answer. 'New Caledonia is…'

'Yes, yes…?'

'Like France. On a Pacific island.'

'Oh. really?' I slouched back, a little disappointed. Still, this was exciting, and I proceeded to grill him. He was an accountant and it seemed that New Caledonia was just like working in Paris. I suppose if you're in an office staring at a screen and a spreadsheet all day you can do that anywhere.

After a hearty meal together, the group dispersed. Finny and Fi hitched a ride back to the next section of trail, and I decided I'd take a day off to rest my ankle. Besides, I still needed to call home. On one hand the events of the Deception river-day-from-hell seemed like an age ago and I didn't want to dwell on them. On the other it had been a defining moment of the journey, and I was still processing it.

I spent the afternoon mulling over the events of the past few days. It'd been a roller coaster. For some reason, after what had happened at Deception River, and the state of my ankle, I just didn't care about being strong anymore. I nervously loaded up my Facebook. I found the video of me crying at the river's edge, along with photos of my ankle taken on my phone, clicked 'Post' and sat back in my chair. I'd just put a little piece of my soul out onto the worldwide web and I was petrified. It felt self-indulgent, but I couldn't not. I wanted people to know I was frightened. I wanted them on this journey with me. Life was never perfect after all. Life was, in fact, mostly a mess. A glorious tumbling, haphazard, last-minute, pooping-my-pants mess – and that's what I wanted to share. Jamie was right – I couldn't pretend it was all rainbows and sunshine anymore.

I was busy basking in the post-share glory and feeling all rather Zen when I remembered something. I sat bolt upright and gasped: 'Mum!' I'd meant to call her before I posted anything to reassure her that I was okay. I called but got no answer. Oh. It was the middle of the night in the UK after all, so I texted her. 'Mum, just so you know, I'm okay. I posted something on Facebook. I had a bit of a…' I paused for thought '… tumble but I'm okay. Call me when you wake up!'

I then spotted a text from Jamie. It read: 'I know that was hard to do. That post of balance you just put out. Honestly, it was great to see. It was real. Keep being you, keep being amazing.'

I replied: 'Oh my good god. I have had a mental few days. I have been to hell, high-fived Hades and come back to the land of the living. Can't wait to tell you all about it! And you can officially do the 'I told you so' dance. You have my blessing, so long as it includes a head spin.'

Any animosity was gone. He had been right, I knew he'd been right. I was done with sulking. I just wanted my friend back.

14

Rodents on the Rampage

'Ugo,' I sighed, 'could you try looking a little less... weird?'

It was 2 p.m. and I was stood on the roadside with my New Caledonian friend. I'd stocked up on seven days' worth of food and was feeling refreshed. We were hitching out of town, and back to where I had left the trail. Ugo had asked whether he could wait with me as he seemed to struggle getting rides, and every time he'd hitched with a girl it'd been no problem. I didn't think he'd affect my chances of a ride too much, so I had welcomed his company.

But we'd now been stood by the roadside for 30 minutes, and I was a little perplexed. I had an inkling that getting picked up as a lone female is always easier, but this was taking longer than I thought. That was until I turned and took a good look at Ugo. He'd paired dark shades with his straw hat and two hiking sticks. He was gently stroking his tufty beard, with hands clad in fingerless gloves. It was no wonder we weren't getting picked up. After I politely requested that Ugo tone down his weirdness, we were miraculously offered a ride not long after. The two events may or may not have been related – I will never know.

Ugo piled out of the van at Windy Gap car park where I'd spent the night two days ago camped next to the river. I hugged him and kissed him on the cheek goodbye before reaching into my pocket.

'I've got you a present.'

I shoved a brown paper bag into his hands with two chocolate bars in it. Over the past two days resting in Hanmer Springs, Ugo and I had really bonded and I'd discovered that these were his favourite treat. I decided that I'd pack him off with a little packet of joy to help him face whatever lay ahead on the trail. Ugo exited the van, and I carried on talking the ear off of our kind driver for a further 15 minutes up the road. It was now 3.45 p.m. and I had 14 km to run to Boyle Flat Hut before dark. I was well-fed, stocked up on good vibes and, as a major bonus, my ankle had halved in size.

I spent the next three days running along the St James' Walkway loaded up with seven days' worth of food. The pack felt incredibly heavy, but the terrain was kind enough. I trotted through beech forest, over rocks, and alongside swampy river plains, often blasting Tina Turner into my headphones to help with motivational levels. Some sections were tough on my ankle, especially with the increased pack weight, and so I checked in with it frequently. The last thing I wanted to do was push it too far, especially as I knew, after consulting the trail notes, that there was a challenging section ahead. To my delight, I met dozens of other hikers on the St James' Walkway. Although most of them weren't doing the Te Araroa, and were out for day or week-long hikes, it was nice to have an excuse to stop and chat, and frequently. On the second day I was belting out Tina Turner lyrics at the top of my lungs when I rounded the bend to find a group of seven middle-aged women in front of me. Through a brief initial chat I discovered that they were out on their annual ladies hike – something that had become a tradition for their friendship group. We'd been chatting for 5 minutes when I noticed one member of the group began to move forwards from the back.

'Here,' she said, 'I almost forgot. We bumped into your friends Finny and Fi yesterday and they passed me something to give you.'

I thought it odd that she didn't seem to be reaching into her pack to give me anything physical... and then it dawned on me – just as she spread her arms open wide.

'Is it a hug?!' I squealed, and she nodded and enveloped me. Finny and Fi had sent the gift of a hug back down the trail, the greatest gift a runner could ask for.

A few days before heading over Waiau Pass, I'd consulted the map. Uh, oh – a dotted line. Dashed lines are good, dotted lines not so much. They meant 'a route' rather than a trail. As in, you can go this way, many do, but be prepared to place your heart firmly in your mouth to negotiate it.

Since leaving Ugo, I'd spent three days running on the St James' Walkway, a popular tramping trail which mixes wide open river plains with forest. The night before taking on Waiau Pass, I stayed at the site of Caroline Creek Bivvy. The Department of Conservation do a pretty good job of maintaining huts, but some get rather neglected. Caroline's reputation had preceded her. Cesspit, hell hole, mouse factory were among the words used to describe it by southbounders. 'That thing needs burning down,' one tramper had gone so far as to say. Another had reported that someone (a human) had taken a dump right outside it. Suffice to say that I wasn't expecting a five-star hotel, but that was okay because I had my very own pop-up palace for just such occasions.

I came upon Caroline at the end of a long day. Nestled just inside the tree line, grey outer shell and a corrugated red roof, she looked kind of, well, cute. Sort of like the Wendy house I used to have when I was a kid. I tentatively slid back the rusty bolt on the crumbling wooden door and peered inside. Huh. Not too bad. The two canvas bunks looked like they'd been well used and possibly urinated in, but it wasn't too bad. Still, experience told me that in places like this it's probably better to pitch your tent, just to be safe. So after inspecting her crumbling innards and writing in her tattered logbook, I pitched up among the trees nearby.

In my haste (and in laziness), I camped a little closer than I should have done, and after drifting off into an early sleep at 7 p.m. I woke to a rustling. I shined my torch at the ceiling and inspected two black things on the lining of the tent, just above my head. Caterpillars? Nope. Mouse poo. Mice had crawled over and then pooped on the ceiling of my tent lining. Wonderful. The sand flies were having a field day with it, doing their very best to drag a turd four times their size homeward-bound. I admired the flies' tenacity. I'm not sure I'd have the balls to take on a poo four times my size.

Another rustle at my feet drew my attention from the poop-haul mission: a mouse was in my tent. 'How did you get in, you little bugger?' I asked, shining the torch at its beady little eyes. No answer (rude if you ask me). I assumed it had got in when I went for a wee. I chased it round the tent with my hands a few times before opening the zipper and watching it kamikaze leap outwards into the unknown. I checked the perimeter for holes. I'd heard mice would eat clean through tents, but I couldn't see anything.

I put my head back on the pillow and drifted off to sleep. Thirty minutes later and I woke to the distinct feel of something on my face. I grabbed out, flung it away, and it squeaked. A mouse had just crawled across my face. Across my actual face. Round two of the tent chase ensued, before a repeat kamikaze exit. And then I found it. Hidden in the sag of the lining near the zipper was a hole big enough for a little mouse to get through. This is how the prison guards in *The Shawshank Redemption* must have felt, I thought.

I pulled some tape from my ankle to patch up the hole and sprayed the outside of it with insect repellent for good measure. I'm not sure if mice like insect repellent but it had to be worth a go. Twenty minutes later I woke again with Micky performing a trapeze act above my head, but at least it was on the outside this time. I flicked its belly and it tumbled off the lining and scampered away.

As my mum always reminds me: 'You do know that mice pee as they run along, don't you?' So ensued a sleepless night, wondering if that taste on my lips was the noodles I had for dinner, or something a little more sinister. Every time I shut my eyes I was convinced I felt the patter of tiny paws across my cheek.

Sleep deprived but in good spirits, I left camp at 9 a.m. Nervous about the difficulty of the next section but excited to get Waiau Pass out of the way, I followed the trail up the river-bed, over boulders and onto lush green slopes, past tumbling waterfalls cascading into azure pools. The valley was filled with a low hanging cloud, and as I climbed the first 100 metres, I entered into a band of fine mist. Not an ideal day to be going up to a ridge line at 1,700 metres, but I employed my favourite fear tactic (pretending it wasn't happening) and ploughed on. The track steepened as it wound upward like a spiral staircase. Every time I got to a pole I'd look on... 'Oh, crikey, it keeps going...' I'd think.

I found myself scrambling up a near-vertical face for 30 minutes. I tried not to be freaked out by the sight of old poles, which had been destroyed by avalanches, and how they clung limply to the rock face, stripped of their orange hats, nothing but bare metal. Sometimes the poles disappeared entirely and there was nothing but a cairn to mark the way. I was growing increasingly tired, and it had now started to snow. My hands were going numb as I clung to rocks. I made it to a ledge wide enough to stand on and placed my pack down to pull on some gloves and more clothes.

'How the hell is this a tramping track?' I thought, now slightly angry at whoever put the dotted line on the map in the first place. I could see how people died up here. In my mind's eye, I zoomed out from the rock face. I saw myself there, in the snow alone, negotiating the climb with a damaged ankle. If my mother could see me now. I knew if I slipped, I'd be in big trouble. The chances were that no one would come by for days.

I decided that this wasn't a productive train of thought, and so shifted my focus solely to where my next handhold would be. I was absolutely petrified, but I needed to keep a lid on it. Letting fear control you is the sure-fire way to enter into disaster. 'Just keep moving. Next foothold. Next handhold. Where's the pole?' I repeated in my brain, channelling and controlling my thoughts. It was now freezing and the snow meant visibility was getting poor.

Onwards I went, until finally the vertical direction gave way to something a little more horizontal and I reached the top. The wind was blowing in from the right, and had stuck snow and ice to the faces of the rocks and poles. This was serious weather. I felt like I was somewhere no one ever went. Just as I reached the crest of the pass the wind took things up a notch and I felt extremely unsafe.

I scampered quickly down the scree the other side, and within 100 metres the wind had stopped. With every step the temperature rose, just a fraction. Ten minutes further on and I was out of the cloud. Not only that, but into some bright sunshine too. It glinted across the surface of Lake Constance, way down below, and I felt safe at last. This side of the mountain was a whole different ball game, and I liked it very much. I looked back to where I'd come from, up into a dark swirling whited-out mess, and I shuddered.

I negotiated the descent to Blue Lake Hut with a mixture of speed and caution. I was tired from the morning's effort and my ankle had started to give out at intervals on the uneven tussock which separated Lake Constance and Blue Lake.

I'd been looking forwards to making it to the shores of Blue Lake for some time. Blue Lake is famous for being the clearest lake in the world, with water which is as optically clear as distilled water. In 2011, New Zealand's Institute of Water and Atmospheric Research carried out scientific tests which put the visibility of the water in the lake at 80 metres. No one's entirely sure why or how the water has come to be so clear. It is mostly thought that it's due to the feeding lakes – all of which are formed of glacial water with little sediment deposits.

I had grand ideas of swimming, naked and free, in the

clearest lake in the world, especially since the sand flies and sludge had robbed me of an expected blissful experience at the Hurunui natural hot springs. Alas, another body of water, another set of dashed dreams. My body, in fact anyone's body, would be considered as water contamination – and so washing, bathing or drinking from the lake is forbidden. I pondered on the shame of not being able to fully immerse myself in something so pure and go for a wild swim. The look-but-don't-touch rule in many natural places around the world was a sad truth, but I also realised that if we imposed this rule on beautiful and unspoilt locations, perhaps they would remain beautiful and unspoilt for longer. Should beauty be preserved or enjoyed, I wondered?

Blue Lake Hut was a 16-bunk serviced facility on the shores of the lake. Partly secluded, and surrounded by dramatic peaks, it was a popular stop-off during the short two-day circuit hike from nearby St Arnaud. Just as with Goat Pass Hut, I had assumed that Blue Lake Hut would be teeming. It was a weekday, but still it was unusual for Kiwis to observe the tradition of only getting outdoors at the weekend, and I was disappointed that I couldn't see anyone inside.

I wrenched the unnecessarily large metal handle upward, and stepped inside. I was rather nonplussed, and walking around, it struck me how cruel a thing expectation and imagination can be. It felt cold and empty, like a deserted community hall. I didn't much fancy spending the night here alone, but I decided to eat lunch and consider my options on a full stomach. The only problem with trying to eat lunch in the hut was that there was an odd smell. One of those rotting-carcass kind of whiffs which feels like someone is trying to suffocate you with a mixture of rotten eggs and death. I put down my peanut butter wrap and moved over to the logbook to read the recent entries.

Before I could even open the book, I was greeted by familiar handwriting. It began: 'Do not drink the water in this hut. We just fished a dead rat out the top of the water tank. It was festering and swollen, and there were maggots in it...' The note continued to explain that there was no cover on the down pipe into the tank and, as a result, a rat seemed to have decided it was a good place to go for a swim, and consequently end its little life.

There was a break in the note and a change of pen. Later that day: 'It's worse than we thought. We drained the tank and found another rotting rat at the bottom, as well as two mice. Definitely don't drink this water!' I looked at the bottom of the page, where it was signed: 'Finny.'

No wonder this place stunk of death. I started to think how grateful I was that the Whio Warriors had made it here before me. I was dying of thirst and would have guzzled straight from the tap given half the chance. I'd grown accustomed to being cautious about drinking from streams and using water tablets where necessary, but checking the water tank nestled on the shores of the cleanest and clearest lake in the world, I hadn't bargained on that one. The irony of the situation wasn't lost on me. Disgusting as it was, I was intrigued, and so went in search of the scene of the crime: the water tank. There, plastered to the front of it was a drawing of a gigantic rat, lying on its back with crosses in its eyes – notifying the viewer, if they were in any doubt, that this rat was dead. Beneath the impeccably accurate artwork was written: DO NOT DRINK!

If Blue Lake Hut's abandoned state didn't sway me from spending the night there, the lack of available drinking water did. Finny and Fi had noted they were headed that day to stay at West Sabine Hut, 7 km further down the track, and I decided to do the same. It was 3 p.m. Sunset was usually around 6 p.m. (or 30 minutes earlier in the bush, as locals always warned me) so I still had plenty of time to make it before dark.

The trail led me yet again to another reunion with Finny and Fi. It ambled gently along the edges of the Sabine River, like a giant, if slightly overgrown, Japanese garden, ducking in and out of bush and over boulder slopes. I enjoyed being able to run freely and bounded off the tree roots, knowing that I was heading for guaranteed company at the hut.

'It's your classic type-five fun,' said Fiona, as we exchanged Waiau Pass experiences. 'Not much fun, and just bloody dangerous.' I tended to agree.

Curled up on the bottom bunk that night, in between Fiona's familiar snores, I could hear the rats in residence here really going for it. We'd all taken care to hang and bag any remaining food, so I didn't mind that I could hear them. In fact, I now only worried when I couldn't hear them – that's when I wondered where they were, and whether they were poised at the edge of my pillow ready to strike as I slept.

THE PANTS OF PERSPECTIVE

15

The Richmond Ranges

I tumbled headlong into the St Arnaud Alpine Lodge. Stopping briefly to allow the automatic doors to slide open, and catching a glimpse of myself in the glass, I looked a state. Entering the large and swanky reception area, I tiptoed across the freshly buffed wooden floor and up to the front desk. The clerk looked up from her screen.

'Hello!' I beamed, grinning from ear to ear through a grimy face. 'I was wondering if you had any space in the… err, backpackers' bit?'

I'd made the call a few days earlier to take a little rest in St Arnaud. The past week had ground my energy levels to a zero, and I knew that the toughest section of the trail lay ahead. I'd left Finny and Fi that morning with instructions to book them into the backpackers' area too, but as it turned out there was only one spot left. I felt a little guilty, but I knew they'd understand. Besides, I had a sneaking suspicion that Finny wouldn't mind one bit that they had to stay in the posh part of the lodge.

Once I'd checked in, I got to what had been on my mind all week: 'I hear you do REALLY good pizzas here.' I had heard from southbound trampers that the pizzas at the

St Arnaud Lodge were beyond compare.

The clerk checked her watch. It was 2 p.m. Had I missed the kitchen? She screwed up her face and I seized the opportunity to sway her judgement.

'I've been running for seven days, and I've just heard so much about these pizzas. I'll be really quick. I promise. I'm, like, a professional fast pizza-eater. I can just go in and eat it now if that makes it easier?'

She looked me up and down, and decided it was best for the whole of mankind that I went and had a shower first. She would order the pizza in the meantime and it'd be fresh out the oven in 20 minutes.

St Arnaud is a strange and beautiful place. Beautiful in that it's nestled on the shores of Lake Rotoiti, an aquamarine expanse of water with a trail running along its shores, and strange in that it has a population of just 400 people.

After a lunchtime refuelling on pizza, beer, coffee and shortbread, I went in for round two at dinner with Finny and Fi. Conversation turned to the fact that the wine, steak, burgers and chocolate cake we were inhaling was terrible for all of our budgets, but wonderful for our stomachs so we didn't care. We then digested the final section of trail that had led us all to St Arnaud. Having already climbed nearly 2,000 metres up and over Waiau Pass the day before, we had all then slept at river level before climbing back up to Travers Saddle at 1,700 metres. It was a climb that had taken me 2 hours of huffing and puffing and there were sections so steep that I had to break them down into ten steps at a time, for fear my calves might explode. But the view from the top had been a highlight of the trail so far. We chatted back and forth about the beautiful blue skies, and the granite mountains with pockets of snow set against them. It had been worth every ounce of energy to get up there.

The joy of making the summit and following it with a 2-hour descent to St Arnaud was saddened by the knowledge that up at Travers Saddle there was a young German lad who had gone missing without a trace last summer – an event all too common in the Kiwi bush, and on high trails. His pack had been found on the saddle itself, laid neatly at the side of the trail, but his camera was missing and authorities could only assume that he had gone off trail to take a picture and slipped somewhere. His family were still desperately searching for his body a year on, and posters lined the huts in the Nelson Lakes. If I thought too long on what had happened to the boy, and how his family would even begin to cope with such a loss, it made me sad, and I didn't like to be sad. I recognised that he was a trail user just like me. He had a family, just like me. I doubt he had done anything reckless to end up missing, and his story hammered home the very real risk of travelling alone through New Zealand's backcountry. Needless to say, I double-checked the batteries in my SPOT safety tracker that night.

The impending nine-day journey through the Richmond

Ranges had stood over me like a dark shadow for the past few weeks. These ranges were revered among trail users as one of the hardest sections of trail. A combination of remote huts, river crossings, infrequently used routes, exposed ridge lines and changeable weather patterns made them a challenge for even the most seasoned tramper. They were now all that stood between me and the final section of trail on the South Island.

Fi and I decided that we'd plan the next nine-day stretch through the Richmond Ranges together. I don't think I openly expressed the relief that that gave me, but I felt it. The next section was rumoured to be the most remote of the entire trail, and the toughest. The thought of going into it alone drained me before even starting. If I could at least know that I would end up at the same hut as my friends each night, well, that made everything just that bit more manageable.

That night, Jamie called. Sitting against the wall at the bottom of the stairs, as it was the only place I could get any signal, I gave him a full breakdown of all the food I had recently inhaled, and explained that I was a bit nervous about the next section. I didn't want to come across too weak, so I played down my concern.

'Is it remote out there? Scary?' he asked.

'Kind of. I'm not sure,' I responded.

'O, maybe you'll cry again. You know people love it when you cry!' he ribbed, referencing the fact that the response to the video of me crying at Deception River had attracted a large amount of attention on Facebook.

I sighed. 'Yes, Jamie, I promise to share it with people if I cry.'

I then moved on to talking about the fact that I missed my family, and he started giving advice on what to think of to ease the longing. 'Think happy thoughts,' he started.

'Happy thoughts? I'm not fricking Peter Pan, J!'

I sensed he was overdoing it with his advice and clocked an ulterior motive. 'Are you trying to make me cry now?' I jibed.

I put the phone down after 45 minutes of giggles and mutual mickey-taking. We were friends, just good friends, and the exchange was a nice little boost before heading into the Richmond Ranges.

The morning I was due to leave St Arnaud, I found myself being unusually productive. Supposing I better start getting ready for the next section, I ripped open the supplies box I'd sent to the lodge from Christchurch. My heart sank. It was the same rubbish I'd sent myself at Arthur's Pass. I ate a packet of mint thins and sat down with a sigh. The first task was to discard the milk powder. I was over milk powder. I didn't even need milk powder. I fondled the jar of peanut butter. I was over peanut butter too, which was a big statement coming from a peanut-butter lover. The thought of placing any more of it in my stomach made me dry retch, and so I made the call to leave that behind too. I loaded the remaining items into my bag: some instant coffee, instant noodles, sachets of tuna fish, a pack of tortilla wraps, another pack of mint biscuits, dehydrated peas, three bars of Whittaker's chocolate, a bag of trail mix and far more packets of jelly sweets than were necessary.

The days in the Richmond Ranges began to settle into a rhythm. Each morning Finny and Fi would leave the hut before me. I'd stay behind, do my stretching exercises, faff a bit (a lot), spend too long reading one of the many dusty copies of travel magazines from a bygone era often left in these huts, and then catch them up mid-morning. We'd have a brief chat, share the genius creative ideas we'd had so far that day (of which there were plenty), question why it was so darn hard, and then I'd bound on to whichever hut was next. There I'd take a nice long break, wait for them to arrive, and we'd lunch. Then, I'd skip off again to the next hut for that night. I'd have time to take a naked dunk in the nearby river, curl up for a pre-dinner sleep before they came through the door, and we could begin digesting the day's efforts.

I enjoyed this game of cat and mouse immensely. It gave me a focus in the mornings to chase them down as fast as possible and, on most days, I had someone to share lunch with too. Once I passed them I would leave them sweets on signposts every now and then, and if I came across a hut I would leave a little note in the logbook which always said: 'Keep going Whio Warriors!'

From time to time I wondered whether I was annoying them by clinging on like a third wheel, but my antics seemed to help break up their days too.

As well as offering up a physical challenge, navigating the ranges proved tricky. The trail twisted and turned at every opportunity, leading me across rivers, through low scrubland and over steep scree-covered slopes. As I began a traverse of Mount Ellis up at 1,600 metres high, a thick fog rolled in, making it virtually impossible to spot the orange marker poles. At each pole I would take off in the direction I thought the trail might lead, trying to keep in mind where I'd come from. If after running for a minute I hadn't spotted the next pole, then I'd realise I'd run in the wrong direction and return to the previous pole to try again. I developed a trick of using my arm span to try to predict where the next pole might appear. Alas, the highly technical arm-span navigation technique didn't work so well when the trail deviated from a linear course. Nor did it work once the marker poles disappeared entirely, and all that remained were cairns placed by other trampers. When I freaked myself out and got lost, I'd have a word with myself, before relocating the trail and spending 30 seconds building a new rock pile in the right direction so that Finny and Fi wouldn't have to stop and talk to themselves too. I relished the chance to be useful on the trail. It was as if I was channelling the spirit of Coach Ron, and that made me smile.

A combination of rain and slippery long grass on certain sections reduced me to a snail's pace, and all sections took longer than I expected. I'd frequently trip and go tumbling down the slope, my sprained and still slightly swollen ankle screaming out with every awkward fall. When Top Wairoa Hut came into view – a bright orange shelter set against a backdrop of lush green – I was overcome with a sense of relief. Finny and Fi came through the door of the hut within the hour, and we chatted as I finished my lunch and watched them prepare theirs. Oh, how I longed for them to tell me that they'd stop there for the day, that the morning section had taken them longer than they expected, and as the next part contained river crossings, they didn't want to risk it getting dark while they were still out. Alas, there was no sign of any intention to stay from the Whio Warriors. So I drained the final dregs from my imaginary can of woman-up, hauled the pack onto my back and slipped out the door, bound for Mid Wairoa Hut.

The trail to Mid Wairoa was exciting to say the least. Some portions of it had eroded away almost entirely, and required that I clung to tree roots to haul myself up and round the already crumbling rocks. At one point, I had grown a little too confident and bounded at speed along a narrow ledge. I lost my footing, tripped, landed on my butt and began sliding uncontrollably down a slope towards a sheer drop. A metre from the edge, I managed to grab a tree root and bring myself to a stop. I sat up and dusted the leaves and mud from my hair. 'Be careful, Anna, you muppet,' I reminded myself, laughing at my own stupidity.

That night in Mid Wairoa Hut the three of us chatted and

laughed about the day's exploits, and inspected the logbook together. There, we found a note from Peter and Andrew, who now seemed to have renamed themselves Mav and Goose. The last time I'd seen them near Lake Tekapo, they had mentioned something about needing trail names, so they'd gone ahead and created them. I think it was an American thing...

16

On Top of the World

Getting up in the dark wasn't something I was used to at all. I'd grown accustomed to waking up with the sun, and most days I didn't even set an alarm, knowing I'd be awake by 8 a.m. at the very latest. I rarely got up before daybreak because there was never any sense in running in the dark. It was dangerous, even with a head torch (which I didn't have), and I deemed it entirely unnecessary. But today was different. The days leading into this one were filled with nervous thoughts. Anxious moments where my mind drifted to tales of hikers missing without a trace on Mount Rintoul's ridge line. The warnings in the trail notes referencing 'steep exposed sections' danced through my brain, frequently and without invitation.

'Feet on the floor, McNuff, feet on the floor, let's go.'

Shimmying out of the toasty warm sleeping bag, I pulled on a jacket, beanie and leggings. Once out of the hut, I tiptoed across the grass toward the toilet. Large droplets of dew freed themselves from the blades as my feet brushed past. I stopped to take in the view. It was rare to have the chance to be in such a remote area and yet have a window into civilisation. We were a four-day hike from the nearest town and I felt a mixture of connection and detachment from the life down there, nestled between the pavements and street lamps, I could be leading.

As we ate breakfast in our tiny elevated palace, I watched the skies come to life through the condensation on the window. The dark navy and violets of dusk gave way to a full pink and orange sunrise, one which lit up the Tasman Bay further to the west. Finny and Fi left at 7 a.m. to get a head start on the day. I rolled around on the floor of the hut for a little longer doing stretching exercises, and 45 minutes later I began the steep climb from the hut up and on to the ridge line.

The trail started in bush before emerging onto open tops and a scree slope. Scree was always a tall order. It was great fun to come down (scree-skiing had fast become a favourite pastime), but a struggle to go up. It absorbed every last ounce of energy from my steps. Heels, toes and even scrambling out-stretched hands sinking into the ever-shifting surface, causing mini avalanches as I ascended.

I hummed the lyrics to the Carpenters' 'Top of the World' as I puffed and panted to the top. The incline eventually gave way to a plateau and I found myself on the ridge line I'd heard so much about. Breathing hard, legs burning, I turned 360 de-grees and a broad smile stretched across my face. It was just… beautiful. The weather had held and I could see for miles upon miles. Peaks of every shape and variety stretched as far as the eye could see. Little jagged grey ones, wide round green ones, big proud reddish brown ones – those in the forefront were crystal clear, and those farther away were just ghostly outlines.

I stood for a minute, taking it all in. Every time I blinked, and looked again, something new seemed to reveal itself. The ridge line curved steadily round to the right. To the left, I spotted an orange triangle on a pole, but I couldn't see a second one further on. It made me nervous when I could only see one. I liked to try to second guess where the trail went – the further ahead I could see, the better. For some reason being able to construct even a shaky and hasty vision of what lay ahead calmed me down. I followed the trail to the pole, perched at the edge of a rocky ridge.

I thought back to the trail notes and tossed a jumble of words around in my mind. I vaguely remembered something about choosing to go directly along the ridge, or skirting around the slope, but I concluded it couldn't be referring to this section of the ridge, could it?! Surely there was no way I would be expected to go along this ridge?! I looked down to the south slope and wondered about going that way instead. It didn't seem to be an appealing option either, as the ground dropped away very steeply and was almost all slippery scree.

I began to doubt myself. I thought back to the challenges of Waiau Pass – how ridiculous that had felt at the time – and I concluded that the trail could well intend to take me along this ridge line. I took a deep breath, dropped down on to the heels of my feet and put my hands out beside me. If I was taking on this route, I was going to do it by staying as low to the ground (or what little ground there was) as possible. I assumed the position of a crab, a very frightened crab with a gigantic backpack. This was going to take some careful progress. Heart beating clean out of my chest, I edged forward. I moved one foot or hand at a time, stopping to regain balance between any progress. The rock dropped quickly away on both sides, and I was clambering on something barely wide enough to take my trainers. Three steps out on to the ridge I spotted two figures in the distance: Finny and Fi. Silhouetted against the early morning sun, the sight of them reassured me. Thoughts that they'd made it this far, so it must be okay, were followed quickly by wondering how they made it. My heart beat harder still and I focused my attention to my breathing. I thought back to the first time I'd tried slacklining. I remembered how amazed I was that bringing your breathing under control had such an effect on how much the line wobbled underfoot. Of course, that was a line strung between two trees in Derbyshire; these were rocks 1,700 metres up in New Zealand. Still, the principle was the same.

Shoving all thoughts from my mind I shuffled a little further along. Still one leg or arm at a time, and still very slowly. I stopped to catch my breath and decided to turn my head to look down the mountain, rather than up and out along the ridge, because looking out along the ridge really wasn't working as a calming tactic. Just as I looked down, I spotted it: 'There you are, you little bugger!' I said out loud. Five metres down the slope to my right was an orange pole. The next pole. The pole I *should* have been following.

'Shit!' I inhaled sharply.

ANNA MCNUFF

The pole is down there. That means I'm not meant to be up here. Up here, limbs dangling precariously on granite rocks – a realisation that suddenly made everything a lot worse.

'Breathe, Anna, breathe…'

I eased myself back in the direction I'd come from. I felt like a bus that'd gone down a one-way street. Turning around wasn't an option. The ridge was so narrow that there was only space for one limb on a section of it at a time. What had been a tricky manoeuvre forwards, doubled in difficulty in reverse. At one point I froze, solid.

'You're going to fall. Don't fall. Just don't fall. For Christ's sake, Anna, don't fall!'

At last I made it far enough back to a point where I thought it would be safe to rejoin the mountainside. I locked eyes on the elusive pole below and supported my body weight on my two arms, lowering myself onto the scree below. As my feet found the floor, it moved.

'Woah!' I yelped, dropping in height as the scree under my feet slid downwards, taking me with it for a little. I grasped a solid bit of granite to my left and watched as a mini rockslide continued below me, gathering up a few larger boulders and sending them tumbling downwards.

I heard a call, and then an echo: 'Anna?!' My name bounced around and off the neighbouring peaks like a pinball in an arcade game. Playing peek-a-boo, I popped my head

242

around the side of the granite that I was now clinging to, and shouted and waved to Finny and Fi, who'd stopped their hike and were facing in my direction.

'Hey,' I yelled, 'I'm here!'

'Ah, there you are!' came the reply from Finny. 'We thought you might have fallen and died,' he added, in his usual matter-of-fact tone. I could hear them as clear as day, even though they were a kilometre further along the ridge.

'Nah, just thought I'd... um... rearrange the mountain a little, you know? I didn't fancy death today,' I called back, using humour to mask the fact that my insides were doing somersaults. 'I'm going to go down and round,' I ventured. 'Is that what you guys did?'

'Yep! That's the way!' they hollered back, before turning on their heels to continue along the ridge line.

After a literal rocky start the poles were kinder from then on. I navigated my way on to the section of ridge where Finny and Fi had been standing and found it wide enough to pick up running again. A little further on I came across them, perched on an open rock, having a snack. They gave a little cheer as I approached and I felt like a child running into the arms of her parents.

'Holy crap!' I exclaimed, throwing off my pack and dropping down to sit alongside them. 'That was gnarly!'

Munching on a square of cheese, I looked around. I could

see Tasman Bay to the west. Atlas-style mountain peaks poked through a blanket of clouds, and the sun teamed up with the bluest of skies to frame ghostly outlines of the ranges already run. Scenes of ineffable natural beauty had mingled with moments of panic, exhaustion, fear and elation. This, I thought, was surely life at its fullest, and the world at its most beautiful. But at the same time, this was also ridiculous. It was insane. Was I really here? Was I really doing this?

I contemplated all the things that might have prevented me from being here: the incessant requirement to earn money, the ease and comfort of a nine to five job, the fear of not being able to complete the run. Yet all at once I remembered how easy the decision had been to come on this run. I'd made it in a split second, before I had a chance to change my mind. And that had changed my life.

It was 2 kilometres from our snack spot to the next hut and there was no sense in heading off alone. Right now, I wanted company. More than that I wanted the company of these two – two people who'd lived in New Zealand all of their lives and understood its backcountry better than I ever would. They calmed me. They were my safety blanket. We walked the next 2 km together and it was the most fun I'd had on the trip so far. I say walked, but, as all experienced hikers do, Finny and Fi moved quickly. I mostly had to trot to keep up with them, especially on the downhill sections. We scrambled across boulder fields and more scree, until dropping down into the bushline, where we paused to brew up a celebratory cup of tea on our stoves. Perched on the side of the trail through cheers-ing and chocolate munching, I felt content. Content, relieved and re-freshed. Their company filled an ache in my heart, a void that had been left empty for far too many months.

The remainder of the day was far less dramatic but no less emotional. Buoyed by the morning triumphs, I felt happy to push on alone again. The trail continued along the tops of the forest, thrusting me once again out on to narrow sections of ridge, but this time I felt safer, more prepared and more con-fident. All I thought was 'just keep moving,' letting the stomp, stomp, stomp of my feet slot in time with the thud, thud, thud of my heart. Every now and then I'd allow myself a glance back at what I'd just run along. Holy heck. It looked badass.

After an hour or so the pathway opened out and through a blustery, tussock-covered hillside was a faint trail winding its way into the mountains in the distance. I could run freely, and it felt incredible. At one point I felt so overwhelmed with happiness that I moved myself to tears. This is what it was all about, moments like these. I felt like a child, free and unshack-led, with no concern beyond the immediate moments, beyond each footstep on the trail.

The trail continued along the ridge, across a scree slope, and then there it was: Slaty Hut. I'd only been running for 90 minutes, and the DoC estimated arrival time said 5 hours! My gaze met the hut with a mixture of relief and sadness. I was proud of myself for making it through the day, proud that I had chosen friendship and shared memories over pride, and proud that I'd kept negative thoughts at bay. I was happy to be headed for safety but, as is the case with all challenges that offer you an opportunity to grow, sad that it was over. I knew that it was days like these that I would take to my grave – those filled with highs and lows, and nothing in between. I sighed a deep but happy sigh and padded off toward the hut.

17

So Long, South Island

Sitting in a cafe in Nelson felt surreal. I felt like a stranger here, like I didn't belong. The world around me was moving in slow motion. I watched as passers-by went about their daily business. Everyone seemed to be moving so fast; everyone had somewhere to go. I felt entirely out of place. That morning I had left Finny and Fi at Slaty Hut. I had run out of the bush and on to the road towards Nelson. Here I was sitting once again in a cafe, filling my face with date and orange scones, and washing them down with a flat white, but this time things felt different. Everything was odd.

I'd been in and out of the bush dozens of times over the past few months, but there was something about this off-trail stop that was different. I couldn't quite put my finger on it. On my second trip to buy more coffee from the counter, the poor guy behind it made the mistake of asking me whether I'd had a good day. I tried to explain that I'd started my day in a hut in the backcountry (blank face) and that I was running the Te Araroa Trail (even blanker face), and that this was all a little hectic in here. He looked around at the two other customers in the I and smiled awkwardly. 'Um… sure… that'll be three dollars fifty… you, um… take a seat and I'll, um, bring it over.'

Back in the bush, things took a turn for the emotional worse, and I hit an all-time and new kind of low. I just couldn't stop crying. It was ridiculous. The rain had turned every element of the trail into a muddy slide. At least once per kilometre I would end up slipping on a tree root, or on a slightly sloping part of the trail, and land with a thud on my behind. I would then cry. Just sit there and sob for anything between 30 seconds and 2 minutes, before laughing at myself manically and setting off again. I could offer up no explanation for my behaviour other than I had gone mental. It was like someone had ripped the control button off of my emotions, leaving them to do whatever they pleased, in any order they wished. I tried my best to pep myself up. I sang, I told myself jokes, I thought of my family, I even sat down at one point and ate an entire 250 g bar of Whittaker's chocolate. When all else fails, chocolate will be there for you.

I left the small harbour town of Anakiwa at 2 p.m. As I was fundraising for the Outward Bound Trust, I'd enjoyed a night at the charity's headquarters there, meeting the school director, Jon, and sharing a few beers with the staff. The Richmond Ranges were now behind me, and I was heading into the final section of the trail on the South Island. Having run 1,400 km to this point, I was now just one section of trail away from the halfway line. I'd learned that Finny and Fi were now a good 55 km ahead on the Queen Charlotte Track, a sub-section of the Te Araroa Trail. If I were to have any chance of making our planned rendezvous for chips at Punga Cove in the evening, I'd have to run a marathon that afternoon.

I sat on a bench overlooking the bay and stared out at the ocean – I'd made 7 km so far today. I desperately wanted to catch up with Finny and Fi, as once they completed the track they'd return home to the North Island. Seeing them was really important to me, largely because I hadn't mentally prepared myself that the last time I saw them would be our goodbye. But I offered myself another option, and it was like a pressure valve released. How about I just take it easy? I don't catch up Finny and Fi, and arrive in Wellington a day late? That way I could actually enjoy the run to the end of the trail at Ship Cove. Would that really be so bad? I decided it wouldn't be bad at all.

I threw my bag on my back and ran the next 7 km to Mistletoe Bay. I'd managed to leave my tent fly (the outer part of the tent that makes the tent waterproof) at Anakiwa, and so I resolved that I'd take a room, over an exposed mesh tent, if they were cheap enough. At Mistletoe Bay, they had a room in a cottage for only $5 more than a camp spot would have cost me.

I was still feeling a bit low, especially now I wasn't going to have the company of Finny and Fi tonight, so I sat in the cottage and stared at the wall. I wanted to call someone. Mum? What would I say to Mum. 'Hi Mum, I'm tired, and just a bit exhausted, I can't really explain it.' My friend Emma? That would only make me feel more sad as she soothed me so far from home. No, I wanted to call Jamie. I stared at the wall a little more, just for good measure. Was calling him now a good idea? I was feeling weak. I swiped open my phone and brought the number up on the screen. My thumb hovered over it. Don't be ridiculous. What are you going to say? I put the phone down and went to make a cup of tea.

Dinner eaten and tea consumed, I was feeling a bit stronger. 'Stuff it,' I thought and I pressed dial. He picked up and we chatted for around 5 minutes. I gave him a tour of my luxury accommodation for the night, and filled him in on my visit to Outward Bound and the journey from Nelson. I left out all the parts where I'd cried and beaten myself up and got frustrated, of course, choosing only to share what I saw as the facts and not the mental narrative that went along with them, but I did want some sympathy. I needed some sympathy. So I tried venturing a little vulnerability, just to see what would happen.

'I'm so tired, Jamie!' I said dramatically, resting my head on my arms on the chest of drawers where the laptop was placed.

'Oh, right!' he said. 'Well, you're tired, and I should go anyway. So I'll speak to you again soon. Ta-ra.'

'Uh, okay – alright. Bye, then.'

I hung up and felt like an idiot. I laughed at myself. He didn't like me like that at all. I felt like I'd put on my best 'damsel in distress, come and be my knight in shining armour' routine, and he'd had to go. That settled it then. We were just friends, and I think I was okay with that.

He loves me not.

It was official; I'd gone soft. I'd caved yesterday and only run 15 km, then taken the (literally) soft option of a soft bed. I knew there was a resort near where I intended to camp the next night at Punga Cove – it was where I was supposed to have met Finny and Fi the previous day – so I bargained with myself that I'd stop for a drink there, before retreating to camp at the DoC campsite 1 km down the road. Under no circumstances would I allow myself to stay in the section for backpackers at the Punga Cove Lodge.

It'd been a long and dusty run from Mistletoe Bay. I'd opted to take the coastal road instead of the trail, because, quite frankly, I'd had enough of dense, enclosed trails. The surrounding islands and inlets of the Queen Charlotte Track were beautiful. Each one was like a little nugget dropped in the emerald and blue ocean, and I wanted to be able to have an uninterrupted view of them as I ran. Running up the final hill to Punga Cove, it was hot as hell. A car passed me and stopped at the side of the road. A woman got out.

'I'm heading up to collect my husband, can I give you a ride?'

'No, I'm okay thanks, I have to run it all. I'm on a charity run. I'm raising money for Outward Bound – but thank you.'

'Are you sure? It's a REALLY long way still to go up there.'

'No, no, I'm okay. Thanks though.'

Was it a really long way to go? I was sure it was only another 2 km to the cove, and even less to the top, but she'd seemed really insistent. I ducked into the bushes for a wee and when I emerged the car was there again, only this time they were coming back down the hill. They pulled over again and wound down the window.

'Here – take this,' they said, handing me a $10 note. 'It's a wonderful thing you're doing. And I still can't believe you're going to run all the way up there.'

Cresting the hill at last I let my legs run freely down the other side. It really wasn't that far at all – just the 1.5 km I had expected – thank goodness. I increased my stride length, bounding from one foot to the other, almost toppling each stride. Whatever happened now, I knew there was a beer at the bottom of this hill. I darted through the Punga Cove complex, moved swiftly past the restaurant and walked straight into the small dockside bar. With my bag still on my back I bought a pint of ale, a can of Fanta, a chocolate bar and a giant slice of carrot cake. I then ordered some sweet potato fries. Just in case, you know, I got hungry on the way from the bar to sitting down. I moved to the sofas on the dock outside and inhaled the first round of food whilst looking out across the bay.

Forest-covered hillsides tumbled into azure blue waters all around me. I never knew there were so many shades of green until I'd visited New Zealand. Palm, punga, pine and beech trees swayed gently to and fro. The odd small sailing boat appeared from behind one land mass and disappeared behind another. Light wispy clouds shifted shape frequently, and moved across the horizon briskly, as if on a mission of their own. White-faced herons and shag birds swooped and glided, diving every now and then into the sea to take advantage of a school of fish that'd just surfaced near the jetty. As dusk arrived, so did the chorus from the birds in the bush. Listening carefully I could hear the haunting cry of the guru and the undeniable sound of moreporks.

A full stomach made me drowsy. I rested my head on the side of the sofa and drifted in and out of sleep. The salty sea breeze flowed over my nose and eyelids, making its way down the back of my duffle coat. My black leggings had soaked up the sun's heat over the afternoon and were now passing it on to my legs. The soft reggae that was pumping out of the speaker system mingled with the voices of lodge guests. I was calm. I was relaxed. This was a little slice of paradise, and I was wonderfully happy.

When I next opened my eyes, the skies had turned to a soft shade of pink, and the moon was out. It was just about full and cast its bright light across ever-darkening waters. There was no way I was heading back and running to the DoC campground, so I decided I should probably go and check-in to a room for backpackers and have a shower…

'Good morning!' said a man's voice just behind me. I

swung around from the viewpoint where I had been enjoying the sunrise to see two guys standing in the car park at Punga Cove. I stepped down from the tree stump I was standing on and moved towards them.

'Hiya. What are you doing up so early?' I asked. It had just turned 7 a.m.

'Off kayaking! Where are you going with that pack of yours?!'

I explained to Gerald and his friend what I was doing. Gerald seemed rather impressed, possibly as impressed as I was of his kayaking tales. I bid them a good morning and sped off down the trail.

I was up bright and early because that day I would run the final few steps on New Zealand's South Island. The only way to get between the two islands (unless flying) is by ferry from Picton in the South Island to Wellington in the North Island. Picton was now actually further south of me, so I'd arranged for a water taxi to collect me from Ship Cove at 4 p.m. and take me back to Picton to catch the Interislander ferry. With no phone signal on this section of the trail I'd had to take a punt a few days earlier on my arrival time at the cove. In doing so, I'd set myself a neat little challenge for the day.

Bounding towards Ship Cove, I was delighted to be passing so many people. I had run alone for an hour before beginning to bump into fellow early morning risers. It was peak tourist time on the Queen Charlotte Track. Today was the first day of the Easter break, and the tour boats must have begun arriving at Ship Cove that morning, unloading hikers on a mission to complete the Queen Charlotte Track themselves. I noted that most of them were travelling light, and worked out by chatting to a few people that their tours often included the ferrying of any luggage between trail sections. I envied them slightly, but then again I was becoming rather attached to my pack. It was becoming a part of me in more ways than one, as welts had started to form on the flesh of my lower back. When I stopped to let a large group pass, a sprightly looking woman in her mid-fifties gave me a good long look up and down as she moved through. 'Good for you, dear! Doing this with your backpack. Good for you!' By 'this' she meant the Queen Char-lotte Track. I didn't have the heart to tell her that I'd 'done it with my backpack' all the way from Bluff. Instead I smiled, thanked her and ran on.

I rounded the bend onto the final downward slope to Ship Cove. A slightly overweight woman in her mid-sixties spotted me and put two hands up, indicating that I should stop. She was struggling to catch her breath and I wondered if I was about to become a part of a medical emergency. Her mid-length blonde-grey hair was plastered to her face with sweat in certain places, and from behind her perspiring glow she placed one hand on my right arm and looked at me with green eyes. 'How. Much. Further?' she gasped.

I looked up the hill I'd just run down and then in the other direction, past her to the foot of the slope. She couldn't have been going for more than 10 minutes.

'Um. It's about forty minutes to the top.'

Her face fell. 'Forty minutes?!'

'Well, it could be thirty-five?' I offered, trying to ease the blow. 'And then, well… it's about another sixty-five kilometres after that.'

'I'll never make it,' she breathed, shaking her head and looking at the floor.

'Yes, you will!' I chirped at her. 'It's all downhill on the other side. And besides, there's a lookout at the top!'

I enveloped her in a hug. For some reason, I just felt she needed it.

At last my water taxi arrived at Ship Cove. I was delighted that I'd made it with an hour to spare. The taxi was to take me to Picton, and to the conclusion of the South Island section of the trail. I looked longingly back at the dock as I moved away from the shore on a small speedboat – the engine turning the turquoise water to white foam – and I breathed a huge sigh of relief. Aside from a 3-hour ferry journey from Picton to Wellington (where thankfully I would be sitting and eating and not running), part one was done. I had run 1,471 kilometres, taking on mountains, forests and river crossings. I had mashed up my ankle and learnt a hard lesson about just how far and hard I could push my body. How much harder could part two be?

North Island

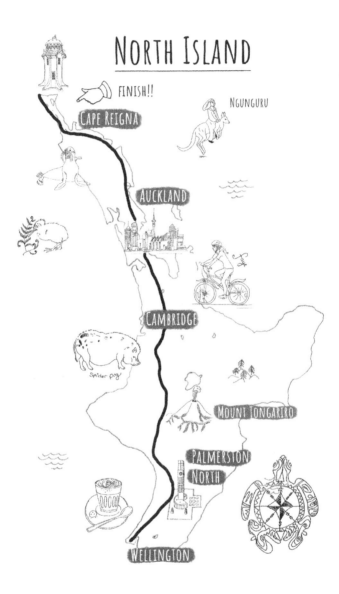

FINISH!!

Ngunguru

Cape Reigna

Auckland

Cambridge

Spider pig!

Mount Tongariro

Palmerston North

Wellington

PART II

18

The Welly Warriors

Whenever I'm asked whether I've been to New Zealand before, the answer sticks in my throat because the honest answer is yes. As a 19-year-old I lived in Sydney for some time, and while I was there I did the typical European thing of thinking I should pop across to New Zealand.

My memory of a week spent in the country's capital city is hazy to say the least. I have absolutely no idea what I did. I wasn't even drunk. I didn't have any money to be drunk. All I remember is that I took myself on a walk, read all three *Lord of the Rings* books, had my debit card declined when I tried to withdraw money for a chocolate bar, and ate cabbage and potatoes for tea every night.

I took a punt that these weren't the only memories I should take away from a city as vibrant and eclectic as Wellington, so this time I arrived with eyes wide open, and on a mission to mix a week of downtime with a visit to as many coffee shops as possible. In between caffeine inhalation I visited the sprightly and hard-working Outward Bound HQ on the harbour front. They made me cannonball into the harbour in order to get a shot for the local paper, a task I was only too willing to complete. I also went on a variety of excursions with Paul and

Lindsey, my rented parents for the week. Paul and Lindsey were on loan from one of my best friends, Emma – the same Emma I would often call during the run in times of need. My rent-a-folks and I visited the inner-city wildlife sanctuary of Zealandia, ate what was voted New Zealand's best pie, went on a windy drive over to Wairarapa Valley and, to put a glistening cherry atop the cultural cake, I also went to see *Shaun the Sheep* at the cinema.

Yet for all the things I did, what I loved most of all were the hidden parts of the city, notably the network of footpaths between the suburbs and the centre. Like a modern version of the Greek island of Naxos, whose crumbling stone-clad walkways take on a life of their own when the sun slides from view, Wellington's myriad of steps, slopes and back alleys are all part of the city's charm. By the end of the week, I'd managed to memorise the route home to the suburb of Karori, plus a few variants, and was feeling exceedingly proud of myself. The fact that I got lost in the botanical gardens on the morning of my departure is really neither here nor there.

Wellington lived up to every expectation I had of it as a capital city, but it was in that city that I also suffered an earth-shattering blow. It was to do with my backpack. My trusty beautiful backpack, which had now served me for three whole months. The straps that broke in Christchurch, and Hamish's attempts to fix them had lasted just about, but the extra movement of the pack as I ran had begun to cause me issues. The foam backing had burst through the mesh at the base and had been cutting my lower back to ribbons since Methven. The area around my lumbar now looked like an angry animal had savaged it, and so in Wellington I finally made the sad decision to buy a new pack. But before I waved the bag goodbye, it had one last trick to play.

Since leaving the UK, I had insisted that my pack weighed an even 7.5 kg. Or rather that's what it had weighed three days before I left, and before I had put 'a few' more things in there. I had some suspicions that the pack could be a little heavier than 7.5 kg, but I chose not to dwell on the matter. What good would knowing the actual weight do after all?

Upon making Wellington, my rent-a-dad Paul became curious about the pack weight and didn't seem entirely satisfied by my '7.5 kg there-or-thereabouts' answer. When I went upstairs for a shower on arrival, he commandeered my backpack… and he weighed it. When I came back downstairs into the living room, Paul was there – waiting.

'Anna, do you want to know how much your pack really weighs?' he asked with an impish grin.

I looked at him, horrified. 'Ah, no, no – don't tell m…' But it was too late.

'Fourteen kilos.'

The damage was done. The backpack lie had been shattered. A base weight of 14 kg meant that with seven days' worth of food and water in there, it would have been up at

20 kg on certain sections of the South Island. I was shocked, but not overly surprised. It did at least explain why there were more than a few days when I felt just a tad exhausted.

It was a sad day when I bought a new backpack from a store in downtown Wellington. I returned home and stood with my shiny new blue pack in one hand, and my old tattered red friend in the other. I felt slightly sad, and would have loved to have given 'Old Red' a proper send-off; to have waited for dark before setting it alight and floating it out on a raft across Wellington Bay. Instead, I folded it as small as it would go and shoved it in the kitchen bin. Practicality over sentimentality.

When the time came to leave with my new pack on my back and new trainers on my feet (names: Butch Cassidy and the Sundance Kid) I made my way nervously to the Wellington cenotaph, in front of the city's Parliament building. I'd put a post on Facebook earlier in the week, letting anyone and everyone who took an interest know that I would be there at 9 a.m., and would welcome any local company. It was a little like sending out birthday-party invites then seeing if anyone turned up. I didn't really expect anyone to be there, and was fully prepared for a solo start of the North Island, but to my delight there were 15 perfect strangers gathered, ready to join me for a run out of town! I was truly touched that these guys had given up a slice of their free time to come and say hello. I affectionately named the group the Welly Warriors and we ran together into the hills beyond the city. After 10 kilometres of company, I packed each of them off with a sweaty hug of gratitude and an oversized high-five. When the time came to trot northwards on my own, I was absolutely buzzing.

The following day, a lady called Sue, who worked for Outward Bound, joined me for the section along the Kapiti Coast. She was a keen runner, although she'd suffered a number of injuries over the years and was even told by a doctor that she wouldn't be able to run again after fracturing her foot. We ducked in and out of the coastline, stopping briefly in a garden store cafe to meet her daughter for lunch and stock up on coffee and cake. We were almost blown clean off the trail a few times, but whooped and cheered as the strong wind pelted sand into our eyes.

Twenty-three kilometres of running later, we padded into the small town of Paraparaumu. Sue's husband had come to meet us for a celebratory finish-line drink and Sue galloped over to him.

'I did it!' she exclaimed. 'I ran the whole way! I was only going to go for 10 k, and we just kept going and chatting. And it was so much fun. I did it!' she beamed.

What she couldn't see was that I was also right behind her beaming. Days like this, seeing Sue's joy at just one day on the trail, rekindled my love for everything about the journey.

I was standing on the edge of the small town of Waikanae. The next section would see me heading into the Tararua mountains, but for some reason I was hesitating. The trails and isolation of the South Island still hung like a lead weight around my neck. I could think of nothing worse than traversing the mountains alone again at this point, and to make matters worse snow was forecast. I sighed, and wondered for the third time in as many weeks whether I'd gone soft. Perhaps I should just suck it up? I had thought that after my days off in Wellington and a good rest that I would be over the hatred of isolation by now, but it was deep-rooted. It festered like a disease, one that had weaved its way into every bone in my body. The Tararuas were Finny and Fi's home mountain range and they had warned me of the severity of the terrain up there, and how quickly the weather could turn.

The alternative option to running through the Tararuas was to stray from the official Te Araroa Trail and head straight down the very busy Highway 1 – a far from glamorous route. Although at 40 km long, it was a similar distance to the trail through the Tararua Range, and it would be all on road, meaning that I could make it to Levin in one day. That would shave two days off the ever-expanding schedule, and that in itself was appealing, even if running down Highway 1 was not. I had to be honest with myself: I didn't want to go into the mountains.

'Stuff it,' I said aloud, setting off and heading for Highway 1.

Days later, I was still being tormented by thoughts of whether I had made the right decision or not, and at last the answer presented itself. Strolling towards me in the trailer park in Levin was a man in a straw hat. His face was in shadow as it was long past dark and I'd just come back from the bathroom to prepare for bed. The guy lifted his head slightly, and offered me a polite greeting.

'Hey,' he said, jerking his head slightly backward.

'Hey,' I said back, smiling. And then I realised. 'Peter?!'

'Anna! No way!'

It was Peter, one half of the San Francisco duo, and I couldn't believe it. I hadn't seen them since near Lake Tekapo and here they were in the tiny town of Levin.

'Right! We have some catching up do!' I shouted at him, extracting myself from what had been an epic reunion hug. 'Beer?' I offered.

'Beer!' he replied in earnest.

That was it, bed could wait. I ran the 2 km back into town, grabbed a stack of beers and some nachos, and returned to the park for some serious catch-up chats with the boys. They'd just come out of the Tararuas, and I was jealous and reassured all at once as they shared pictures of the snow-covered mountains they'd battled through.

'We were frickin' freezing!' Andrew bellowed, before taking another swig of beer.

'Oh man, I've never been so cold. Someone had used up all the firewood. I swear my pee actually froze inside me that night,' continued Peter.

'Totally froze, bro. Like solid,' added Andrew in his laid-back Californian accent.

Finny and Fi may have left the trail, and Coach Ron was now long gone and back in Canada, but I still had two of my pack with me. The stories the boys had told me, and knowing that they would be on the trail, somewhere – that was enough to help me through the second half.

19

Kindnapped

I'd spent the past 48 hours laughing. The kind of belly-ache laughs that you just won't ever have on your own. Hanging out with the San Fran boys just about filled my soul right up to the brim, and so, after three more coffees I'd mustered up the courage to surrender my efforts to camp alone in the bush that night. Instead I'd decided to follow the boys' plan – I'd called the Makahika Outdoor Centre to ask if they'd be able to take in one more waif and stray from the trail that night. The answer was, of course, yes.

It was 3 p.m. before the boys and I parted ways that afternoon. They went to do some errands in town, and I started the 15-km run to the Makahika Outdoor Centre. The trail beside the road out of Levin was a dream – well-graded, separated entirely, and full of walkers and cyclists. I was approaching a group of young lads, when they spotted me and started chatting amongst themselves: 'That's a really big backpack. Is it a dude? No, it's a girl…!'

As I passed them they saluted and yelled in military fashion: 'GO, Navy SEAL! GO!'

I smiled. I took it as some form of respect, and growing

up as the middle sibling with two brothers, I thrived on respect from boys.

Five kilometres out from Makahika, Andrew and Peter (or Mav and Goose, as I'd now started calling them) drove by in a 4x4. They'd opted to be collected in what they'd deemed a 'trail-legal hitch' and they tooted and cheered, before pulling over to check whether I was sure that I didn't want a ride.

'No, thanks!' I chirped. 'I've got these motors!' I continued, slapping my legs. 'And I'm really enjoying myself out here.'

They drove off, and I was left in shock because I'd meant what I'd said. I was actually enjoying running today. After a day off in Levin my legs craved the sick monotony of movement once more. The thud of thighs and how the tarmac came up to greet my soles at every step is something I didn't realise I'd missed. I was back in the game. I ran on, singing and smiling, entirely in a world of my own. I was just about to start motoring past a large house to my left when someone called my name:

'Anna?!'

'Yes?' I said, swivelling round to see a man who'd just got out of his car in the driveway. How did he know me, know who I was?!

'I spoke to you earlier on the phone!'

'Oh, John, hi!' I said. 'I'm carrying on up the road here, right?'

'Well, not if you want to stop in with us tonight… We… uh… we live here.'

Oh my, how embarrassing. I was about to run clean past the house.

Sally and John were a formidable couple. They'd met in the military and, according to Sally, John's bum looked pretty darn fine in a jumpsuit back then. It was a *Top Gun* love affair. Sally was extremely pretty, with short dark hair and cat-like eyes, which were a deep brown and sparkled when she spoke. Her pearl earrings and pearl necklace added an air of femininity to her otherwise direct attitude. She was undeniably a femme fatale. I could tell that she wouldn't take any crap, and I liked that about her immediately.

Beneath the strong exterior, Sally had a softer side. She loved to look after people and more than that to feed them, especially those on the Te Araroa Trail. Sally let us in on her strategy to lure unsuspecting trail users into her home. She would spot the trampers coming, and grab a couple of cold beers from the fridge. She would then walk to the roadside and literally dangle the beers in front of them. She was a hiking-schedule assassin, and beer was her weapon of choice. Sally told the tale of one particularly tricky customer who said he must walk for 16 hours that day, and so when Sally offered up beers, he paced up and down outside the house for 40 minutes until his 16-hour shift was up, and he could 'legally' come in. Trail rules – everyone has theirs and as I've told you, they are ridiculous.

On Christmas Day the previous year, trail users from all surrounding sections had flocked to the outdoors centre, many of them collected by Sally and John. By the time Sally and John had finished their pick-ups, they had 15 around the table for a turkey dinner. Over the next 72 hours I would learn that Makahika was like the Hotel California; you could check out any time you liked, but you could really never leave.

In between hosting and caring for random vagabonds, Sally and John ran a fully functioning and very successful outdoors education centre. Something which I didn't know how she had the time and energy to do, especially considering the feast she laid on that night. Cheese and crackers with grapes, apricots, quince and nuts to start, followed by fish, chicken, greens, steak, potatoes, sweet potatoes and roasted beetroot for main. Then there was a plum, pear and rhubarb crumble with cream for pudding, followed by chocolates and coffee. Then port for afters, naturally. Peter, Andrew and I rolled from the table to our bedrooms that night feeling incredibly satisfied. I had no idea how I was going to run in the morning with all of that in my belly.

And so I didn't. One night at Makahika turned into two nights. We were invited to their neighbour's house for dinner the following night, and so we all accepted. On day three Sally made an offer to dish up lamb and pavlova the following day, and proceeded to invite over half of the neighbourhood to join us. I decided that this was getting silly, and that I definitely needed to get running now. Then Sally threw a curve ball: 'Stay tomorrow and you can go on the flying fox.' The flying fox was the long, fast zip-wire that ran from the forest out the back of the outdoors centre to the area of grass just outside the main house. There was no way I could refuse such an offer, and Sally knew it. I was done for.

Four nights after arriving at Makahika for a 'quick stopover' I eventually ran out and into the forest. I estimated I was 2 kg heavier and I knew that I had been well and truly 'kindnapped'. That is, taken in by strangers and subjected to untold levels of kindness, against my will. I vowed to go back one day and allow it to happen again.

The pub on the corner in the small town of Shannon had an old-English-style charm about it. Well, perhaps more East End boozer than Sunday lunch bistro. The decor was fresh out of a 1970s episode of *Coronation Street*. The carpet was a zig-zag red and brown – the kind of pattern you might find on the underground or on chewing gum-encrusted coach seats. The kind that hides things. Vomit, broken glass, secrets – things. Pictures of local rugby teams, which were faded and tea-stained around the edges and dated back as far as 1903, adorned the walls. A date that by new-world Kiwi standards was archaic. A long wooden bar at the back of the room led to two well-loved pool tables, complete with lampshades hanging overhead. There were three TVs on the wall, showing a mixture of horse racing and greyhound racing, and some kind of machine that allowed people to place live bets and two betting game machines stood against the far wall. It was a familiar surround in an entirely unfamiliar place; I felt at home and at odds all at once.

I entered the pub looking less Lycra-clad than usual, thanks to a quick baby wipe n' change in the public loos opposite. I set myself down at a table in the corner, adjacent to a group of older men, each with their own ale warming in hands. Settling in to my very own pint of ale, which I felt was deserved after the 17-km run completed from Makahika that day, I overheard the table of older men opposite talking about me. I say overheard – they were as good as having a conversation as if I wasn't there.

'Oh, she's tramping I tell you. Tramping. On the move. Everything in a bag.'

I looked over at the group and smiled. They seemed a little shocked that I'd heard their quiet patter, but raised their glasses and nodded in my direction nonetheless.

Over the course of the next hour, I enjoyed an array of exciting horse races, and became rather transfixed with one particular character in the pub, a rather irate middle-aged man. I watched (albeit as subtly as I could) as the man spent his time moving back and forth, from the bar to the betting machine, back to his stool, and shouting obscenities at the TV screen in between. Wherever he was, whatever he was doing, there was always, without fail, a cigarette protruding from his face. He was a man who wore his heart on his sleeve, clearly – the losses and gains with every hoof print were etched upon his weary face.

By the time one of the men at the next table came over, I'd reached my one-pint alcohol limit and switched from ale to Diet Coke. It was clear that Bruce was of Māori descent, if not entirely pure Māori. He had a twinkle in his eye and smiled with his bottom teeth, a bit like Muttley from *Wacky Races*. Dressed in what I would call classic Kiwi attire, he paired a rugby shirt and shorts with bare legs and gum boots (wellies).

He put his hand on the table in front of me and leant in. 'Say... You, ah, you got somewhere to stay?'

'Yeah. I'm okay, thanks. I'm just going to pitch my tent,' I announced, wondering whether my honesty was a good idea after seeing the shocked look on his face. I blamed the ale.

'You what?!'

'My tent. I've got a tent in here.' I patted the backpack. 'I was just going to pitch it up, um, somewhere, tonight.'

'Well, where ya gonna pitch it?! Not round here I hope?'

'Yeah, the small park, round the back?' Any patch of grass was a campground to me by this point.

'Oh, no, no, no. Oh, no, no, no, no,' Bruce repeated, shaking his head violently. 'You'll come home with me. We can't have you in your tent. Let me just call my wife.'

He came back 5 minutes later. 'Good as gold,' he winked. 'We'll have you stay at ours.' Bruce winked again before returning to his pint and his friends. Intrigued, if a little bemused by my intention to camp in the local park, the 'lads of Shannon' then began grilling me. It could seem odd that I felt entirely at ease chatting with a strange group of men in a pub in a town where I knew no one, but I always trusted my gut. I'd met my fair share of strangers on my travels to lead me to believe that these guys were harmless, and my gut told me as much. They were just curious, and better than that they were real characters. And I loved meeting characters. Gordon, the oldest member of the group, seemed to find my story especially amusing. He regaled me with tales of his trips to England, Scotland and Wales, before crossing his arms and looking down at the ground. Gordon was thinking. He looked up.

'You're running?'

'Yep.'

'You're game, ain't cha?!' I felt this was a rhetorical question. I wasn't entirely sure what 'being game' entailed, but interpreted it as a Kiwi way of saying I was 'game for anything' and 'up for life'. And in that case, I was 'game'.

'On your own?' Gordon continued.

'Yep.'

'I told you she was game!' he guffawed, turning to the others.

'And you were going to sleep in a tent?!'

'Yes, Sir.'

He leant back on his stool and laughed. 'Oh, she's game I tell ya!' he said again, throwing his arms in the air and shaking his head.

At around 8 p.m., Bruce slugged down the final inches in his glass and, with a nod of the head, indicated it was time to leave. It was at this point that I realised Bruce might be drunk. I thought he smiled and winked (and perhaps swayed) a little more than usual, but I took it just to be his nature. My first clue came as he backed out of the parking space, continued to reverse across the entire road, and collided with the grass verge on the opposite side.

'Oops!' he exclaimed, looking sheepish.

'Hey, Bruce, take it easy won't ya?' said fellow drinking-buddy Paul, in the passenger seat.

It was then it dawned on me: Bruce had had a skinful. I would have scrambled out of the car then and there, but I had a feeling that we weren't going far. The town was only a kilometre from one end to the other, after all. Besides, Bruce seemed to have a top speed of 10 kilometres per hour, something which I was extremely pleased about and didn't feel could end in fatality.

Of course, there was no regard for the correct side of the road, and so Bruce simply took the corner on whichever side he saw fit. It was a relief when, after dropping off two friends, Bruce announced: 'This is us,' and pulled into a driveway.

I was introduced to Bruce's wife, Claire, or more I was passed over to her, as Bruce muttered and waved a bit, before moving to the couch at the end of the room by the TV to lie down. I immediately felt at ease with Claire and she greeted me like a long-lost daughter.

Bruce and Claire had a relationship which was clearly built on a foundation of love, and that love included a love of winding one another up. The next hour mostly consisted of Bruce saying inappropriate things, or insisting that I eat an avocado for dinner (I'm not sure why either) and Claire insisting with equal force that he pipe down. Bruce would pipe up again, giggle at Claire's despairing look, and return his gaze to the TV. I couldn't help but laugh.

'Where's your pie tonight, Bruce?' Claire asked, crossing her arms.

'Well, you know, I thought it wouldn't be appropriate to bring a pie home for dinner, seeing as we have a guest n' all,' he winked.

'And why don't we have any dinner, Bruce?'

'I don't know, Claire. Where's our dinner?' He grinned, let out another Muttley-style laugh, and I sensed there was more to this story. Claire rolled her eyes at Bruce, sighed and turned to me.

'Yesterday I cooked this one a lovely roast chook and he arrived home with a pie. A bloody pie!' She looked back at Bruce, who just grinned harder and shrugged. 'So I told him I wasn't making dinner tonight, and then he bloody brings a guest home!'

She threw her hands up in despair, before turning to me: 'Sorry, dear, it's not you. It's lovely that you're here. It's him that's the problem.'

Ten minutes later Bruce resumed the avocado crusade, until I eventually accepted some leftover pizza, alongside the avocado, and sat down in front of the TV with them, watching the Kiwi version of *The Bachelor*.

By this point Jake, Claire and Bruce's grandson, had arrived home. He seemed to have inherited all of Bruce's cheek and as much of his charm too. He was doing an equally good job of winding his nan up.

'Jake, how about you get a job?' Claire sighed.

'Na, nana, I've got a job,' said Jake, rummaging in the fridge.

'Have you?!'

'Yup… Driving you two nuts.'

'Oh, Jake!'

'I'm pretty good at it,' he grinned.

I spent the rest of the evening watching TV and chatting

with Claire. Bruce roused from where he was half asleep on the sofa opposite me, and interjected every now and then. It all felt very 'normal' – safe, comfortable and a world away from a night camped out in my tent. At around 10 p.m. Jake left to go possum shooting with his mates (quite the young male Kiwi pastime, it would seem) and Claire made me up a bed in the corner of the living room. After a little more chatting, she moved off to bed, leaving me alone in the living room to gorge on just a little more TV. Five minutes later, she came back out in her nightie. She smiled at me and walked to the kitchen cupboard, returning with a tin and placing it on the table.

'In case you have a bedtime drink of chocolate milk, you're going to need some biscuits to go along with it, aren't you?' She smiled.

20

Running with a Record-breaker

I'd agreed to give a talk at a small country school on my way from Palmerston North to Feilding. For some reason beyond my understanding, and despite the principal saying I could come at any time of day, I had arranged to give the talk at 9 a.m. The school was a 2-hour run from Palmerston, which meant I had a disgustingly early wake-up call. I found myself outside the school, bleary-eyed and doing all I could to prepare to entertain some kids for an hour.

I was sad to be leaving Finny and Fi for yet another time in this trip. I'd run from Shannon to their home town of Palmerston North yesterday and we'd had the most rockin' reunion dinner. Andrew and Peter had even turned up to make it a full 'pack' house, minus Coach Ron. We laid him a place at the table anyway and sent him a video to make up for it. It was now almost a month since Finny and Fi had left the Queen Charlotte Track on the South Island, and it was strange to hear about how they had begun to settle back into 'normal' life away from the trail. Their journey was complete, and yet I still had 1,200 km and another two months to go. Out here, these guys were my family. But in a strange way, I found that when I left them, as with all good friends, it was more 'so long' for now than goodbye. I knew we'd meet again someday, on their travels or mine, or perhaps both of ours. Still, I was sad. Thinking about not seeing the Whio Warriors again made me well up, so I tried not to think about it as Fiona ran with me for 10 minutes until we picked the main trail back up. She seemed to dislike goodbyes as much as I did, and so after a brief hug and one long last exchange of take cares, I ran on and didn't look back.

Having nipped into Bunnythorpe School to deliver the talk to a 30-strong register of kiddywinks, I was back on the road by 10 a.m. and feeling decidedly less sleepy. The trail to the modest town of Feilding was modest in itself. Mostly it required that I ran on the verge of a busy road. It was a scorcher of a day and as I shuffled my way along a not-so-pleasant highway, my mind was now firmly focused on the bottle of ice-cold Fanta that lay in wait, just a kilometre down the road.

It was then that I spotted another runner who had stopped at the side of the railway track just up ahead. He had on a cap and shorts, with a hydration belt and knee-high compression socks. He'd turned to cross the railway line, but had stopped and was now looking directly at me. I was also looking back at him. Seeing as we were both looking at one another, I thought we should probably converse some. I smiled as I ran toward him and stopped to say hello.

'You must be going one heck of a long way?' he yelled over the roar of passing traffic.

'Yes, Sir! All the way to the lighthouse at Cape Reinga.'

'Ah, you're running the trail?'

We chatted for a minute or so about what I was doing here in New Zealand, before I decided that I'd like to learn a bit about him too. I asked him what kinds of runs he liked to go on, and whether he enjoyed long-distance running.

'Yeah, I've done some long stuff,' he said, trailing off at the end of his sentence. The next sentence was even quieter and I had to strain over the traffic to hear it. 'I mean, I ran around the coastline of New Zealand a few years back.'

'I'm sorry, you what?!'

'Yeah, actually the biggest one was a run across the states last year. I did that in fifty-one days. Averaged about ninety-four kilometres a day on that one.'

'Are you serious?!' I couldn't believe my ears.

'Yeah, broke a world record…' He tailed off.

Now, in my experience, exchanges with legends are often tricky. Most true legends are quite self-deprecating. They don't want to shout or boast about their exploits, but at the same time, during a roadside exchange there's really often only a couple of minutes to fully explain who you are and what you do. Thank goodness I'd asked! This, as it turns out, was Perry Newburn and I just so happened to catch him while out on a training run around his home town of Feilding. We chatted for a few more minutes, during which I asked: 'So how do I find your blog?'

I pulled out my phone as Perry directed me to his Facebook page – a Facebook page which had 27,000 likes. Bloody hell, this guy was practically famous.

I looked again at Perry's face, and this time I saw him in a new light. This wasn't just some guy I'd bumped into at the side of the road. This was a man I admired and respected. His face was one which had clearly seen life. Blue eyes twinkled beneath the peak of his faded black cap, and long blondish-grey hair cascaded from beneath it, just far enough so as to touch the tops of his shoulders. I put him in his mid-fifties. He had a soft manner, very straightforward but very level with his emotions. There was no doubt that Perry had tales to tell.

'Say, Anna.'

'Yeah, Perry?'

'Can I come run with you tomorrow, as you go out of town?'

'Of course you can!' I smiled, delighted if a little petrified that he might annihilate me with his ultra-speed. We exchanged numbers, as I promised to keep him updated on the plan of action.

At midday on the following day, I was waiting for Perry at the clock tower in the centre of Feilding. I'd been up since 7 a.m. to catch the Anzac Day service with my lovely host family, the O'Brien's.

'Sorry I'm a bit late,' said Perry, striding the last few paces towards where I was sitting under the clock tower. 'I had to go running.'

'You what?! Err… Perry, we're about to go running?'

'Yeah, but I've got things to sort this afternoon, so I can only run out with you for say twenty ks. So I did twenty-five kilometres just now to get it up to a sixty-five kilometre total for the day.'

'Blimey, Perry!' I exclaimed, but I wasn't entirely surprised. In my Google-stalking the night before I'd learnt that in addition to the accomplishments he'd already told me about, he also ran from Auckland to Christchurch to raise funds for the victims of the earthquakes, and then took on the challenge of running for 72 hours straight around his local motor racing circuit, just to see how far he could go. Suffering from hallucinations and exhausted, he crossed the finish line having covered 500 km. That was another world record, by the way.

Setting off, Perry's pace seemed a good match for my own. I felt entirely comfortable and, more importantly, reassured that this was the speed that awesome long-distance runners moved at. We talked some more and I asked him a ridiculous amount of questions. I learned that he had a wife who was battling with cancer and a 22-year-old son with severe learning difficulties. Running, he said, was his escape.

Running with Perry was an absolute joy. We moved steadily along quiet back roads in brilliant sunshine. Some were gravel, some were tarmac, but either way the going was easy. The air was still as we glided past lush green fields. After 20 km we took a break at the side of the road and chatted a little more, before Perry turned around and headed home.

'See ya, Anna! Come run with me sometime, won't cha?!' he hollered as he ran away.

I trucked on, grinning from ear-to-ear and reflecting on that chance meeting with Perry. It wasn't just his accomplishments that made me smile. What buoyed me the most was that two perfect strangers, from two different generations, living on the opposite sides of the planet could find so much in common. And what I loved even more was that Perry insisted he wasn't anything special. He genuinely believes he's just a normal guy who likes to run. And in a way, he is. It just so happens that he has the mental capacity to keep going far, far longer than most.

'Hola! You got time for a chat?'

'I've just woken up. Give me ten?'

'Are you getting your chest hair out again? Make sure you prune it this time. No one likes a rogue chest-bush, you know.'

'You love it.'

'I do, now hurry up!'

I used the 5 minutes that followed the conversation with Jamie to find myself a streetlight in the campground on the edge of the small town of Bulls. Not just any streetlight, of course, a streetlight which presented my face in the most flattering way and made me look anything a little less like I'd been running for four months. I sat down by several before finally choosing 'the one'. I still looked as rough as a dog and so pulled a beanie over my head to hide as much of my face as possible, and contain my wild locks.

For some reason, as the finish line crept ever-closer, the back and forth between me and Jamie had become more fun. Largely because it was becoming more real. I felt like I wanted to invest some energy into whatever it was we were doing because I would soon be home and would find out if it would or wouldn't turn into something. I found that our chats went in phases. I ended some confused, some convinced he liked me and others convinced that we would just be friends.

Jamie's face popped up on my tablet screen and I began regaling the events of the few weeks since we had spoken last. 'You're doing amazingly,' he would say at intervals, often swiftly accompanied by 'That's beaaaauuutiful'. I told him about Perry, and staying with Finny and Fi and about Wellington and the little trail gang who had run me out. The retelling of all my stories was accompanied by grandiose gestures and a deluge of swear words. I was over-excited that evening, to say the least. I'd like to say that I was subtle with my affections, reserved and demure. I was about as subtle as a juggernaut. I got off the phone and wondered if I had overdone it with the flirting. Then I decided that I just didn't care. The poor lad. He had experienced the full force of my advances.

I crawled into my tent as a final message appeared on my phone: 'Great chats, McNuff. I especially enjoyed the swearing. I think you should bring that into your school talks, for the kids. Seriously, you're beautiful.'

He loves me.

Running into the town of Whanganui was terrifying. It was pouring with rain as I left my camping spot at Koitiata Beach. I'd overslept massively and had woken up at 10 a.m. I made a conscious decision not to beat myself up and decided that I must have needed the sleep. After 10 km I hit a very busy State Highway 3. Now where? I wondered, before checking the map. Oh, for God's sake. The map was telling me that I had to run down State Highway 3. I looked at the volume and speed of traffic.

'You've got to be kidding me?!' I said aloud.

I started to run and the rain continued to pour. Over the last few weeks I'd been reading the book *The Chimp Paradox* by Professor Steve Peters – a book that had helped me to understand what began to happen next. *The Chimp Paradox* theory states that our thoughts and subsequent actions are a result of the interaction between two very different parts of our mind: the 'chimp' part, which is animalistic, reactive and driven purely by emotion, and the 'human' part, which is more rational, takes time to consider past experiences and is generally calmer. Standing at the edge of Highway 3, the chimp part of my brain was going nuts. It was in fight or flight mode and screaming at me: 'Danger, Anna, danger!' (although I felt less like a chimp and more like a sitting duck).

I could barely see where I was going and the frequent debris left by rockfalls meant I kept having to hop off the verge and into the road to make my way forward. I was terrified. But more than that I was worrying about what people were thinking as they drove by. I wanted to hold up a big sign that said: 'I know this is bloody dangerous! I don't want to be here either!'

I thought back to my equally ugly run into the town of Levin along State Highway 1 and how I promised myself I wouldn't run on a busy road again, because it was just plain stupid and unnecessary, especially when there was usually another perfectly good, albeit slower, way around. But this time there was no other way around. Short of clambering through farmers' fields, hopping fences and scaling bluffs, State Highway 3 was the only way to go.

There did look to be a turn-off on the main highway, a few kilometres further on. I could follow a minor road and take a sidestep north to pick up another road that ran parallel to the highway. I wondered why the trail hadn't gone this way in the first place? Perhaps it was because that road I was heading for was narrow and winding, and having space on a busy highway was better? Or it could be that it was going to add an extra 5 kilometres to the journey? If I took the detour it meant that I would be running 39 km that day. I made my mind up. I didn't care what was on that detour road, I was getting off this highway as soon as I could, even if it meant running extra kilometres.

'This is not bloody fun!' I yelled at the top of my lungs, breathing hard as yet another camper van passed that little bit too close. My stomach turned in nervous knots, and so I started singing to distract myself. This was a finely honed technique and a tactic I employed when riding a bike downhill, which I hated. It seemed to calm me down as I focused on the singing rather than the task at hand. I started regurgitating portions of Ed Sheeran's latest album *X*, and ran on.

At last the turn-off loomed into view. I waited for a break in the traffic and darted across the road. A hundred metres along the deserted, quiet side road, calm and order returned to my world. I slowed my pace, found a rhythm, slotted into a groove and breathed a huge sigh of relief.

The problem with not taking any breaks in a 39-kilometre day was that my shins and knees started to suffer. I found that even a 5-minute break every hour helped to keep pain at bay, but I hadn't taken those breaks today. I'd just run straight for 5 hours. As Whanganui town loomed into view my ankles began to creak – my still recovering right ankle especially – and the front of my shins started to groan.

Entering the small suburban metropolis of Drury, I found myself high up above Whanganui, the river weaving its merry path below. I could see the entire town from up here, and it was a majestic view. I checked the map, and then I checked it again. My route seemed to take me straight ahead, but there was no road. I began running down another road only to real-ise it was a dead end, and so I backtracked a hundred metres and scratched my head.

Ahead of me was a large two-storey bright orange building. It looked entirely out of place in a residential setting. I moved closer and read the sign: 'Welcome to the Drury Hill Elevator!' What was this elevator?! I went inside and let my eyes adjust to the darkness. I was in a small, dark entranceway – there was just a closed wooden door in front of me and a buzzer to my right, nothing else. I pressed the buzzer. This was like some-thing out of *The Rocky Horror Show*. Just when I thought Dr Frank-N-Furter might make an entrance, a woman appeared with no sign of suspenders and (rather disappointedly) looking entirely normal.

'Down?' she asked in a deep voice, handing me a leaflet as we stepped inside a lift to the right-hand side. I nodded, keep-ing my eyes fixed firmly on her as I shuffled backwards into the lift and the doors closed. This had the makings of a great start to a horror movie.

As it turned out this elevator was a direct route into town. It took me 66 metres down to a long 250-metre tunnel which ran under the Whanganui River. I thanked the nice lady in the lift (mostly for not murdering me) and skipped along the tunnel, shouting and singing and enjoying the satisfaction that can only come from multiple echoes. The tunnel surfaced in the centre of town – the diversion I'd taken had landed me smack bang where I needed to go! It had saved me from being squished by fast moving trucks and included a quirky run through a tunnel. Why the official Te Araroa Trail didn't go this way was a mystery to me. I made a mental note to ask Rob, the trail CEO, about it at some point.

It was Anzac Monday so many cafes were closed, but I managed to find one open. I shuffled inside, laid down my pack, changed out of sopping wet clothes in the toilet and proceeded to fill my face with ginger beer, chicken pie, a chocolate milkshake and a large flat white. In that moment, heaven was a place on earth.

21

A Visit to Jerusalem

In Whanganui I was given a high-vis vest by a friend of a friend whom I'd stayed with in town. I really should have had one before now, but it'd felt surplus to requirements to carry one through the bush, and I'd not intended to run on quite so many roads from Wellington to here. In honesty, I'd been lazy. I could have done with it running into town on the Highway 3 of death, that's for sure.

I thought it'd be nice to use the vest to tell people what I was doing. Not that they'd be able to read it, but I felt like the vest was a blank canvas, and I, an artist. I took out a permanent marker and scrawled in big letters on the back: 'Anna. 3,000 km run for Outward Bound.' At least that way if I found myself running down a busy highway, I had something to offer up as an explanation to the bemused drivers.

I turned off the main highway out of Whanganui and took the river road toward the town of Jerusalem. My body felt incredible and I clocked up 30 km with no effort at all. Running along the road, I thought ahead to the Tongariro Alpine Crossing, which had become my next point of focus. As an exposed mountain pass, which goes up to 1,120 metres high, it was the final place in the trip where the weather could turn nasty and affect my progress. Each day I winched the crossing higher and higher onto its pedestal until it cast such a shadow over my mind that I could no longer think beyond it. If anyone talked to me about places after the crossing, I zoned out. I just had to get there. To get there, to get over it and down the other side.

If I were following the Te Araroa Trail to the letter, I should have kayaked the Whanganui River, but instead of a five-day kayak I opted to run the 90 km along the river road. Because, well, despite all my protests, I really do like running. That and the fact that I couldn't be bothered with the logistics of arranging a kayak. I soon learnt that the Jerusalem river road was one so steeped in history that it made me gasp and giggle with glee. Meeting folk along the road, I learnt more about it and the town of Jerusalem itself.

Previously a fishing village, Jerusalem became the site of a Roman Catholic mission in 1854. It was here that Sister Suzanne Aubert later founded The Order of Compassion, which offered sanctuary to abandoned Pākehā (fair skinned and non-Māori) children from Wellington. In the century that followed, Jerusalem attracted its fair share of celebs – most notably the poet James K. Baxter, who established a commune in the town in 1969.

Chatting to those who live along the river today I discovered some more exotic tales about Baxter's commune. Legend has it that each year, dozens of women would make the pilgrimage up the river road, just to 'be' with the poet. The postman on duty during Baxter's residency reported getting quite a shock when delivering mail – as several bare-breasted beauties would emerge from the grounds to greet him. Then there's the story about a driver who was unable to continue along the road, because Baxter was in the middle of it, making sweet Whanganui love to one of his lady friends. I discovered first hand that Jerusalem's glory days have long since passed, and it's now a hidden gem – home to a modest Māori community and frequented by small groups of tourists. It's an undoubtedly special place, and I could see why an artistic soul like Baxter's would have felt so at home here.

It was a crisp autumn day, and as I approached the town from the south the sight of the evening sun wrapped around the spire of the hilltop church was breathtaking. Rumour had it that the grounds of the church were still beautifully maintained by two sisters of The Order, and the sizeable St Joseph's convent remained immaculate, offering a bed to those who might be in need as they pass through. Running through a backstreet of what seemed to be a largely deserted town, I approached the church. I meandered through its manicured gardens, which were in stark contrast to the ramshackle homes that surrounded it. Next to the church was a large building. Clad in white painted wooden panels and a red roof, it matched the colour scheme of the church – that had to be the convent. I ran around to the front and peered in through the window. This place was huge! A large kitchen led through to a living room area with chairs and cushions, many of which were straight out of the 70s. Children's toys were neatly stacked on simple bookshelves and a lone teddy sat in one of the armchairs. It had an eerie feel to it, a cross between a home and a hospital, but I'm sure that was just my imagination, and an overexposure to Hollywood horror movies. Still, it looked clean and enticing for a night's kip. If I could manage to stay here, and control my imagination, it'd be a sweet deal. I contemplated a plan B, which would have been to pitch the tent on the front lawn, and then went looking for the sisters.

There were a few houses close to the convent, but all seemed empty. Where was everybody?! I wondered. And then I spotted a woman though a window. She was rather large and sitting in a chair, watching the TV. I thought for a moment that it might be rude to disturb her, but I really fancied getting into the convent, so I knocked on the window. She didn't move. I knocked a little harder still, and put my apologetic face firmly in place. No movement. I tried one more time, this time at the front door, before running back around to the side window to watch for signs of movement. Nothing.

I returned to the front of the convent, disappointed. I had wanted to put another piece of the Jerusalem puzzle in place and to immerse myself in the history of a convent I'd heard so much about, but the sisters were nowhere to be found, and so it became apparently clear that I wouldn't be piecing together any history puzzle that night. I considered my options. I could run on, but I had quite settled on the idea of staying here, and I wasn't sure where I could camp further down the river. It was then that I spotted a small outhouse to the right of the building, with a sign that said: 'The old convent.' I tried the door and, to my surprise, it was open! I slid inside and started an exploration.

There was something in the kitchen that resembled a torture device, or a giant pasta maker, I couldn't decide which. Perhaps this is where they tortured people and then turned them into pasta? In reality, I concluded that it had something to do with washing clothes, but it was clear no one had been to this laundromat in a good 50 years. I backtracked into the living room and inspected a large couch lined up against the wall. The hefty brown single cushion looked like it'd seen better days, but it was comfortable enough. I pulled a few cobwebs from the felt-like surface and lay down. Perfect. Long enough for me to stretch out on, and good enough for a bed.

I lay down, doing my best to ignore the 15 spiders I'd counted crawling up the wall next to me. I looked at one square in the eyes. Did spiders have eyes? I didn't know, but I was trying to find out. So long as they stayed away from my face, ears, nose, eyes, or any orifice for that matter, we wouldn't have a problem. I think we understood one another. Every now and then a car would rumble past on the gravel driveway outside. I could hear music coming from a house nearby and, in the early hours of the morning, the odd shout from kids, but I left the town the next day having not seen a soul. Well, unless you count the lady in the living room chair – but I couldn't really be sure if she was actually still alive, so I didn't count her.

I was now on the final day of the 90-km run along the river road, and was on my way to the next town, Raetihi. The day had started off rather solemnly, and my mojo levels were low, but I had a feeling they had the potential to climb, and so I kept an open mind. I left the old convent at 8.45 a.m. and ran on through a misty valley. The sun hadn't yet hit and it was colder than I had felt in a long time. Stopping to pull my gloves on I looked up and realised that I had happened across an incredible view. The dark river snaked its way through a deep gorge. The clouds were hanging low enough so that the peaks either side of the river poked out above them like little pirate hats. This was stunning. The only problem with it all was that I felt nothing. No joy. Just… nothing, yet I knew that was wrong. In fact, I was starting to get annoyed by how disconnected I felt to everything that was going on around me. I decided I needed a little music to brighten the mood as I set off, and boom! I snapped out of my funk immediately. For some reason, actually admitting to myself when something felt crap always seemed to help.

My tactic for the day, as always on tough days, was to break the distance down into chunks. I had a total of 38 km to make. My strategy was to restart the day at the turn-off at Pipiriki, which was a distance of 13 kilometres. I'd get there and pretend I hadn't run at all. Then I'd tell myself I only had 25 km to run, and wasn't it a lovely day to be on a 25-km run? I used to do this kind of thing all the time in rowing training and in races. We'd do a 20-km loop on the river, passing the boathouse halfway through. At the boathouse, I'd always stop and pretend I'd just got in the boat. I knew I was lying to myself but for some bizarre reason it seemed to work.

In my new music-fuelled, crap-accepting state, I made the corner at Pipiriki without too much drama. I continued with the chunking technique and ran the next section just one hour at a time. The majority was uphill, and so I plodded on rhythmically, singing along to whatever my MP3 player chose to throw out. To my surprise, I was making faster time than I'd expected and I was managing to keep quite an even pace up the hills. I had journalist Richard Askwith's words in my head as I ran, from his book *Running Free*: 'Gravity is not your friend. Take small steps and wait for the top to come.'

With 10 km to go, my energy levels began to falter. And then, right in front of my very eyes was the most beautiful mountain I had ever seen. Mount Ruapehu was in full view, clear and dazzling, with its pure white peak and granite slopes set against a clear blue sky and rolling green fields. There was no other word to describe it other than majestic. It looked like a painting, and I found there to be something wonderfully calming about an enormous mountain, as old as time, watching over me. Ruapehu wasn't alone out there. Scanning the horizon to the east, I saw a perfectly formed, snow-capped volcano. That was Mount Ngauruhoe (Na-ra-ho-e), also known as Mount Doom. Ngauruhoe is heavily featured in *The Lord of the Rings* films. It is the centre of evil and where Frodo is bound for glory as he makes a bid to drop that pesky ring into oblivion. From where I was standing, it was far away and so small, but no less beautiful than Ruapehu. It was two for the price of one at the majestic mountain store today, and I just couldn't stop staring. I started to run off then stopped again, and stared. I stared for another 5 minutes. Then even as I ran, I stared at both mountains. Beautiful, just beautiful.

Sat in a cafe in Ohakune, I stared at the floor. I had well and truly lost it, and I wasn't sure I could actually bring myself to leave. I was sick of everything. Of unpacking and packing a backpack that could only just about house its contents. Of explaining to people what I was doing and have them look sideways and not really know what to say. Of being away from my family. God, how I missed my family. Of the cuts on my back and the pain every time I heaved my pack on to my shoulders. Of the mindless monotony. Of living my life in hourly chunks. Of eating. Of being hungry.

I wanted to cry, but I was even sick of doing that. I knew this was too early to hit a low like this and I knew it was because I'd let myself start thinking about the end. I was two-thirds of the way through the trail and still had 1,000 km left to run. I had reached saturation level. Despite yesterday's incredible mountains, I realised I didn't care for another breath taking view or another once-in-a-lifetime chance meeting with a fascinating individual. I just couldn't see what lay ahead that I hadn't already experienced. Had the adventure become dull? Predictable? All I wanted was to be home. I was jaded, like a rusty penny. Still shiny somewhere underneath, but worn, oh so worn.

I'd woken up that morning with tiny painful slits in the corners of my mouth. I knew from my rowing days that this was a sign of being run-down. The slits usually took about a week to heal, and would split painfully back open each time I tried to smile. Which was a good job, I guess, because I wasn't doing too much smiling right now.

I was sick of my own company, of my own mind and of my own stupid thoughts. I felt I knew how I would feel each day, like my mood for the rest of the adventure was a foregone conclusion over which I had no control. I was running away from one town and the next one couldn't come fast enough. What kind of life was this? What could I do? I wasn't going to stop. I would rather be miserable for the final two months and complete what I set out to do than give up and go home. But it was like trying to climb out of a gorge in the middle of a landslide. Every move I made forwards, I slid backwards, and at pace.

I tried a change of location and took myself for a walk to sit in a different local cafe. There I resumed staring at the floor. Tears welled in my eyes and a lone drop escaped down my cheek. I didn't move. I just carried on staring as more tumbled after it. I was very aware that there was a guy sitting on the table right next to me, and as hard as I was staring at the floor, he was now staring at me. I must have looked entirely odd, but

I didn't care. After an hour of wallowing in self-pity and dehydrating my eyes sockets, I pulled myself together. I knew I just needed to find something to snap me out of it... I looked out the window. The clouds were shrouding Mount Ruapehu in a thick sludge. I took a deep breath, wiped my tears and slung my pack over my shoulder. There was nothing left to do but to go towards it.

Taking the track around the mountains in Tongariro National Park was beautiful. The Martian looking landscape was punctuated with pockets of dense native bush. Boulders, grey dust and spatterings of red and orange rocks stretched as far as I could see into the horizon. I'd hit the trail in the early morning and found it to be icy; the rocks were unstable underfoot and progress was slow, especially when clambering over boulders, but my spirit had improved a little overnight. Although I still felt somewhat jaded by the trail and the challenges it offered up that morning, I was at least enjoying small sections – a reminder that the flame of happiness was still lit, somewhere underneath it all.

Striding on through the Martian landscapes, I spotted a large mountain to my left. Poking through clouds in the distance, I knew that Mount Taranaki was some 200 km from where I was standing, and still it looked masterful. I turned my head further to the left and spotted Mount Ruapehu, and turning back to the right, in the direction I was headed, there was Mount Ngauruhoe, now much bigger than it'd been last time I'd seen it on the road to Raetihi.

I knew now that I was only a few kilometres from the next village, called Whakapapa. Yes, for the non-Kiwi among you, you read that right. Although it might seem to be pronounced as if you were planning to brutally beat any fathers in the area (*Whak-a-papa*), it is, in fact, pronounced in a far more sinister way: *Fuk-a-papa*. I repeatedly struggled with pronunciations of New Zealand's town names, which were once upon a time named by Māori , and usually for a reason. *Whakapapa* literally translated means 'genealogy' – it describes knowledge of your ancestors, or the foundation which your family and current life is built upon. An understanding of *Whakapapa* allows people to locate themselves in the world in relation to their human ancestors. Compared to some other towns in New Zealand, I'd got off lightly with my pronunciation lessons by planning to run through towns with names such as Whakapapa, Whanga-rei, and even Maungakaramea. At least I wasn't running through the town Taumatawhakatangihangakoauauotama-teaturipukakapikimaungahoronukupokaiwhenuakitanatahu, which literally translates to 'The summit where Tamatea, the man with the big knees, the slider, climber of mountains, the land-swallower who travelled about, played his nose flute to his loved one.'

I made great time on the climb to Whakapapa. The fa-miliar orange poles switchbacked up a steep volcanic slope ahead of me, and instead of opting to follow them, I pow-ered directly up it. I felt amazing. My lungs burned, my knees ached and my calves threatened to explode but I was nailing it! And I nailed it right up to a road, which would take me into town where I knew there were places to fill my face with food. Within 30 minutes I was bounding into the tourist centre and checking the weather board. The last time I'd checked a few days ago, there had been a storm forecast. To my delight, it read for tomorrow: 'Light cloud, turning to drizzle in the afternoon.' And the day after: 'Showers and reaching gale force winds in the afternoon.' Score! The storm had moved back by a day and that meant I was just going to sneak over the Tongariro Crossing before it arrived. I bounded out of town and along the trail to Mangatepopo Hut, at the foot of the Tongariro Crossing. What a difference a day makes. The previous day, I couldn't possibly see how I would move forward feeling the way I did, but with a good day of running under my belt, a clear weather forecast and a new challenge lying in wait tomorrow, things were on the up again. The old saying is true – no storm lasts forever.

22

Taking on the Tongariro

I managed to catch my alarm on the vibration just before the music started blaring out of it. I was like a sleeping Jedi – half asleep, yet with cat-like reactions. Something about sleeping at the foot of the Tongariro Crossing had done that to me. I had spent the night in the most content mood in Mangatepopo Hut with 11 other people; ten of them French and one Brazilian. I'd been safe, warm and surrounded by lots of noise. It was a superb hut environment, and one that led me to conclude that it was simply the lack of company and people on the trail, which led me to bouts of sadness and confusion.

I threw my pack on to my back and bid goodbye to all members of the Mangatepopo Hut. I then stood for a moment, enjoying the quiet on the deck and staring at the full moon still in the sky, before setting off to join the main trail to the crossing. I felt great about my chances today; like I could smash it up and over the crossing early, and gain some time back, as I was starting to get a tad concerned about not making the finish line before my six-month New Zealand visa ran out. I'd just expected everything to be a little bit more straightforward than it had been.

I stifled the moans from my stiff lower back and joined the

steady stream of tourists who had started to trickle in from the trail to my right. The crossing gets around one million visitors a year – its spectacular views, challenging climb and good accessibility (you can drive to a car park either side) makes it one of the most popular one-day hikes in the world. Thankfully there didn't seem to be many tourists this morning, which is exactly what I was hoping for with an early start. I felt almost embarrassed as I pounded past seven tourists on the climb to the top. I wanted to stop and explain that I wasn't trying to impress, to get up there first, but I was running the country and that this trail was a part of it. I found that if I screwed up my face a little, and was incredibly polite as I asked them to move to one side to allow me through, this helped to alleviate my fear of judgement.

Although disgustingly steep in parts, the trail up to the Tongariro Crossing from the south side really is a treat. I learned that there are some benefits to running on a tourist trail, and that is that the trail is made suitable for those tourists. Beautifully graded, suitably wide, the Tongariro crossing boasted steps, an en-route toilet and large sections of boardwalk.

'You going up there?' asked a boy from Manchester whom I had befriended on the middle section of the climb. He nodded toward Ngauruhoe. 'We're going to try to be the first up it,' he said. 'I hear it's a nightmare with all the rockfall if you're not one of the first up. Some guy died last year, you know. Hit on the noggin by falling rock.'

I'd considered taking a side trip to climb what was arguably New Zealand's most famous volcano, but a trip up Ngauruhoe was going to add at least an extra 90 minutes to the crossing time and I didn't fancy getting caught up with a load of tourists. I stood at the foot of the volcano for 5 minutes, just staring, in a complete state of indecision. One side of my brain was screaming at me to grab life by the balls; the other half was telling me that I just didn't care and I could appreciate its beauty from down here. I looked back on the string of tourists that I'd passed, who were, on account of my procrastination, now rapidly catching me back up again. I must have looked fully unhinged. At last I let it go.

'You'll have to wait, Ngauruhoe. See you next time.' I said aloud before trotting on up the trail.

The crossing was a many-staged affair. A snaking, steep pathway wound its way up Mount Tongariro and led me at last to the most beautiful plateau. At 7.45 a.m. I was alone up there. In stark contrast to the blustery climb, on the plateau, sheltered by Ngauruhoe on one side, and the half snow-dusted crater of Mount Tongariro on the other, it was calm and windless. My deep panting slowed to longer intakes of breath. I dropped my run down to a walk and then stopped and stood entirely still. Turning 360 degrees around I felt a sense of peace and calm I hadn't encountered since coming down off the Mount Rintoul ridge line almost a month ago. This place was stunning, and to be up there without a soul in sight was hugely satisfying. A feeling which was rather confusing considering I had spent so much time yearning not to be alone. My brain made little sense of this point, but I was too happy to care. I hadn't a care in the world, in fact. There was something rather spiritual about the plateau and being up there alone meant I could give it the attention it deserved. It was just me and the mountain, and, given the number of tourists who passed through here every day, that felt rather special.

I looked ahead and saw that the plateau ended some 200 metres further on. I padded on slowly, longing for it to go on forever, but I could see there was still a higher section of trail to negotiate. The more time I spent down here, the stronger the winds got up there. And boy-oh-boy they were strong! Up on the highest point of the crossing the winds swirled around me, making such a roar that I could barely hear my own thoughts. Over the crest to the north-west were two lakes, one a pale turquoise blue, and the other a mesmerising shade of emerald. Mountains poked through clouds in the distance to the north-east, and I had a better view of Ngauruhoe up here too. Even though the sun had long since been up, soft shades of peach and lilac mixed with scarlets still suspended in the sky, a welcome remnant of the sunrise.

'Jesus!' I yelped as a chill ran all the way through me, right through to my bones. I'd stopped for a minute too long up on the crossing and I was now officially freezing my tits off. I threw my bag on the floor, dragged out another layer of clothing for all areas of my body – gloves, hat and leggings – and (tits still intact) set off along the sandy and rocky ridge-line trail.

At last I hit the descent. The trail snaked like a grey ribbon down the mountain in front. I stopped to take a picture, which I was going to send later to my cycling buddies back home. It reminded me of my favourite road climb in the world, Sa Calobra in Majorca. If only they allowed bikes up here. Still, without wheels, the descent was a runner's dream. A beautifully graded, wide footpath, meandering down an open plain. Watching the sulphur gas escape from gaps in the black rocks of the Te Maari craters, I took great delight in passing signs warning that I was entering a volcanic hazard zone. Within this zone I was to 'keep stops to a minimum and be prepared should an eruption take place.' I wasn't entirely sure what being prepared entailed, but I had been a Girl Guide once upon a time, and I was hoping that my sash full of badges counted for something.

I knew the eruption warnings were a real risk. In August 2012, the Te Maari craters on the northern side of Mount Tongariro had blown their tops. A second eruption in the November of that year had sent scorching hot rocks flying into the air, rocks which had then landed on the track I was running on, and also on the Ketetahi Hut, which had just now popped into view. I looked at the hut and wondered if there had been anyone in it when the explosion had taken place. How frightening would that have been? What do you do when you're making your noodle surprise and the earth just decides to blow up?!

I knew the hut was out of official action thanks to the

flying fiery rocks incident, but for some reason I had assumed that I would still be able to get water from there. When I arrived I found that there was indeed a large water tank, but it had run dry. I'd just get some at the bottom, I resolved. There must be some kind of water tap at the bottom. It's a tourist destination after all and tourists need water.

At 11.20 a.m. I arrived at the car park on the north side of the crossing. Tongariro was over with and out of my way! It'd taken a little over 4 hours to run the crossing, which I was pretty stoked with considering I had stopped for around an hour of that. Alas, there was no water. What I didn't account for is that most tourists were bussed in from surrounding hotels, which had perfectly good water supplies, and they didn't walk or run to the foot of the crossing. Sensible beings, these tourists.

Over the past few weeks the thoughts about the trail section beyond the crossing had steadily piled up in my mind. Since leaving Wellington I'd not been in the bush alone for more than a day at a time and I was growing well-accustomed to running on quiet gravel roads, enjoying the consistent pace they allowed me to maintain. The gravel was softer on my knees than tarmac, and easy enough to make good time along. I liked being able to predict how long it would take me to complete the miles that day, a confidence which had mainly led to late starts and arrivals into towns just before dark. The problem was that once you've tasted speed, and I'm talking 10 minutes per mile here (motoring, I know), it's hard to go back to the slower terrain. North of Tongariro, I knew that I would enter sections of bush again, and I wondered how I would cope.

It all started perfectly well – the road from the foot of the crossing was a whole heap of nothing, but allowed for fast progress. A few cars passed before I turned off the first highway and onto a new one. My mouth had started to get really dry and I could taste beer once again, which I knew meant I was dehydrated. And then there it was like a mirage in the desert, a holiday park! Oh, happy days! That meant water! I padded in and looked in on the office but I couldn't see anyone around. I looked left and saw that there was an open kitchen with a tap. Hallelujah! A man appeared from across the field.

'Can I help?' he asked.

I swivelled around. 'Oh, yes, I'm running... I've come over the crossing... and... I've still got twenty kilometres to go and well... I've run out of water. I just wondered if I could fill up with some from the tap over there?'

He looked me up and down.

'This water is for our paying customers,' he said.

'I'm sorry?'

'It's not free, you know. We have to pay for everything on this site. We pay a water bill every month and we pay to get it filtered, so the water is only for paying guests.'

I was a bit shocked. Was this guy actually refusing me

tap water? I looked back at him. Yes. He was. I started to feel something boil inside of me. I wanted to scream at him and ask what had happened in his life that had led him to become such an arsehole, but the fact was, I still needed water.

'Well, can I pay you for the tap water then?' I offered through gritted teeth.

'No, you can go and buy some bottled water from the office over there.'

I wanted to cry.

'Okay, thank you,' I said. Lips trembling, hands shaking, I packed my stuff into my backpack, turned around and ran off. There was no way I was giving that man a penny. I'd rather die.

I took a small unmarked bush trail off the road to the right and headed into the forest. Much of the ground was a thick clay, which made it wet and slippery underfoot, so much so that on the downhill sections it made more sense to sit down on my butt and slide to the bottom, than try to stay upright. All the while, through the slipping and sliding, I paid close attention to the GPS on my phone. The Tongariro Forest was like a maze, and trails shot off in every direction.

I managed to at last find some water from a nearby river before the trail became obscured by bush and rocks. I had spent 10 minutes relocating the trail, then whooped and cheered at my own achievement. I was a trail warrior! I had food, I had water and I had found the trail.

'Warrior!' I screamed, as I beat my chest and raised my arms aloft.

By the time I crawled into my tent that evening, I had run a full marathon. I concluded that it was probably the first and last time I would run a marathon with an 18-kg pack on *and* take on the Tongariro crossing. One to tell the grandkids, I reminded myself.

I looked down at my legs which were a certifiable mess. The trails were lined with flax grass, a special kind of long-bladed nemesis whose leaves are coated with a sticky substance. As I ran past them, the main area of each blade would stick to my leg, and then flip the blade sideways to allow the sharp edge to slice through my skin, like a giant paper cut. My legs were covered in these tiny cuts, my ankles especially, and they were now stinging like mad.

I always forgot how bright the light of the moon could be – a side effect of living in a city at home. It was rare to be able to see its luminosity without the dull throb of light pollution, but I could see it in full glow that night as I munched on noodles in the porch of my tent. I turned on my e-reader and loaded up Alastair Humphreys' *Thunder & Sunshine*. I had read this book twice already, but I tended to reread books I liked, because I knew what to expect. I found that I frequently read tales from other adventurers in my tent during the evenings, often to keep me sane. I found solace in our common experiences, the emotional roller coaster, the longing for home, and all at once the desire to continue. In short, their stories made me feel less mental, and anything that could do that was most welcome.

After a week of staying in small towns and passing through tourist areas, it felt odd to just have my own thoughts (and Kiwi Kev the mascot) for company once again. A return to isolation triggered an experience which had now become very familiar, and part and parcel of sections of trail where I was alone. That night, I thought I could hear people just down the way, or coming along as I was setting up camp. I really believed that I could hear them talking but, of course, there was no one. Just me, camped alone in the bright light of the full moon, and relieved that the final high-mountain pass hadn't defeated me. Strangely, although I knew in the end that these imaginary people were never real, the voices or the feeling of someone being nearby never bothered me. I just accepted it as a quirk of the adventure. It was like a secret I kept between me and the trail. I talked to my stuffed toy Kiwi Kev, I heard voices in the distance every now and then, I imagined that I wasn't alone, and I was okay with that. With my imaginary people, just down the way, I curled up in the forest, and drifted off into a dreamless sleep.

23

The Great Battle of Bog Inn

I ran around the front of Hauhungaroa Hut and peered through the window. I could see two blokes milling around inside. Score! There were people, and I liked people. Best of all there seemed to be equipment everywhere, which meant they were DoC workers, and I liked DoC people even more than normal people. A conversation with a DoC worker was one without ego. It was one without agenda. It was a conversation with someone who loved and appreciated how they spent their days, and saw little distinction between work and leisure time.

I was delighted to find the hut and, in fact, I'd quite liked to have found it an hour or so earlier. After making it through the Tongariro Forest, I'd set off from the small town of Taumarunui late that morning. I'd run 32 km along hot, dusty and mostly deserted roads before beginning on a bush trail for 6 km. At the start of that bush trail, I'd had to have a little sit down and cram some all-too-essential survival cheese into my mouth. I was low on energy and well and truly ready for a lie down.

Opening the door to the hut I was overwhelmed by a smell that can only be described as man. A perfumery of dusty armpits, wet woollen socks and freshly cooked beef steak. Checked

313

shirts, camouflage and fluoro hunters' jackets, boots and all sorts of electrical odds and ends were sprawled across every surface. There were four bunks, a small bench in the corner, a wood burner and a steel work surface up against one wall. I gave it a solid six on the hut-o-meter. Structurally, it'd have been a five, but the view over the Hauhungaroa Ranges and the Pureora Forest beyond had delivered a bonus point.

The older of the two workers stood up. He was clearly flustered and was behaving as if I'd just walked in on him on the toilet.

'Oh! Hi. Hello,' he said, jumping to his feet and wiping his grubby hands on an even more grubby shirt.

I smiled, hand outstretched. 'Hello. I'm Anna.'

Nick and Russ were DoC employees doing work to monitor invasive species in the area. That is, their job was to keep tabs on the number of different types of animals that roamed the bush around the hut. It helped them to keep a handle on how effective the 1080 pesticide drop in that area had been – 1080 is designed to kill possums – and to detect the presence of other invasive species, such as mice, rats and stoats, which were a threat to the natural environment. Nick was busy in the corner of the room, filling in some kind of hideous-looking form. I pondered the absurdity of form-filling in the middle of the bush, sought out one of the few available and visible sections of floor and put my pack down. I was like a kid in a candy shop; their equipment may as well have been cola cubes and strawberry bonbons.

'What does this do?' I asked, picking up a pad of black things sitting on the bottom bunk.

'We put those out for the rats to run over,' said Russ. 'We can keep tabs on the species by the shape of their footprints.'

'Oh my. Now that's clever… and how about this?' I said, holding up a piece of plastic piping. 'Are you building toilets for the rats?'

'Ha! No, those are the tunnels. We lay them out in grids and put the black pads in the tunnels. The rats run through them.'

'And these! What are these?'

'Those help us mark out the grids.'

And so it continued. When I had exhausted every possible piece of oddly shaped material, the conversation turned to me. We went through the usual where I was going and how long I had been 'walking' questions. Then I would shuffle my feet and awkwardly look at them as I introduced the fact that I was running the trail.

'With that pack?! You're running with that pack?'

These were always funny exchanges, and it was like I needed to remind myself every time I told people exactly what I was doing. On some days, I'd be like: 'Yeah! I'm running this trail. I'm running it SO HARD it's begging me to leave it and go home.' Other days I'd opt for humour in a bid to deflect the incredulous onlooker: 'Yeah, I'm running with the pack, that was a stupid idea, wasn't it?' Other days I'd feel rather embarrassed, nervous and unsure. Was I actually running this trail? 'Umm, yes? Yes. Yes. I am. I'm running it with the pack.'

'Where you headed to tomorrow?' Russ asked.

'Bog Inn Hut,' I said, hoping it wasn't as vile as the name suggested. The men looked at one another.

'Bog Inn? Are you sure?'

'Ye... yes? I'm sure?' I said, now actually feeling quite unsure.

You see, the thing was, even though I was the one running this thing, even though I was the one who'd run 2,115 km to this point, battling snow, rain and swollen rivers, I was still convinced that others knew better about my project progress than I did.

'That's quite a way from here,' said Russ. 'Here let me show you.' He led me outside. 'You see that ridge over there. Bog Inn is right on the other side of that.'

Crikey, that ridge looked a long way off. According to the trail markers, it was only 30 km away, but by the looks of what was between me and that hill over there, it would all be through dense bush and that would mean the going would be slow. I was more keen than usual to make it through to Bog Inn in one hit, as I was only a few days from the next town of

Te Kuiti, and beyond there were more towns and more people. Spending another day in the bush on my own wasn't really something that appealed to me. As I cooked dinner and settled into bed, Russ and Nick began chatting via radio to the other workers dotted around the hills.

'JG 79 this is NC 88. All good over here and copy the weather, over.'

I listened intently to the forecast. It seemed that there was a storm headed in within the next few days, and I hoped I could make it to town before that hit.

By 7 p.m., it was pitch-black outside. The hut was filled with a thick haze, a mixture of fire smoke and evaporated sweat. You had to love hut life. The simplicity of it. The fact that I felt completely comfortable in the company of two strange men I'd just met, and they in mine (or so I assumed). Nick rustled around in the corner a little while longer, filling out forms by the light of headlamp, before clambering into the bunk below me. Russ was already long gone into the land of nod. His deep snores reverberating off the hut walls. I read a little more, before shutting down my e-reader and drifting off myself. Judging by the terrain Russ had pointed out, tomorrow was going to be a big day.

I ran away from Hauhungaroa hut at 8 a.m. The sun was just starting to peek over the hills in the distance, and it was still cold. According to the DoC time, it would take me 17 hours to reach Bog Inn Hut. If I was to make it there before dark, I needed to do it in 9.5 hours. In theory that should be fine, but I'd learnt that *should* be fine, often meant it *could* be fine. I never really knew what lay ahead. I hoped for a smooth trail and easy passage; something I quickly learned was a pipe dream.

I decided that today would all be about mental strength so, as I had done on the banks of the Jerusalem River, I broke the day down into sections in my mind. Waihaha Hut was 11 km away and, even though the DoC sign said it'd take me 7 hours, I figured it'd take me around 4 to get there. I found I could usually run for around 50 minutes lost in my thoughts, until I 'came to', so I just needed to do that four times, and I'd as good as be at Waihaha Hut. Simple.

I felt an immense sense of pressure. It was more than just making Bog Inn Hut before darkness fell; it was to do with making it out of the bush and to a town in as few days as possible. What was I even looking forward to in that town? I wasn't sure. If the past few towns had been anything to go by there wasn't much going on in towns in these parts, but at least there were people there. For the first hour of running I was calm, confident and composed. I had a plan; I just needed to execute it. Then my GPS began to fail. The trail started to twist and turn through dense bush that made running a challenge. In many places the trail was so overgrown that I couldn't see where my feet were landing, and the long grass snagged my leggings and grabbed at me as I passed. At one point, the trail disappeared entirely, and I found myself running up a gully which just didn't feel quite right. I stopped to check the GPS app on my phone, which failed repeatedly. So swore repeatedly.

'Well, you're useful, aren't you?! Just sitting there in my bag, and then I get you out to use you and you don't work. You can shut up too (now I was talking to the trail). Why would you go changing direction like that? Where am I supposed to go from here?!'

According to the chimp management theory, I was at this point 100% chimp and 0% human. I shouted a little more at my GPS app, and eventually it kicked back into life. I had headed off east, when I should have gone north. I moved my little location arrow in the direction of the dotted line on the GPS, ducked under a few trees, and pushed through some head-height bush. Emerging on the other side I could see a ground trail reappear and I caught sight of a pink ribbon tied to a tree. I didn't often see pink ribbons, but I'd noticed in the past that they were tied in places where the trail might take a sudden turn. They weren't official trail markers, but they were put in place by either other trail users, or kind locals. I was back on the trail and I'd only lost 10 minutes, but distractions like that not only cost me time, they jolted me from the flow of the run and my predetermined mental strategy of only having to 'think' every 50 minutes and instead brought me back into the present, where I was on a trail on my tod and still a long way from home.

But then I made Waihaha Hut, and when I realised that

I'd made it in just 3.5 hours I was absolutely delighted! I couldn't quite believe that I'd made faster time than expected. Getting to Bog Inn today was possible, I thought. I was going to make it. I sat down and inhaled a cheese wrap. I was soaked in sweat, and so I started to get cold quite quickly. After just 15 minutes of rest I set off again into the bush, prepared for another chunk of running. The next section said a DoC time of 10 hours. I'd halved the last section so figured I could do the same here too. That meant 5 hours of running. That was still a long time, but really it was two 90-minute sections, with an hour on the end. All I had to think about were those blocks, one at a time.

With every incline I hit, I began to get anxious. Every section of uphill slowed my pace dramatically, and so the more uphills I encountered, the longer it was going to take me to make the hut. When the anxious thoughts would well up inside of me they'd start at the very base, at my feet. Gradually over the next 10 minutes they'd work their way up my legs, into the pit of my stomach before shrinking into teeny particles to work their way up my wind pipe. When they reached the top of my head, I exploded. At myself, of course, because there was no one else to explode at.

It became a day of ups and downs, in every sense. I fell over lots and spent an unusual amount of time on my arse. The floor was covered with blackened leaves, slimy and slippery from the recent rainfall. There was just so much mud. Not the nice kind of mud, but the stuff that smells of rotting animals and has purple oils formed on the surface. Several times I went calf-deep in it. There were rivers to cross too, but they barely bothered me now. I would flit between enjoying my frequent slips and trips into the mud, and at the other end of the spectrum, I would end up being genuinely hurt. It was a roller coaster of cursing and manic laughing.

I was just thinking about what would happen if I fell and hurt myself here in the middle of nowhere – morbid day-dreaming, let's call it – when I slipped. My right hand was holding on to a tree slightly above me and to my right and, as the ground dropped away beneath me, my shoulder snapped backward with a loud crack. Then my arm went numb. I landed on my butt with a massive thud.

'Oh, shit!' I thought. Had I dislocated it? I knew this is how people dislocated things. I sat for a minute until I had some feeling back in it. I tried to move it, and I could. Phew! It was really painful, so I ran with my arm cradled across my chest for the next 30 minutes until I got all the feeling back. I resolved to go a little more carefully from then on. This was only a run after all, and coming back home in one piece was far more important than anything.

Out in a clearing and up at just over 1,000 metres above sea level, I had an incredible view of the surrounding land-scape and I felt at last like I could breathe. I checked the GPS app – just 10 km to go! I celebrated with a little dance before remembering that my shoulder hurt, and I whooped, half in pain, half in joy. Less than 10 km, I thought. Imagine if I'd set off for a 10-km run this morning – wouldn't I be feeling that that's a positively short distance to go, and be delighted? So I took off again with that mindset.

At 5.30 p.m. I squelched and slipped my way across the final bog, and saw at last what I had been working towards all day: Bog Inn Hut. I had been running for 9.5 hours with two 15-minute breaks. I was destroyed but elated to have made it to this modest and humble hut, and to be one step closer to the next town. I threw my clothes and sleeping gear out of my pack, made a brief affair of dinner and crawled into bed. It was 6.10 p.m. A runner's bedtime by all accounts.

The following morning I was still feeling exhausted, but I was content. My shoulder was now really beginning to ache, but I'd become accustomed to the pain, and it didn't seem to affect my running too much. The only noticeable disadvantage was that each time I picked up my pack I had to do it exclusively with my left arm. I checked the map for information on the days ahead. I was sure that I didn't have far to go until the next town of Te Kuiti, but, I'll be honest, planning for this section had been minimal. I had roughly thought that I'd just throw a few days' worth of food in and it would be fine. Much to my horror, I still had 74 km to make Te Kuiti. My heart sank.

That meant two more 37-km days. On the plus side, it was at least mostly on gravel roads. There was the option of doing the distance over three days instead, but I was keen to make town and worst of all I had only packed enough food for two more days. All I'd eaten the previous day was two cereal bars, a cheese wrap, some nut mix and a pack of noodles with cheese for dinner. I was so tired that I didn't even eat any of the chocolate I had left. I must have been seriously tired, as I'd eat more than that on a day I sat on my arse in the office.

I decided to make as many miles as possible that day and clocked up 41 km before bedding down for the night in a forest just off a dusty track. I still relished the challenge of wild camping, and so enjoyed spending the final 5 km of running, selecting the perfect spot in a pine forest.

Pine forests were my favourite type of place to camp – the soft spongy needles made a mattress of their own and the wide spaces between the trees were perfect flat ground. The only thing that worried me slightly about camping under pine trees tonight was that it was windy, and pine trees tended to move about a lot in the wind. Still, it was always a toss-up between cover and safety, and this really was the best spot I'd found. I waited for darkness to fall before setting up the tent, just to be safe. I was still almost visible from the gravel road and, although there was only a car going by every few hours, I didn't want one of those cars to be that of a farmer and to be discovered. Perhaps they would permit me to stay on their land, but then again perhaps they would ask me to move, and the thought of packing up everything and running on further just wasn't worth the risk.

The last thought that went through my mind that night was of Andrew and Peter. I'd popped into a pocket of signal at the 1,000-metre saddle and got a message from them saying that they'd just bashed out a 40-km day and were now in Te Kuiti. I knew I wouldn't catch them any time soon, but I felt satisfied knowing that we were still just a few days apart on the trail.

It was now light and even though it was bucketing with rain, I decided to leave camp. A storm had raged through the night and the creaks and groans of the forest around me had led to a range of disturbing and vivid dreams. I thought about the day ahead – it was 34 km to Te Kuiti, and it looked set to rain all day. The storm that Nick and Russ had learned about on the radio back at Hauhungaroa Hut had well and truly arrived.

This was a day when I didn't want to leave my tent. I wasn't entirely sure where I was going to get the mental strength for the day ahead, but I was used to it now. 'Just start running,' I told myself. Once I started running everything always fell into place. Sitting in the doorway of my tent, I started a morning video which I intended to upload to Facebook when I made town.

'I'm in a tent in the forest. It's cold, and it's windy and it's raining. Still. At the other end of today is a big cup of coffee. A giant cu…'

My words were disturbed by a loud crack. What in the

THE PANTS OF PERSPECTIVE

world was that?! I leapt out of my tent just in time to see the tree next to me split in two and come crashing to the ground. It landed 2 metres from where I'd been sitting.

'Holy crap!' I stared in shock. Adrenaline pulsed through my veins. I felt sick. I looked up at the trees; they were swaying to and fro in the wind, bending and flexing in the gusts. I suddenly felt incredibly unsafe. If I needed motivation to get running – this was it. I packed up as fast as I could, hands shaking, and decided that I probably wouldn't post that video after all – it'd only make my poor mum worry.

Running away from the forest, the rush of adrenaline subsided and gave way to manic laughter. That was close! Oh, my days, that was close! What a way to kick-start the day! The rain continued on and off for most of the morning, and by early afternoon I was facing a full-blown monsoon. A strong wind drove the rain sideways into my face and I went into a trance. I took myself away from my body, from the trail entirely and escaped into my mind. I was struggling to see, cocooned in the hood of my rain jacket, but I managed to angle my hood down just enough to catch glimpses of where I was headed.

After 4 hours I was well and truly soaked to the skin. I approached what I knew to be the final junction before Te Kuiti at long last. My phone had been reduced to a slippery mess and so I'd worked out based on guessing 1-km squares on the map that I had just 7 km left to run to town. I spotted a yellow sign that I now recognised as giving distance and direction, and as I closed in I saw a number that made my toes curl. Nine kilometres to Te Kuiti was almost enough to break me. It was only 2 km more than I'd expected, but those 2 km might as well have been 20 km at this point. I was pooped. I took shelter in a small corrugated iron shed, on a little wooden bench. I threw my pack onto the straw-lined floor and sat down. I knew I just needed to press the reset button. I gave myself a talking to and sucked in a huge breath of air. As I exhaled I erased everything that had happened that day so far from my mind, and pretended once more that I was just out for a 9-km run. I turned my exhaustion into anger and determination and set off again.

I was in that final 2 km to Te Kuiti, and on my last legs. I'd run clean out of energy and was forcing myself to focus on one roadside bush at a time in a bid to break up the final 1 km to the centre of town. A cyclist in a high-vis jacket turned onto the road from a side road and started moving toward me. I realised I hadn't seen a cycle tourist since just before Queenstown on the South Island almost three months ago, and considered that perhaps they'd stop for a chat. The cyclist made a beeline directly for me, and it was then that I spotted a red ponytail protruding from beneath her helmet. She crossed the road and pulled up in front of me, just as I recognised the face framed by the helmet.

'Anna McNuff!' she shouted, pulling hard on the brakes to stop the bike in the downpour.

'Faye?! I can't believe you found me!' I said, hugging her, trying my best not to drag her off her bike. This wasn't just any cycle tourist. This was Faye Shepherd.

Every now and then on the road, I'd receive an email or message from a stranger to let me know that they'd felt inspired to go and do something off the back of watching the run unfold. I found these messages both overwhelming and humbling. Every single one made me smile, buoyed me and made me feel that little more like what I was doing was worthwhile. I'd taken inspiration from so many people over the years, and to think that I was doing that for someone else made me feel, for want of a better word, validated.

One of the women following the run was Faye, and she had taken post-inspiration action to the next level. She'd been following the journey on Facebook from her home town in Cornwall and decided that my pictures of the South Island were just too stunning to miss out on. She'd taken extended leave from work, hopped on a plane from the UK and come to cycle the length of New Zealand. Even though we'd not met and only spoken through a few messages, I liked this girl immediately. I knew she was a girl with balls. Big, fat, hairy lady balls.

In that final kilometre to town, Faye had absolutely made my day. She told me that she'd bought me lunch, and sorted me out with a room at a local backpackers' lodge. She'd also bought supplies for dinner, including a bottle of wine. I absolutely loved this girl – her actions were beyond kind and I was completely blown away. Faye was an angel. The rain miraculously stopped a few minutes after our meeting and suddenly I had my mojo back. I felt full of energy again. Faye's energy was now mine too.

We trundled on slowly, Faye pedalling at my side, and as we reached the main street of Te Kuiti, I turned to her and said: 'Faye, there's just something I really need to get before we go any further.'

She looked concerned. 'What's that? Are you hurt?'

'No, but I need Fanta.'

I didn't know what it was about Fanta, but I craved it, always, on this run. There was something about the slippery sickly sweet liquid gliding down my throat that was addictive. It quenched thirst, it gave me energy, and I needed it.

We stopped briefly to allow me to buy a litre of the orange stuff. Given that I'd been running on minimal food the past few days, I also went a bit OTT on everything else. All I'd eaten was a packet of porridge that morning, and a handful of nuts – to be honest, in the wind and rain, I couldn't be bothered to break my running rhythm to eat. Laden with food, which Faye kindly offered to put in her panniers, I was ready to rock.

'Now. Where's this place?' I asked.

'It's about another 2 km up the road. And sorry, it's up a

really steep hill,' she grimaced.

In stark contrast to my toddler tantrum about the previous 2 km, this was 2 km I didn't mind at all, especially when I found out we were travelling in the right direction, which was an unexpected bonus! Fuelled by Fanta and smiles we set off; Faye on her bike again as I ran alongside. As it turned out, Faye had done a stellar job of finding the best backpackers' accommodation in town. Well, okay, it was the only place for backpackers, but it was awesome nonetheless.

I peeled off my sodden clothes and scuttled into a steaming hot shower, still with Fanta in hand. I sat on the floor of the shower, clutching the bottle of Fanta and letting the warm water trickle over my head and cascade down my weary body. I'm not entirely sure why I decided to take the Fanta in with me, I just wanted to. It felt right and so I rolled with it. My relationship with this soda was getting serious. I breathed a sigh. That section was done. I had run 2,193 km and now had just over 800 km left to go. I knew it was mostly minor roads and gravel tracks all the way from here to the next big milestone of Auckland – no more bush-bashing for a while. Lovely.

After the Fanta shower, we shared a proper girls' night in. Faye whipped up a stir-fry, with apple pie and ice cream for dessert, and we cracked open a bottle of New Zealand wine. On inspecting the rather dubious VHS collection we opted not to watch *He Died with a Felafel in his Hand* (apparently not some kind of food-fuelled porno, but in fact a dark Australian satire), and just chatted instead. Faye was another Instafriend – kind, adventurous and wholly in search of herself.

I'd decided that I was enjoying my hilltop view from the hostel so much that I'd take a day of rest. My shoulder was giving me a bit of jip, and pulling the pack on and off was painful, so I decided to use my rest day to arrange a few more school talks and catch up with friends.

One of those friends was Laura Kennington, who was in the middle of kayaking Europe's longest river, the Volga, solo. She was having a really tough time, and was feeling so alone in a country where she could barely speak the language. I tried to distract her with gossip: 'So... There's this boy. Well, there's *a* boy.'

'Anna! There's *a* boy?! There's never a boy. Who is this boy?! TELL ME!' she barked, as only excited girlfriends can. 'And how the heck is there a boy when you're running across New Zealand?! Did you find one in a bush?!'

'It's a boy from home. I think we're just friends, but I don't know. It's sort of, I mean, I think I quite like him. But it's weird...'

I tried to condense four months of friendly and sometimes bizarre exchanges with Jamie into the space of 15 minutes.

'Ah – you lurrvve him!' Laura chirped.

'Oh, shut up! I do not love him. It's probably nothing. I

just, well, he just… Oh, whatever.'

After we'd hung up, I tried to analyse my feelings towards Jamie. I didn't think I loved Jamie, but after years of being footloose and fancy-free, there was a stirring in my heart that I couldn't quite explain. My stomach turned in mini somersaults when I thought about talking to him. Heck, I wanted to talk to him most of the time. The only times when I didn't want to speak to him was when I was feeling weak, exposed and fragile. And, in truth, those were the times when I needed to speak to him the most.

The truth was it had been five years since I'd been in love, and the prospect of loving someone again was confusing to say the least. My last relationship had ended in heartbreak, and it was mine that got broken. Someone once asked me what it feels like to have your heart broken, and so I told them that it hurts – it physically hurts. And once you've got over the fact that you've lost your best friend, you have to deal with the fact that somehow you were not enough, for them at least. To give the whole of yourself, to choose to show someone every possible part of yourself, only to have them say, after five years together, 'thanks, but no thanks,' is the deepest cut of all.

From the rubble of a once happily-ever-after relationship you are forced to reconstruct what it means to be you. To rediscover what it is that you love so much about yourself that it doesn't matter if someone else doesn't love that bit too. Because you love you, and that is enough. That's what adventure had allowed me to do in the past five years, and perhaps, just perhaps, I was ready to let someone in again.

24

SpiderPig

The torrential downpour that had escorted me so kindly into Te Kuiti continued for a further three days. When it came time to leave the campground at the next town of Otorohanga I kept delaying the day's run, hoping, wishing and praying for it to stop. The weather gods weren't listening and so I started on my merry way in my rain gear. I'd been in high spirits ever since Faye had appeared on the edge of Te Kuiti and I didn't plan on stopping now. As droplets hammered on my arms and were forced sideways onto my face, I pulled out my phone to take a video.

'Here's the thing,' I screamed over the ever-rising wind. 'It is absolutely tipping it down. I can hardly see. I can't feel my hands, or my toes. Or even my face for that matter. Feeling your face is overrated, anyway… But I've decided that there's two ways to do this. You can either get miserable about it, or you can get happy. And I'm going to get frickin' happy!'

The rain was what it was. I had no control over it, that much was true. The only thing I had control over was my reaction to its relentless presence. Recognising that I had the ability to choose my mood, I resolved that today would be a good day, rain or no rain. So I continued to smile, to talk to the cows, and to wave at the sheep and at cars that passed me by. I probably looked insane from the outside, but it was working. The determination to remain upbeat allowed me to glide above conditions that could have dragged my mood into the underworld. Besides, my next major stop-off was in a town I'd been hoping to visit for a while now: Cambridge.

I'd first met Mahe Drysdale when I was twenty-one. He would spend half his year training at one of my local London rowing clubs, Tideway Scullers. There he'd train with arch-rival and friend, Alan Campbell, who was at the time GB's fastest single sculler. We'd all stop and watch as Mahe glided past us on various stretches of the River Thames tideway. Our coach would make us take note: 'Look at his catch, you see how he applies the power?' We oohed and aahed and one day hoped we might shift our boats as fast as Mahe could. Other than those fleeting glimpses on the river, I had mostly been in Mahe's company during legendary Tideway Sculler's parties or parties at Henley Royal Regatta – a solid basis for a friendship, if you asked me.

I was often asked along the run whether I knew anyone in New Zealand. I had a few friends from home, and a couple of other friends of friends, and then there was Mahe and his wife, Juls, whom I sort of knew but really we were more acquaintances than friends. I didn't think I'd ever met Juls, although I had a photograph of us with our arms around one another at a rowing after-party in Boston's Head of the Charles rowing race. Neither one of us has any recollection of the evening, or remember the other being there. Any Kiwi I told about Mahe and our friendship was gobsmacked. I hadn't realised that, given the small population and their national love of sport, the Drysdales were as good as Kiwi royalty. I would officially be staying with the Wills and Kate of New Zealand.

I trudged up the driveway to the Drysdale's farm in the suburbs of Cambridge and within spitting distance of Team Kiwi's training ground, Lake Karapiro. Juls' mum greeted me on the driveway with a gigantic hug.

'I'm Penny!' she said, engulfing me in her arms. Oh, how I loved to be engulfed.

'Nice to meet you, Penny!' I mumbled from inside the hug.

'Oh, we've met!' she said. I was a little confused. 'From your videos, Anna. I've watched them all and I feel like I know you already.'

'Oh!' I smiled. How nice was that. I was always a little amazed when people watched the things I put out on social media.

I spent a couple of days with Juls and Mahe, getting to know them better, and their adorable new baby Brontë (also known as Brontë-bear) too. On day two of my stay, I was introduced to another important member of the family.

'Um, Juls…' I said, staring out the window. 'Who or what is that?!'

Juls looked up from chopping fruit. 'Oh, that? That's

SpiderPig.'

'SpiderPig?' I enquired, continuing to stare out the window.

'Yeah, some of my teammates gave him to me as a birthday present four years ago. They said he was a micro-pig when they handed him over. But they also laughed as they said it, so I wasn't really ever convinced. And now he weighs one hundred and ten kilograms.'

'One hundred and ten kilograms?!' That was some serious pork meat there.

'He's really very friendly,' said Mahe, getting up and moving to the door. He stepped outside and into the paddock. 'Here pig, pig, pig, pig, pig, pig!' he called in rhythmical fashion.

There's no way that pig was going to… yes, it was! Spider-Pig galloped (as much as pigs can gallop) across the paddock towards Mahe, before he proceeded to rub its trunk, and then its belly as it flopped onto its side like a dog.

I took two full days of rest with the Drysdales and Spider-Pig. They put me up in my own little cabin, a little way from the main house, and fed me up as only professional athletes can. I used the downtime on those days to visit a couple of local schools to speak to the kids, and went to the rowing lake to watch Mahe train one morning, something which made me pine a little for my younger days on the water. When the time came to leave the Drysdales's farm, I was really rather sad. Juls and Mahe were my kind of people. They understood the need to challenge yourself. I didn't need to pull the charity card to explain why I was doing what I was doing – they just got it.

For the 30-km run from Cambridge to Hamilton, I'd managed to score myself a couple of wing women. Wing woman number one was a girl named Hannah. I'd never met Hannah before, but she and her husband, Campbell, had walked the trail southbound earlier in the season. I couldn't resist the chance for a natter with someone who knew the trail well, and from her emails she seemed right up my street. We arranged to meet on my final morning and for her to run me out of her home town.

Wing woman number two was Nikki. I'd met Nikki at Leamington Primary, a school I'd been in to speak at the previous day. She was a teacher there and had been following the run since the beginning. Nikki had asked whether she could run with me for a few miles out of town, and of course I said yes.

'Oh, well, I'll just come for a bit. I run really slowly, and I've never run further than ten kilometres before. Are you sure I won't slow you up?' Nikki asked.

'Nikki,' I said in the tone of a mother that was about to tell her child off. 'Don't be silly. No, you won't slow me up. It'll be lovely to have your company, and we'll go at whatever pace you like. I'm in no rush. And I've got a big backpack remember! We'll make it by nightfall and that's all that counts… and if we don't, I'm prepared. I've got a tent and everything!' I grinned.

She smiled back, and I could tell that she knew it was definitely happening. She was excited. Nikki had some teacher duties to fulfil so she wouldn't be joining from the start, but the plan was that she'd follow my GPS tracker and join in when she could.

As I shuffled my way out of Cambridge with Hannah, I enjoyed exchanging trail experiences with her, and relaxed somewhat when she confessed that she hadn't followed the trail to the letter in many places either. Hannah and I had been running together for about 10 kilometres when a lone figure appeared at the side of the highway, and she was waving. It was Nikki! We slowed up for a hug.

'You made it!' I exclaimed, locking her in an extra-strong embrace.

'Woo, yeah! I mean, I had to ask special permission to get let out a bit early from school, and then I was worried I wouldn't find you, and then I was worried where I'd leave my car, but here I am! Oh, gosh. I can't believe I'm here!' The entire mass of words came out as one sentence and stream of consciousness. She was extremely excited and her energy was infectious. 'Now, if I go too slowly, you just tell me, okay?'

'Nikki, we've talked about this! You'll be fine, but I promise to tell you if we're going too slowly, okay?'

'Okay.'

Hannah had set a rather blistering pace for the first portion of the run, and like any days that followed rest days, my legs were heavy and the large jumble of belongings on my back felt most unwelcome. I was glad Nikki had joined us and brought along with her a desire to take it steady, something which would allow me to slow up a little.

'Okay. I'll probably only come for a few ks anyway,' Nikki reiterated.

'You come for as long as you like. We might even make it all the way to Hamilton,' I winked at her. We still had 20 km to go to make Hamilton.

'Just a few more ks and then I'll call for a pickup,' Nikki piped up after we'd run 8 km from where she'd joined us at the roadside.

Hannah and I looked at one another. I said, 'Okay, Nikki, whatever you want,' and proceeded to distract her with chatting.

At 15 km, she said, 'Okay, just a few more then, and then I'll call for a pickup.' This was already 5 km further than she'd ever run in her life.

'Nikki…' I said slowly. 'You know we've only got five kilometres to go now. Why don't you come the whole way?'

That was it. The challenge was set. Nikki fell silent. She gritted her teeth and shuffled on. Five kilometres later Nikki,

Hannah and I arrived on the outskirts of Hamilton. Nikki was glowing with pride, Hannah looked as fresh as a daisy, and I was doing my best to hide the fact that I was completely shagged. We hugged for an extended period of time, chatted a bit more then hugged again, before waving one another off and back to our various homes, or at least my home for the night with a brother of a friend in Hamilton.

Watching Nikki walk away, I became acutely aware that she was the perfect example of what this run was about. I often found my journey reflected in the lives of others. It had been a real privilege to watch Nikki today. To observe as she told herself she wasn't capable of something, to be gently convinced that maybe, just maybe, she could do it, and then to watch her come spinning and grinning out of the other side. It was days like this that filled me right up to the brim. Had my five-month journey been condensed into one day, then it would have taken on the same range of emotions (although with perhaps a few more tears) that Nikki's did today.

25

Back to Where it all Began

'So, um, like, where do you poop?' The room was filled with giggles. The kind of high-pitched giggles that only 30 teenage girls could create.

'Oh, I just take a plastic bag, do it in there and carry it with me. I hang the bags off my backpack like trophies.' I kept my face dead-pan. The giggles stopped. Every girl's face was now adorned with a look of horror. I knew this group was soon to be heading off to spend five weeks on Great Barrier Island, and the girls were on the hunt for tips and tricks to help them survive their own adventure. I left it a few more seconds.

'I'm only kidding!' There was an audible sigh of relief. 'I poop in holes in the ground.'

'Eww!' came the second reaction and one I was used to from school kids by now.

I'd done seven school talks in the past three days: two at primary schools in Cambridge, and five in a mix of primary and secondary schools in Hamilton. I was utterly exhausted, and all at once completely revitalised. School talks were one of my favourite parts of the journey. To speak to a room full of excited faces and minds that had yet to be tainted by the constraints of reality was a complete joy. It was the groups of teenage girls that I enjoyed speaking to the most. In the hour sessions with them, we would mostly sit around in a semicircle and discuss everything. My adventure, but also their hopes and dreams. I would tell them what it was that made my heart sing, and ask them if they had discovered that 'thing' yet themselves. During these sessions, such as the one I was in with the 30 girls at that moment, I would watch as even the shyest girl crept tentatively out of her shell and divulged what she'd really like to do with her life.

I was standing at the edge of a field, shouting at a small orange triangle: 'Well, you're bloody useful, aren't you? All hidden away there behind the bush. Ridiculous. You could have at least said something.'

Fifteen minutes earlier, I'd gotten lost. I'd missed the marker, the one that I was now hurling abuse at, and found myself in a dead-end field surrounded by 3-metre-high fencing. I had now, and even before the time-wasting episode, well and truly lost my trail mojo.

It had been four days since leaving Hamilton and it had poured with rain for much of that. The energy stored up from the school talks had run low, and I was starting to feel a little under the weather. On this particular day, I found that the trail at this point, well, it had no point.

You see, I wasn't in the middle of nowhere, enjoying jaw-dropping scenery and cascading waterfalls, as to my right was State Highway 1. I could see it from the trail quite frequently, and although the trail was keeping me from running along Highway 1 (for which I was very grateful), it slipped and slid alongside the river, sometimes disappearing into the river entirely, and would require me to move inland and scramble over electric fences, or have a face-off with a paddock full of angry bulls. As it was, I seemed to have lost my love for running on anything other than a surface that would get me from A to B in the fastest possible time.

It probably didn't help that I was dehydrated. In my rush to leave my host's house that morning I had forgotten to fill up with water. They were on their way to church and running late, so I'd bundled myself out the door without a second thought about water. I'd also neglected to buy any extra food. So here I was, screaming obscenities at an orange triangle, having run 27 km on a packet of trail mix and zero water. There was no doubt, I was an idiot.

With 5 km to go, the trail joined up with State Highway 1. After double-checking the map to affirm that I definitely should be running down the side of a state highway with traffic moving at 100 kilometres per hour, I began to enjoy the thrill of it – the different feel of the hard tarmac beneath my feet, and the toots from passing cars as they spotted the 3,000-km mission scrawled in marker pen across the back of my high-vis jacket. I also amused myself with what passers-by in their cars must think to see a girl with a high-vis vest and oversized pack running down the side of the motorway.

The heavens opened and began to pelt with rain again. Just then a car passed and pulled in 500 metres ahead of me. 'Oh, crap,' I thought. This happened a lot if running along a road. Quite often cars would stop to see if I wanted a ride somewhere. Subsequently I would receive baffled looks from drivers when I replied: 'No, no, thanks – I'm doing this out of choice.' I'd normally opt for the line: 'I have to run, I'm doing a charity challenge.' Somehow this implied that there was a force greater than my own will making me do what I was doing. I knew this was my choice, but it seemed a stretch for many people to understand that it was a choice, and phrasing it as 'I have to' seemed to be something they could comprehend and accept.

I began waving at the woman who'd climbed out of the car in front. She was wrapping a jumper around her head to keep the rain off, and now rummaging around on the back seat. Oh, no – she's clearing a space for me to sit in the car, I thought. I began shouting: 'I'm fine! No, no, you'll get wet out here. Really – I'm okay. I have to keep going, I have to run it, it's a ch-ar-i-ty chal-len-ge…' I shouted over the wind and roar of the passing traffic. It wasn't until she got right up close, and I peered inside her makeshift hood that I recognised the face.

I'd last seen that face (attached to the body of a woman named Judith) standing at the side of the road at Arthur's Pass Village, as I scoffed down a customary date and orange scone. Waiting for the rain to subside, Judith had been hitching a lift back to the trail, to continue on in the opposite direction.

'Anna!' she yelled. 'You might not remember me...'

'Judith! How in the... what the...?!' Before I could finish she shoved something into my hands. 'Here – take these!' She hadn't been rummaging around on the backseat to clear a space, she'd been rummaging for cookies! All hail the cookie rummage!

'I knew you were in the area, I've been following on Facebook. I was on my way back to Auckland, just thinking, I wonder where Anna is, and there you were! Running down the side of the highway!'

Now. I know statisticians out there will probably tell me that there is no such thing as a coincidence. That the chances of Judith driving by in the 2 kilometres during which I was running along the highway, on that day, at that time, were actually rather high, but statisticians can jog on. I thought it was ruddy amazing, and I still do. There had to be a 10-minute window in that day when our paths could cross, and they did. See? Amazing.

We had a brief chat about her journey south, and about my 'day from hell' at the hands of the Deception River. It turns out that she'd busted her ankle too on the trail south and had to quit a few days later. It became difficult to hold a conversation on the side of a windy highway, and it was raining harder now, so we said our goodbyes and off she went.

Two kilometres down the road, at the turn-off to the next section of trail, there she was again. Judith had parked up in a side road. She'd gone up ahead and bought me a choco-late milkshake! A chocolate milkshake, I tell you! I could have kissed the woman. In fact, I did.

'Let's have a bit more of a chat,' I said, gratefully slurp-ing on the milkshake, throwing my pack onto the grass verge and clambering into the passenger seat of her car out of the rain. Ten minutes later, milkshake inhaled and feeling satisfied with having had a proper natter, I emerged from the car feel-ing like a new woman. Thanks to Judith, I was full of cookies and chocolate milkshake and equipped with a bit of knowl-edge about the next section of the trail. I waved her goodbye, shrugged my pack back on and set off on my way again, to the small town of Mercer.

Running into Auckland I felt like the same person who had left there four and a half months earlier yet completely different all at once. In the 2,400 km I'd covered, things had changed. My heartbeat fluttered gently when I saw the lights of Mission Bay come into view. There was the coffee shop I'd stood outside and spoken to Jamie from the day before I left in a state of angst. It was like coming home, but I still had so much further to go, in every sense.

For five days I almost forgot I was in the middle of a run across the length of New Zealand. It was lovely. I spent almost two days solidly curled up in bed, recovering from some kind of vomit-inducing, head-throbbing virus I'd picked up on the way into town. But after that I felt myself slipping back into the big city lifestyle, and the inevitable odd social nuances that come with city life, such as shifting my gaze as I passed someone in the street to avoid any kind of eye contact. God forbid our eyes might meet! Cities, I had realised, offer us permission to live in our own shells. Millions of people, cocooned inside their own mind, their car, their office, moving from one place to another, not looking, not observing, not breathing in, not stopping. In reality, there were a lot of similarities between the trail and a huge city, such as London or Auckland. You can be very lonely in a city, surrounded by people, so perhaps it is better to be lonely in the bush: in the bush, at least, the loneliness makes sense.

I was sitting in my friend Becky's Mission Bay apartment again – the very apartment I would return to when I had finished the run in a month's time. It would be like running past my front door. The exit was there. The airport, my passport. I was ready to be done. I was ready to go home. I missed my family and my friends. I missed walking over Waterloo Bridge at night, the curve of the Thames from Richmond Hill, whizzing through Westminster on my bicycle, dodging angry cab drivers and absent-minded tourists. I missed *BBC Breakfast*. I longed to stop, to pack up my suitcase and fly back to London. But what was I flying home to exactly? It sure as heck wasn't the kind of freedom I'd enjoyed for the past four and a half months. I'd be flying home to normality, a job and my friends. But would it be to greener grass? I didn't think so. I knew that I would miss this beautiful country and its wonderful people. I would miss the freedom and simplicity of the trail, and the life that it had allowed me to lead. A life I knew I would dream of next month when I was staring at my tattered trainers wondering where on earth to go from here.

I had sat on this same bed back in January, fretting about whether I could even make a week of the journey, and here I was months later, battered, bruised, and sick, but so proud of myself. I had transformed from someone who had little knowledge or understanding of how to navigate through the backcountry to a woman capable of crossing rivers and spending days alone in the bush. I knew that even if I failed now, I had still succeeded. But I also knew that I needed to finish what I'd started, and reach Cape Reinga, or I'd always regret it.

I acknowledged that the reality of entering the final month of a six-month journey was messy. My mind was a tangled web of thoughts, feelings and emotions – enough to give my hormonal 15-year-old self a run for her money. My body was weary, and the wheels on this one-woman wagon were starting to fall off. My hips ached, my knees crunched and I was pretty sure that the vertebrae in my upper spine had given up on any form of salvation, opting instead to fuse themselves together in self-defence. The tiny muscles that surrounded my shins were in revolt too. I'd spent the first hour of each daily run wincing as I waited for the pain to subside. Then there was the hotspot on my left ankle, which I daren't prod any more. For each time I did, just to remind myself it hurt, guess what? It bloody hurt.

But I also knew that the pain was starting to rear its ugly head because I knew I was near the end. I knew I was in dangerous territory. From the moment you allow yourself to think that you're almost there, well, it's then that it becomes inexplicably difficult to keep moving forward. I knew my body would keep going; it was now a running robot set to cruise control. I could run 35 km with a 14-kg pack without a second thought, and I had to remind myself that this wasn't 'normal'. The first time I put five 1-kg bags of sugar in my pack and ran 5 km, I'd nearly passed out.

These two opposing trains of thought had clouded my mind since the Tongariro Crossing, and they had officially begun to drive me nuts. Why would I wish away the final kilometres, only to savour them in hindsight? In the month since they had turned up, I'd tried using a few of the mental tools in my armoury to help me out. I tried denial first, that well-worn method of tricking myself into believing I only had a little bit further to go, or that I was starting afresh. So I tried treating this last month as if it were the start of the trip. 'Woo! Let's go, McNuff. Hup! Hup! Hup! New Zealand, here I come!' It held up for a day or two, then fell flat on its face. One level of denial too far for even my brain to cope with, it seems.

Denial having failed me, I tried to buddy up with my other friend, distraction. This I found came in the form of stunning landscapes, kind hosts, fundraising, school talks or even a conversation with friends back home – where we would spend an hour chatting about anything and everything except my run.

Alas, in the past month, I found that someone had stolen my bountiful distraction bucket and replaced it with a limp sieve. The things that buoyed me, inspired me and spurred me on now slipped through the saggy perforated bottom faster than I could grasp on and use them to their fullest. That made me sad. And then it hit me. The fact that I didn't know how to deal with this mental battle was a challenge. Not the one I'd expected to face when I began, but a challenge nonetheless.

The questions were no longer 'Will my body give out?' or 'Can I run that far?' Instead I asked myself could I make it to that lighthouse at Cape Reinga with eyes wide open – having enjoyed, relished and treasured every last drop of the journey?

As far as I could gather, this was just about the best practice for 'real life' that I could get. I refused to spend the final month waiting for the end to come, because it felt suspiciously like those working weeks where you live only for the weekend. And balls to those weeks, I say.

26

The Auckland Army

There was a small cheer as I walked out of the Devonport Ferry terminal on the north shore of Auckland. I smiled and cheered back, moving along the line to hug each and every one of these beautiful individuals who had turned up to run me out of town and kick-start the final 600 km of the journey. I had put out a post on Facebook and Twitter, encouraging anyone and everyone to come and run with me up the coast if they fancied. I hadn't expected a soul. Well, perhaps just Natasha, who was a friend of a friend from home and had escorted me around the city for the past few days. I hadn't expected anyone because it was, once again, tipping it down with rain. And I mean biblical, 'grab the animals, line 'em up two by two and get Noah on the blower' kind of biblical. Yet here they were: 15 shining faces all willing to brave the deluge on my behalf. We had 23 kilometres to run to make it to Long Bay, and having retired Frodo and Sam, I would be running out in a shiny new pair of yet-to-be-named trainers. 'You ready team?!' I yelled, doing my best to drown out the noise of the rain beating down on the ferry terminal roof.

'Yeah!' came the resounding reply, and we were off! The first few kilometres passed with little effort at all. We were all riding high on the euphoria that comes from the chitter-chatter between a group of overexcited and exercise-loving Lycra-clad strangers. I strode alongside a lad named Ashwin for the first few hundred metres. He was not Lycra-clad but had instead come dressed as if he were ready for dinner – in khaki shorts and a short-sleeved shirt. He looked far too dapper for our ragamuffin run-gang.

A few kilometres later I took great joy in handing the pack to Darren, who was also part of the group. Darren and his girlfriend, Arnya, were the super-buff, mega-fit kind, so I was delighted as they passed the backpack between the two of them for 4 km, huffing and puffing the entire way. 'How the heck have you run all the way to Auckland with this thing?! I've done 1 km with it and I'm dying!'

After 4 km I thanked them both for the assistance and threw the bag back on my shoulders where it belonged. I had loved having no weight on my back, even for a few kilometres. I'd relished in the freedom and the ability to bound more than usual with every stride.

'You're a bit wonky, aren't you, Anna?' ultrarunner Jen said, appearing alongside me.

'Oh, that? Yeah, I think I am. Not much I can do now. I figure I'll just cling on till the end!' I was fully aware that I had begun to lean to my left as I ran, mostly because my lower left back was permanently jammed up. I'd given up with any form of stretching by this point – everything hurt so much, that when I tried to move it, it hurt more the next day than if I just let it be – so I opted to let my wonky body be, and would drag it to the finish line in whatever state I could.

'Anna!' Ashwin pulled alongside, relieving me from the chat about my wonky back.

'Yes, Ashwin?!'

'This is me. I'm done. I'm off to catch the bus home. Thanks for the chance to run with you, it's been a pleasure.'

'See you later, Ashwin!' I yelled, after hugging him good-bye. I looked back at him for a moment as he ran off, his sodden clothing clinging to every part of his body. I thought about him sitting at that bus stop for anything longer than a few minutes and hoped he'd be okay.

With the running spot next to me now vacant, I moved to be alongside Lisa-Joe. Lisa-Joe managed the PR for Outward Bound Trust. She had sorted me out with some local PR as I passed through Auckland, but also arranged for me to speak at her daughter's school. Lisa-Joe was lovely. Of Asian descent, she had the most wonderful smiley face, a beautiful daughter whom I had met during the school talk, and the most Kiwi accent ever. She looked fabulous, always, including when she turned up for the run in pouring rain, dressed in a leopard-print top and bright pink shorts. She had the bounciest running style, which filled you with joy just by watching her run. Lisa-Joe made it 10 km before bidding us all farewell.

Gradually all the other runners dropped away, until there was just Jen and her two friends Liz and Bryony. This was it. We were the hardcore four, in it to win it for the full 23 km together. The next 90 minutes were brilliant, as we chatted and laughed, hopping along the coastal pathway and bouncing over rock pools and slippery rocks. When the finish line came, I was delighted. It was only a short day by all standards, but I was still pooped, and ready for Jen and her husband, Pete, to transport me to their home for a big feed and a comfy bed.

I was snuggled deep beneath a duvet in a warm bed and I did not want to get out of it. I looked at my phone and noticed that today was the first of June which meant the first day of the Kiwi winter. By my calculations, I'd be done by 28th of June, which meant I now had less than one month left to run. I could hear the voices of Jen, Pete and their kids moving around in the kitchen downstairs. After several minutes of self-talk, I managed to extract myself from the heavenly cocoon in their spare room and present my ravenous tummy for breakfast.

'Nah, I'm only doing the fun run...' said Jen between mouthfuls of toast, as I asked whether she had entered New Zealand's legendary 100 km Tarawera Ultramarathon.

'Oh. How far's the fun run part?' I asked.

'Only sixty kilometres. Pete's doing the full one hundred.'

This is everything that I loved about Kiwis. Kiwis were nails. I had learned that they thought nothing of spending days trekking in the bush and crossing rivers, just as they thought nothing of running 60 km.

After a breakfast of kings, it was time to get going again. Jen and Pete had offered to run with me to the start of the Okura Bush Walkway. As I paced along behind them, through fields and along the coast, I smiled. I loved that these two frequently went running together. What a nice way to spend your days, I thought. I'd learnt that although they entered races together, they mostly ran them separately. But when it came to training runs, they did those together. I looked on in envy at Jen and Pete in the same way I did at Finny and Fi's relationship, and their ability to adventure together. I added another requirement to the tick list for my future Mr Right, and that was to one day meet a boy I could go running with. At the start of the bush track, I hugged Jen and Pete goodbye, promising that I'd try to catch them before I flew out from Auckland in a month's time.

The Okura Bush Walkway was everything I could have hoped for on a morning where I continued to struggle with energy levels. I had been in high spirits when running with Jen and Pete this morning, but those spirits had gradually slipped away now I was on my own again. The trail was well-graded and easy to run along as it wound gently through native bush. Popping out onto the estuary, I found myself alone but for a couple just up ahead. I was concentrating hard on the placement of my feet as they squelched through the freshly exposed mud. I looked up at intervals, and as the couple moved closer towards me, I noticed that they were staring somewhat. Fair enough, I thought. I'd be staring at me too, if I were them. What kind of fool runs along an estuary with a gigantic backpack?

'Hello!' I smiled, stopping just in front of them.

'Are you Anna?' said the man.

'Er… yes, that's me. How on earth…?!'

'I knew it!' he exclaimed, now entirely triumphant. 'I just knew it! I saw you way back there, and I thought there can't be too many girls running with backpacks around here, and so I says to Mary… this is Mary by the way…' I nodded and smiled as he gestured at the woman to his left. 'I says to Mary… I know that girl, I think that's Anna McNuff. I've been following her on Twitter!'

As it turns out, this couple were from Lancashire in the UK, where Paul had been watching my journey unfold from the UK for months. They'd come on holiday to New Zealand for a few weeks, and somehow we'd managed to cross paths. Isn't life just grand sometimes?

'I mean, we're on holiday so I haven't checked your tracker for a few weeks. I knew you were somewhere in the North Island, but… wow! Just wow! Can we have a picture?!'

'Of course you can have a picture!' I laughed, moving in towards him. 'Selfie?' I offered.

'Oh, yes! A selfie!'

We spent a few more minutes chatting, and I found it incredibly flattering how much of the run he had actually followed. It was like reliving it all again, even though I was still in the middle of it.

'I mean, when you busted your ankle on that river, I thought that was it, I thought you were done…!' Paul shook his head, as if he'd felt the pain of those few days in the bush too. 'And those river crossings. How do you cope with those?!'

'I just cry, Paul,' I grinned. It was said as a joke, but it was far truer than he knew.

When the storytelling and reliving was done, I gave both Paul and Mary a huge hug each, and thanked them: 'You've made my day you two, really you have. I'm going to be running on smiles from here on in!'

'And you've made ours! Go steady in the last section, won't you? And look after yourself.' And with that we parted ways.

Trudging along the main street in the small north shore town of Orewa, I felt a little sluggish. My legs had yet to regain their energy, but I ploughed on in the hope that some form of sprightliness would reappear soon.

Checking the map, I realised that I'd clocked up a neat 30 km. If I could run 30 km with a sluggish-feeling body, then I had to be happy with that. Pulling my phone out of my bag, I started a new text message: 'Hiya Rob, just rolling into town. Where's a good local meeting spot? Tell me and I'll be there, on a street corner, on a park bench… somewhere!' A reply came swiftly back: 'Sweet! See you then. Meet you on the entrance to Pak'nSave? You'll find it!'

I'd been in touch with Rob, the CEO of the Te Araroa Trail, sporadically since his first message to me in Lake Tekapo, which read: 'Anna! I've just found out what you're doing. And it's amazing! You're amazing! Call me or message me if you need anything, anything at all. And you must come stay with us on your way north from Auckland.' I had felt that staying with the 'guardian' of the trail that had offered me a life-changing adventure was something that simply needed to be done. Besides, from our small exchanges, one thing was clear: Rob was a dude.

I found my way to the Pak'nSave and sure enough within 5 minutes a 4x4 turned up and tooted at me. Rob drove me to his house, which was a beautiful, split-level home set up in the hills, with a sweeping view of the Pacific Ocean. I had my own room and a marshmallowy soft bed on the lower floor. I only stayed one night, but welcomed the injection of family life from Rob, his partner, Lucy, and her two teenage kids. Staying with Rob was like a Catholic going to confession. As he explained the many efforts that went into marking and maintaining the trail, and especially the laborious process of obtaining permission from land owners, I felt that I needed to tell him of every time I had deviated from the trail, and to ask for his forgiveness.

Rob was a passionate man who was keen to please and do the best he could with the funds and resources he had available for the trail. He had taken on a tall order, inheriting the job of CEO from the very man who had founded the trail, Geoff Chapple, but I could tell immediately that Rob was business savvy. He had an incredible drive and ambition for the trail and he knew what he needed to get there. I offered Rob what feedback I could on the sections that I had found challenging, and answered other questions about areas he wanted more information on.

I knew it could have been all-too-easy to moan and pick holes in what had been a labour of love for Rob for many years. After all, I had heard loads of trail users say, 'this section is badly marked' or 'they've picked such a stupid route for the trail in that section', but instead I said: 'The truth is, Rob, the difficulty of the journey is what makes this trail unique. If it were like every other trail around the world, it wouldn't be the Te Araroa.'

'I'm glad you've said that, Anna, because I think so too,' said Rob in reply.

I thought for a moment, and began to get slightly emotional. For all the ranting and raving I had done along the way, for all the swearing at orange triangles, talking to poles and cursing the weather, I still adored this trail. It would beat me to a pulp, grind my body to pieces, turn me into a blurring wreck, and yet I truly loved it. The highs, the lows, the companionships it had offered me. The challenges it had laid in my path to allow me the freedom to grow as an individual. I felt very proud to be among the few to have travelled along it, and to have a deep connection with the land it passed through.

27

Knock, Knock...

I was standing on the doorstep of a house full of strangers. My fist was clenched, poised in a position to knock on the front door; something which I had tried to do repeatedly for the past minute, but failed miserably, each time backing out at the final moment. Had anyone in the house been watching out of their front windows over the past 5 minutes, they would have seen me stand at the edge of the driveway and pause, then walk up to the door and back to the edge of the driveway, before walking back up to the door again. I would have looked certifiably insane and wouldn't have been surprised if whoever was inside the house had already called the local psychiatric hospital and reported a clear danger to society loitering in their front garden.

I really hated asking for help. I just didn't want to be a bother, but I'd run clean out of options. Well, I still had the option of finding a camping spot, but it was getting dark, I was tired and the weather was getting really rather vicious. The wind had picked up gradually over the past few hours, and the clouds had made a steady transition from white fluffy friendly things to sinister looking dark, bulbous evil things. I could hear the rumble of thunder in the distance, and I knew it wouldn't be long before it descended on me. I'd been looking for a camp spot for the past 5 kilometres but there was nowhere 'off trail' to pitch up. Most of the trail had been a rough pathway through an area littered with old tree stumps and broken branches, and above all, on an exposed hillside. I stopped for a while at a passing place on the final forestry road I'd been running along and considered camping there. But it was right on the trail, and goodness knows if trucks came down there at night. The last thing I fancied was being woken up by a logging truck squashing me to death, and so I had run on.

Reaching the end of the forestry track I had come across a house, which was the very house I was now standing on the doorstep of. To the side of the house was a near-perfect patch of grass, and I say 'near-perfect' because it was rather sloping, being on the top of a hill. 'I'm sure whoever is in that house wouldn't begrudge me a night on their lawn,' I thought.

I pulled off my visor and grasped it in my hands, just in front of my lower stomach, as if I were a Georgian suitor about to ask for a damsel's hand in marriage. I put on my best apologetic face, took a deep breath, and knocked. Twenty seconds passed before the door opened. A woman stood in front of me, her immediate expression one of surprise and mild confusion.

'Hello. Um, I'm Anna. I'm um… running the trail. The Te Araroa Trail. It's getting dark and I was looking for a place to camp. And I wondered if you wouldn't mind if I pitched my tent in your garden for the night?' I paused and waited.

There was a long pause during which I thought, 'Oh, dear! She thinks you're a weirdo! No chance, Anna, no chance…!'

'It's not really a good place to camp,' the woman said at last, accompanied by a friendly tone. 'I mean, it's on top of a hill. There's a storm coming and it gets real windy up here. And the garden's on a slope.'

'Honestly, it's fine. I'll be fine. I just need somewhere. I don't mind the wind. Or the rain. Or… anything.'

'Well, okay then, if you're happy. Go on and set yourself up over there. By the bench should be the best spot.'

'Thank you so much! I really appreciate it. Thank you. Thanks again!' I said, moving away to the garden.

Twenty minutes later, after chasing various layers of my tent and groundsheet around the garden, I noticed a car pull into the driveway. A man got out, called over a hello and went into the house. Five minutes later, the woman came out of her house again and over to where I was wrestling with the final section of the tent fly.

'My husband's just come home,' she said. 'We've had a chat and… why don't you just come on in the house? We've got a room with a floor you can sleep on.'

Although it happened often that strangers took me into their home, I was always amazed. I mean, I would take a stranger in, but I'd never actually had one knock on my door. Sandra and her family were everything I loved about travelling. The level of trust required to have me set foot over that threshold was what I believed the world was like. I gave up watching the news years ago because, well, it's all a load of baloney if you ask me. Yes, bad things happen in the world and people do dark deeds, but I preferred a more measured view of the human race. I believe that we are innately good individuals, and things happen in our lives to make us lose our way. There's no way that the human race would have made it this far if we were all a bunch of hateful, bomb-dropping, gun-wielding murderers.

'You hungry?' said Sandra, as I reappeared in the living room after a nice warm shower.

'I'm always hungry!' I replied, following it quickly with: 'But, I've got some noodles I can cook up?'

'Don't be silly. How does beef stew sound?'

'Like heaven,' I grinned, rubbing my very empty belly. Moving over to the window I looked at the hilltop view onto my next destination, Dome Forest. Even from the comfort of Sandra's living room the forest looked a little intimidating. Densely packed pockets of bush rose upwards from the valley floor and spread across the horizon like the waves of the sea. I knew I needed to run up, over and through that jumble of green, and that I may well not see anyone until I made it through to the other side of the forest, but still there was a bubble of excitement in my belly. It wasn't far to the next section of trail along the east coast now, and the beaches I would

THE PANTS OF PERSPECTIVE

encounter were rumoured to be stunning.

That night a thunderstorm raged around the little house at the top of Kraack Hill, and instead of sitting it out in my one-man tent, praying the outer fly would cope with the deluge, I found myself sitting on the Wight family's couch, watching *The Italian Job*, with a belly full of beef stew and ice cream.

A few days later I awoke in my tent on the opposite side of Dome Forest, in a campground at Pakiri Beach. I'd been woken by the notification of a message: 'My mum just did a slut drop, and she wanted me to send it to you.' It was from Jamie and attached was a video of his mum doing the very move we had enjoyed together at the family Christmas party. I rolled over in my sleeping bag, just as the continuation of messages came through: 'If you're knocking around, it'd be nice to chat!'

I replied: 'Your mum is a HERO! Give me 30 minutes. Just got to pack up the tent.'

'Just packing up are you?! Did you have a lie in, you lazy biaaach?! Gotta drive a few people home, but I'll call soon.'

I packed up the tent with that little buzz in my tummy which comes from knowing you're about to speak to someone who lights up your day. Calls with Jamie had become more and more frequent over the past month, and we were now speaking every few days. A few weeks ago he'd sent me a message that had changed the game, for me at least. He had messaged me about the fact that his mum had forgotten her suitcase for their family holiday and that she kept screaming, 'I won't have any clean knickers!' Although it might not seem like anything significant, it was the first time he'd let me in to any side of his life beyond the charity foundation and our 'official' connection. He didn't need to tell me about the knicker saga, but he wanted to.

'Okay,' I messaged him. 'Ready when you are. I'm by the beach waiting for the tide to go out so that I can avoid a swim across a river!! I'll be here for another half hour I reckon, before I get bored and just go for it!'

Pakiri Beach was just about the most beautiful stretch of white sand I had ever clapped eyes on. Last night I'd wandered out onto the first section of beach to watch the sunset. The skies glowed in the most amazing oranges and reds, turning the reflection on the thin layer of water near the ocean the most fabulous shade of indigo.

Between the campground and the next section of beach was Poutawa Stream, which flowed from the land and into the sea. It wasn't a large stream, but when the tide was in it was over chest-high. I didn't fancy a swim, or getting soaked to start the day, so I was waiting for it to drop until at least waist-high before setting off. I was normally a little conscious of finding a spot where I looked as attractive as possible before I chatted to Jamie, but today I didn't care. Today he could see me just as I was. We chatted about the events of the past few days, and I gave him a tour of the beach, or as much of it as I could, and we talked about the finish line.

'Are there gonna be loads of people there to cheer you in?' Jamie asked.

I explained that this was a bit different from his 8,000-km run across Canada. He had been surrounded by a media storm when he finished in February 2014, but mine, well, mine I was glad would be different.

'There'll just be me and the lighthouse,' I explained. 'And I'm glad about that. It sort of feels like, I dunno, like a very personal journey. Does that make sense?'

'Yeah it does,' he replied.

That day I had the most stunning run so far. I plugged in my music, tied my still yet-to-be-named trainers onto my backpack and ran barefoot for 17 kilometres of beach. I loved the feel of the sand between my toes, the strike of my heel as it pounded the harder sand toward the water's edge and the clean footsteps I left behind as I sung at the top of my lungs. I'd come a long way since my first sandy run in the first week of the trip and I felt like a different woman.

I didn't see a single soul on the beach that day, but I was okay with that because I knew I would be surrounded by people at the end of the day. I even didn't mind that I had to cross the Pakiri River along the way. The surge and pull of the open ocean on the river flow presented a new challenge and I had to work hard to control my thoughts. My imagination still had a tendency to run wild, just as it had in previous river crossings, but I was more confident now. I knew myself and my abilities better and I felt far more at ease than I ever had with the river crossings. In the final hour of the day, I took my phone and messaged Jamie: 'Ended up having the best day EVVVAAAA!!! Thanks for the pre-run motivational pep talk. You should start charging for that… It's priceless.'

I got a reply a few hours later. 'Just so you know… I woke up this morning buzzing too! I can't stop thinking about how beautiful the end of the run will be. I think it's the right way to finish it. Up there on your own.'

He loves me.

At Mangawhai Bridge, sand in my shoes and a massive smile on my face, I met Gerald Mannion, whom I had last seen in a car park on the Queen Charlotte Track two months earlier on the final section of the South Island. He took me back to his family farm, and over the next few days it became my home from home. Every day Gerald dropped me back to the point I'd left the trail, and would come back and collect me from the end of the day's running. He was on full-time Dad-duty and I was so very grateful. He knew the area well, and so each time I got back in the car and his dog hopped on my lap for the ride inland to his home, we would chat about the section I'd just run and he knew every nook and cranny I was talking about.

The trail from where I had originally met Gerald at

Mangawhai to the southern side of the Whangarei Heads was a real treat. I ran along swooping clifftops, where I'd find myself at eye-level with the birds and looking out on the Pacific Ocean, before diving down to well-graded forest tracks, and then trotting along yet more deserted sandy beaches. The running was easy and the scenery was everything I had expected of a journey through New Zealand's northland area. Every evening I was surprised to find Gerald at our agreed meeting point along the trail, and he was always bang on time. He had a daughter, Sarah, who liked to enter ultramarathons, and he said he was used to being the support wagon for her, which explained why the logistics of dropping me off and collecting me for those three days were second nature to him.

Each day I woke up still in a little bit of disbelief that Gerald would be so kind as to take time out of his life to help me, but it was something I should have known to accept from the Kiwi people by now. I felt truly at home in the days with the Mannion family. Davina, Gerald's wife, loved to ride horses and so over dinner one night she let me into the world of her passion. She talked of going riding in America, another country that had captured my heart a few years back.

As Whangarei loomed into view on the final days with the Mannions,' I was passed like an adventurer-baton to the next host. I was still getting used to being hosted so often after all the isolation in the south. I had realised that while the South Island was about beauty and vastness, the North Island was all about the beaches and the people. Gerald had handed me over to the city of Whangarei, and I, in turn, handed myself over to a day off and a night with an old university friend in the city centre, before moving to base myself at Parua Bay for two days. There I stayed with a local keen runner named Kirsty. Kirsty had been in touch the previous month and asked if I would come into Parua Bay School to give a talk to her kids and the others there. Not only was she going to put me up and feed me, but she also wanted to escort me out of town – what a doll. I duly went into Parua Bay School and, after a lively chat with the primary-aged kids, the conversation turned to my trainers – they were horrified that I hadn't yet named them, so I invited the kids to pitch in their ideas. I later received an email from Lynfa, a teacher at the school, titled 'naming your shoes', which read:

'Hi Anna,

The kids and teachers have decided to name the right foot 'Live' and the left foot 'Life'!

Lynfa'

I couldn't think of a better name for the final pair – the kids had nailed it.

On the final night before my run continued, I was sitting in a bedroom in Kirsty's house at Parua Bay, going through the usual process of planning the next two-week section. I took a moment to look over the 300 km that remained of my journey. After months of never-ending planning, my final calculations had now been reduced to one page of my notebook. Just one tiny page. I knew the end was coming, and fast, but it all seemed so concrete now that it was down there in black, or rather grey, and white. I ran my fingers gently over the pencil marks, as if they were an old friend I was yet to meet, and sighed. The deepest of sighs.

28

Nuns Riding Kangaroos

I had no idea how to pronounce Ngunguru. Whenever someone asked me where I was headed, I tried to look vaguely knowledgeable, screwed up my face and ventured a stab at the name of this small town. So long as I went up at the end of my sentence and smiled, this seemed wholly acceptable. No matter how many times someone would tell me how to pronounce it correctly, I'd repeat it back to them and thank them. Then I would immediately forget what it was, and I'd be back at square one.

As it turns out there are several ways to pronounce Ngunguru. 'Nun-a-Roo' was a favoured local pronunciation, while 'Nung-a-roo' seemed to be the more widely used version. Then there was my own attempt: 'Ng-goo-rah-goo'. I actually quite liked the first, local pronunciation. I found it far easier to remember than the others, largely because all I had to think about was a nun riding a kangaroo, and boom, the correct pronunciation would pop into my head.

Kirsty had run with me for 13 km that morning, and she had destroyed me. The woman was fit, and in a sick way I'd enjoyed the pace she'd set from Pataua to the edge of the Mackerel Forest Track. In contrast to the beautiful clifftops and beaches that led me to Whangarei Heads, the trail now included a fair amount of road running. Kirsty and I ran side-by-side on the flats, chatting away in the sticky heat of the morning as we passed small villages and clumps of native bush. Running on tarmac wasn't always the most exciting of tasks, but it did mean that I didn't need to concentrate on the placement of my feet and so could dedicate all available brain-power to chatting. When we hit a hill, there was no way I could match Kirsty's speed (well, no way short of hyperventilating) and so she would pound ahead and wait for me at the top of each one. When the time came for her to turn around and head back, I was very sad to say goodbye, but her absence did at least mean that I could slow down a little, and for that my body was grateful.

As a result of Kirsty's power hour, I made good time on the 34 km I'd set myself for the day, and arrived at my 'nun-a-roo' hosts' house at 1.30 p.m. I was 3 hours earlier than I'd said I'd be, as I had intended to stop for a longer lunch break, but after sitting at the side of the road and cramming some non-descript meat and cheese into my mouth with cars whizzing by inches from my legs, I'd decided that I wanted to just crack on.

Linda and Jim weren't my original intended hosts in Ngunguru. It was their neighbours, Melva and Hilton, who had been following me intently since the start of the run. I thought about how often I'd received one of their enthusiastic messages: 'We're waiting for you up here in Ngunguru, Anna…' or 'We hope you have time to stop in up here at

Ngunguru, Anna…'

Each time I'd read the town name, I thought: 'I have no idea how to pronounce that', looked at where it was on a map and thought 'Dear goodness, that's a long way north. I won't be there for ages'. And now here I was, almost four months after they'd begun with their string of encouragement. Sadly, I'd missed Hilton and Melva, who were in Australia as I passed through, and so I was met by Jim, their neighbour, instead.

Jim welcomed me into his home as if I were a long-lost grandchild. We hugged hello and he held on to my hand tightly as he looked at me. 'I'm so glad you're here,' he said, immediately making me feel rather precious. Jim was 5 ft 6 in with a round face and piercing blue eyes that welled with emotion when he spoke about his little home town of Ngunguru.

He explained that his partner, Linda, had given an interview on the radio that week, and that she'd spoken about how 'anchored' she'd felt here. He started to well up, and apologised.

'I'm sorry,' he said. 'It's just we're both so happy here. It's a very special place.'

Jim loved everything about this little town. He talked about the many 'moods of the estuary' and even stopped us mid-conversation at one point to go outside onto the balcony to look at the way the light was hitting the water. He loved the birds and the unique sand spit that he and Linda were working so hard to preserve. He loved the school his grandchildren went to, and the way they ran their annual cross-country along the clifftops and on the beach.

I liked the idea of being 'anchored', a feeling you get about a place when you finally feel like you've found home as Jim described it. Perhaps it felt like that to Jim and Linda because they had one another to share it with. I certainly hadn't found my home yet. I mean, my home in London would always be *a* home, but really I felt I could live anywhere, so long as I was surrounded by love and filled with a sense of purpose. I hoped that one day I'd be anchored somewhere too.

Jim's voice was always measured and calm as he regaled the story of his life. These were the favourite moments of my journey – moments where I was given the opportunity to look through a window into someone else's existence. To cross my path with another's and have the chance to look back at where they'd come from to get there.

Jim told me about the way things used to be, and what he saw to be the 'real' New Zealand. 'We used to be eight-wire people,' he said. 'Everyone knew someone who could fix whatever you'd broken. The old guy who lived next door to the fish shop would rummage in his tool box and pull out some scrap he'd picked up a few months back, and that'd do the trick. We've lost that now. There's no need to fix things anymore. Now people just buy new things.'

Both Jim and Linda had travelled extensively through Asia and Europe. When I asked Jim whether he found Hong Kong claustrophobic, he said, 'I suppose you could, but I did the one eighty.'

'What's "doing the one eighty"?' I asked.

'Doing a one eighty is when you turn yourself a full one hundred and eighty degrees and take another look at the situation. You realise there must be another way to see things. Normally, a better way. As soon as you "do the one eighty" life becomes a lot more fun.'

I stored that idea in my back pocket for the days when I thought I might need to 'do a one eighty' on things myself.

At 6 p.m., with cuppa number four in hand, I heard footsteps on the stairs. Linda entered through the sliding doors. Linda had had a rubbish day, and so she, Jim and I decided to go on a wee picnic. We fired up their camper van, stopped by the local fish-and-chip shop, stocked up on wine and drove to the edge of the estuary. There we continued our chats by candlelight, with some of the best fish I'd ever had the pleasure to eat, shrouded in batter and hanging limply from fingers and faces.

Later that night I was getting into bed on the pull-out sofa in the living room when Jim remarked how much he'd enjoyed the 8 hours we'd spent chatting. I said it felt like I'd known him for years.

'That's what happens when you don't have long to get to know one another,' Jim said. 'You get straight to the good stuff.'

The clock struck 12 as I began to run out of town, with Linda at my side. It was only 11 km to my next stop at Matapouri and so I was in no rush to get going. Somehow, I'd managed to get a day in hand, and so I had decided to spend an extra night between Ngunguru and Whananaki, at the small beachside town of Matapouri. It was a good choice; the Tutukaka Coast was stunning, and after leaving Linda at the local sacred puriri tree, I ambled slowly along the trail through fields and light bush before arriving at the tiny general store in Matapouri.

I'd loved being hosted so much over the past few weeks. I'd needed it and I felt fully refreshed, but I also craved the freedom and solitude of my own flimsy walls once again. My body had also missed its recovery sleeps – arriving at my bed for the night and crawling in for a nap. This wasn't really so socially acceptable when staying with hosts, and besides, I wanted to stay awake and chat to them. I made a mark in the sand as the trail hit the main road and spent an hour exploring around Matapouri, trying to suss out a good spot to pitch my tent. The main bay had looked enticing, and offered a slightly more secluded spot – but it was a popular thoroughfare to get to the coastal trail, and so I went to investigate Whale Bay on the opposite side of the headland.

Whale Bay is the most beautiful little inlet. Dense bushline met the ocean in a way I'd only experienced before up at Cape

Tribulation – on the very north of Australia's East Coast. Alas, there was an onshore wind at the bay, and on inspecting the high tideline I wasn't entirely sure that my tent would survive the night without being washed or blown away. Instead I back-tracked to Matapouri Bay, and set up camp just back from the waterfront, next to a dead seagull. I didn't make a habit of sleeping next to dead animals, but the seagull was occupying the only spot on the beach that was both secluded enough and flat enough to house my tent for the night.

As I put up the tent, I had a pang of nerves. I had chosen a pitch which was a little more exposed than usual. Being on a public beach, I was out in the open, and could be happened upon quite easily. I considered why it was that I suddenly felt so nervous. The only thing that really ever made me believe I would come to any harm was other's beliefs about the world. 'Oh, I'd be careful in northland – lots of dangerous people up there,' I'd been frequently warned. One guy had even gone so far as to write to me about the dangers of local crystal meth addicts. Much to my irritation, my brother's Māori friend back home was filling his head with stories about 'Māori people in northland being deluded and irrational and that they would see me as a threat'. Still, these weren't my beliefs and that wasn't the way I chose to live my life. As I cooked dinner and watched the sun slip into the ocean from the open door of the tent, I reminded myself of just that. I fought against sleep for around 10 minutes before finally crawling into my sleeping bag, and letting my heavy eyelids drop. It was 5.45 p.m. – a new record.

At 8 p.m., I awoke after my 'first sleep' and ventured out for a pee. The sand was now cold beneath my toes and I craned my neck upwards as I walked away into the bushline. The stars were incredible. Like scattered diamonds suspended in a sea of black – there were so many that they oscillated. The Milky Way was clearly visible, and its presence began to make me feel very emotional. I thought about how lucky I was, about how many people got to see this, to experience this. I'd read so many adventure books. Books where people had pitched up on beaches and fallen asleep among beauty and nature. That was me tonight, and I couldn't quite believe it. A tear escaped from my left eye and rolled down my cheek. I felt so grateful. I took one last look up and glimpsed a shooting star before crawling back into bed.

Was that?! That was definitely voices. I could hear voices, and they were coming toward the tent. How many were there? Two? Three? No, four – I could hear a fourth. I checked my watch. It was 2.30 a.m. Who the heck was out here at 2.30 a.m.?! Now they were shining a light in my direction and their voices were getting closer. I tensed and stopped breathing.

'Kia ora. Beach patrol,' said the loudest one. Oh, shit. I'd heard about this. The fine for camping illegally on beaches in NZ was $250. Was I about to get slapped with a massive fine?

'Hiya,' I replied, moving to the exit of the tent to greet my fate.

'Just kidding! You mind if we light a fire here?'

Kids! They were bloody kids! Phew. I remembered the fire pit which was tucked up against the rock face, not too far from where I was pitched. It was clearly a local hang-out spot. I wondered how many teenagers had escaped the watchful eyes of their parents and come and hung out here. Ewww. Was I camped on a local make-out spot? On the site of awkward fumbles and first kisses and… I shuddered… of popped cherries? I hoped not.

'Sure. Go for it,' I replied, and rested my head back down, knowing I wouldn't be getting much sleep, but relieved I'd escaped a fine. At least they'd asked permission. That was nice. They must be lovely kids.

I drifted in and out of consciousness for the next 45 minutes. Tuning in every now and then to the increasingly inebriated and highbrow conversation going on around the fire pit. Suddenly there was a loud whoosh and a blaze of light. What the heck was that?! I could smell gunpowder. Then it happened again, followed by laughter. Oh, crap. They were throwing fireworks. They were drunk and throwing fireworks. I lay there, heart beating fast, wondering what to do, when I heard them start discussing whether to throw one at my tent. I froze, petrified, thinking about the plastic that surrounded me and how that would melt nicely onto my skin if it started to burn. My heart beat fast. They wouldn't actually…

Whoosh. Another firework shot past the tent missing it by

a few centimetres. It was followed by an eruption of laughter. This wasn't cool; I wasn't up for burning to death. I had to make a human connection with these little shits, to show them I was a real living breathing human being, and to dissuade them from throwing anything else with gunpowder at me. I climbed out from the tent.

'Hi there,' I smiled.

All four of them fell silent, looked sheepishly at the floor and giggled. I wandered off, as if I was going to the toilet. I didn't feel like I needed to say much more – they looked suitably embarrassed and I crawled back into the tent feeling much happier. Besides, I'd just heard one of them say that they'd run out of fireworks. Thirty minutes later the sound of their voices drifted further and further away. I thought for a moment about these kids, and how they'd burst my little happy bubble of belief that the world was filled only with loveliness. Then again, perhaps it was my fault. I really shouldn't be camping on a public beach, but in my last few weeks on the trail I was getting reckless with my choice of camping spots. On one hand, the end, which was now just 200 km away, felt like a foregone conclusion. But what had happened tonight shined a light, a big explosive firecracker of a light, on the fact that there was still a lot more that could happen before I made that lighthouse at the cape. At last, and once again, thinking about that magical lighthouse, I drifted off to sleep.

29

'And to Make an End Is to Make a Beginning'

I was staring down at a seemingly endless bridge of wooden planks. It moved away from me in perfect perspective like a train track disappearing into the horizon. I'd seen this bridge a thousand times in pictures. It was the longest footbridge in the southern hemisphere – one that crosses the Whananaki Inlet and connects the two sides of the town – offering holiday go-ers an on-foot alternative to the 12-km drive around the inlet. I knew that on the other side of this famous bridge was the equally famous (at least amongst Te Araroa users) Whananaki holiday park.

It had been the most stunning run from Matapouri to here. I'd made my way along several white sandy beaches (one of which I'd stopped on for an hour-long nap), and then along a lonely paper road which skirted the coastline, offering up the most amazing views of the bluest of blue Pacific Ocean and its surrounding farmland.

'Ah! Here she is!' said Matthew in his thick South African accent, turning away from the couple he was chatting to in the holiday park and taking a few steps toward me. 'We've been waiting for you, girl. What kept you so long?' He grinned and opened his arms for a hug.

'I can't believe I am actually here!' I said, emerging from his bear hug.

'Come! Meet Tracey and my boys.' Matthew took me inside and introduced me to the whole family. I met Tracey, who also delivered a stellar hug, and his two sons, who looked up awkwardly and smiled where they sat on the living-room sofa. We had a brief chat about my days leading up to here and how the trail and my body had treated me – something I couldn't even begin to cram into a few minutes, but I tried my best.

'Okay, enough chit-chat.' said Matthew. 'Let me show you to your special home for the night, Anna…'

Walking out of the house and through the front garden, Matthew turned sharply right. 'Ah! I must show you this first!' he exclaimed before leading me to a big pizza oven. 'We built this for the trampers,' he said. 'We know they've had a long hard week through those forests and…' He stopped. 'Are you going into the northern forests?'

'Umm… I'm er… not sure yet.' I tailed off.

'Okay, well anyway… we know they've had a long week through those forests and most of them, in fact all of them, are broken! Some have run out of food because they've had to wait out rain, or got lost a bit in there. And others, well, I think the others are just a bit shocked! Ha! It's all a bit much for them at the start of the journey. So we like to offer them something nice to eat when they get here. And pizza is really popular.'

'So you built that oven just for TA walkers?!'

'Yup!' said Matthew, beaming with pride.

'And it's not *just* that we built. Come.' He began to walk off and motioned for me to follow. We stopped in front of a small green, wooden half-hut. 'Your palace for the night.'

'Cool!'

'Go on, take a look.'

I pulled open the hut door to find two bunks on the right-hand side. It was barely big enough for me to stand next to the bunks, but it was all you'd ever need for a good night's kip. On the back wall were the scrawls of trampers who had passed through here, including notes on the direction they were headed in, their nationality and a small message.

'You'll have to leave us a note before you go,' insisted Matthew, before a short pause. 'Well, I'll leave you to it. When you're scrubbed up I'll take you for a drive around the coast.'

I laid my stuff on the wooden floor and sat on the bottom bunk. I smiled. These guys were wonderful. I don't know if you've ever met people who you immediately feel connected to, but Tracey and Matthew were that type of people. Matthew's embrace wasn't just a literal one, it extended far beyond that. Over dinner they told me the tale of how they'd met. It was a love story fit for a Disney film. Matthew and Tracey had first dated in South Africa when they were sixteen. As most young relationships go, they had broken up a little way down the line, had other romances and, aged 37, bumped into one another again. From there they rekindled their romance and the birth of their two boys had followed, as had a move to New Zealand to give those boys a life they deserved. That night Matthew cooked us up some big juicy steaks on the outdoors barbecue, before I bid them goodnight and returned to my bespoke Te Araroa hut. Flicking on the small bedside lamp, I reached for the marker pen to leave my own message on the wall. I chose a few words from my favourite T. S. Eliot poem, *Four Quartets*: 'And to make an end is to make a beginning.'

I used the morning of my departure from Whananaki to go into the small school across the road from the campground. Upon arrival I was serenaded with a Māori welcome song by nervous-looking children, Matthew and Tracey's sons included, who were all barefoot – just as kids should be. As they sang, a small ukulele played in the background. Surrounded by beautiful song, I realised how much I would miss this. I had been treated to Māori songs by kids in the schools so many times. I knew that this would be one of the last school talks I'd give before the journey was done. And that made it even more special. I'd calculated that I'd spoken to around 4,000 kids since leaving Bluff. Far more than during my US journey and something that I was immensely proud of. I considered for a moment who had had more impact on whom. I resolved that perhaps it was equal. Although the kids and teachers never knew it, their limitless dreams and boundless energy had brought light and purpose to even the darkest days on the trail.

Out of sight from the park, on the trail just around the Whananaki Inlet, something stirred. When I realised what the emotion was, I smiled. I was sad. So very sad. Not only to be leaving Tracey and Matthew, but knowing that this journey would soon all be over. It was the feeling I'd been hoping for over the past few weeks, but all I had felt was homesick. Now I was sad to be going home, and that meant that I had created something truly special to be so sad about leaving it behind.

The days from Whananaki to the foot of Ninety Mile Beach passed in a haze. I enjoyed a reasonable amount of road running, and ran a few extra miles to spend the night camped alone at the beautiful Mimiwhangata Bay. I spotted several wild pigs on the trail that day and, on a beach of small shells, watched the sun dip into the ocean and the moon rise gently in its place. It was so calm and peaceful there. Better still, after the time spent with Matthew and Tracey, I felt entirely nourished. After leaving Mimiwhangata Bay, I had then opted to take a slightly different route via the small town of Russell to the northland mecca of Kerikeri.

A niggle which had been bothering me on my left shin for the past two weeks had now upped its game to a new level, marked 'beyond painful', and I began to get concerned that I might be doing some lasting damage. As I turned over in my sleeping bag at night, I would accidentally touch my right foot on my left ankle. No matter how light the touch, I'd wake up and hit the roof in pain. Then my left foot would be sent into a powerful cramp, which left me swearing, clutching my foot and trying to wriggle out of my zipless sleeping bag in order to stretch it.

Deciding that I couldn't employ my usual tactic of ignoring it and ploughing on after all, I began to ice it at every opportunity. The pain felt too close to the inside of the ankle to be shin splints, and so I assumed it must be some kind of inflammation. The only thing to combat inflammation, other than rest, was ice, so I raided any store I could find along the route in that week for frozen peas, carrots, sweetcorn… you name it, my shin got treated to it. On the final icing session, I even indulged the pain with a full melange of golden vegetables. One particular day, running through the Waitangi Forest on the way to Kerikeri, the shin pain had really got to me. I cracked, and cried for 2 solid hours because it was so acute.

Doing my best to distract myself from the increasing pain in my shin, I squeezed in one final school talk at a secondary school in Kerikeri before making a decision that had troubled me since Queenstown. The Herekino, Raetea, and Omahuta–Puketi Forest Tracks had been playing havoc with my mind. I had asked for an opinion from almost every southbounder I met, because I couldn't decide whether to take the 'official' Te Araroa route through these forests, or to run the road to the foot of the final section at Ahipara. The forests were renowned among trail users. Matthew had mentioned them earlier that week and they were the very reason he had gone to the trouble of building a pizza oven to feed weary souls who emerged from them. Many trampers reported scarce or unreliable water sources, slow progress, poor markings and thick knee-deep mud. The latter forest trail especially concerned me. According to the trail notes, one section included canyons which were subject to flash floods. In large capital letters it then read: 'DO NOT ATTEMPT TO GO FURTHER IF THERE IS HEAVY RAIN IN THE REGION.'

My reason to run these trails was that they were part of the official route, and I was trying to stick to the official route as often as possible. But the very thought of entering the four to five-day forest stretch drained all energy from my body. It made my legs feel like lead and my mind feel like jelly. I could run it, of course I could, but I had a feeling it would make me miserable. I wouldn't enjoy it and I would only be running it to tell other people that I had done it. On top of that, I had to seriously consider what this run was starting to do to my body: to my back, my hips and to my sore and angry shin, especially. Although running along the road would mean more impact and strain on the injury, it could also mean less time on my feet and a quicker passage to the finish line.

I stood at the turn-off to the first forest track, just outside of Kerikeri, and gave myself 5 minutes to decide. I thought again of the trail notes, about flash floods, and the advice not to go in heavy rain. It had been pouring for the past few days and was set to continue. I told myself it was unsafe, which I actually think was true, but I also had to be honest that I was making a conscious choice to run the road section. Taking the road would only mean three days of running to get across the country to the west coast. It was a slightly longer route, at 110 km as opposed to the 98 km through the forests, but on predictable surface like tarmac I knew I could make faster time, which would mean I could be at the lighthouse within the next week. I resolved that I would enjoy the road more. Although the impact on tarmac would take its toll on my legs, I could set myself to cruise control. I could run without anything to think about except that lighthouse.

30

Ninety Mile Beach

I opened my eyes and I was shaking. I was in a room by myself, on a single bed with two bunk beds at the other end of the room. I tried to remember where I was, but all that filled my mind were the dreams that'd rocked my sleep through the night. I'd dreamt about trying to pack up my backpack, but everything kept exploding back out of it. I'd also dreamt that I was up on a mountain and the wind kept picking me up, so I was clinging to rocks and roots to stay grounded.

The mind fog cleared. I was at Ninety Mile Beach Holiday Park and I now had just 87 km left to run. I stared up at the 1970s-style ceiling. The pit of my stomach bubbled and fizzed with nervous energy. Why was I so nervous? Excitement, yes; sadness, that'd be understandable; but nerves? I struggled to understand exactly what it was that I was nervous about. I should be leaping out of bed, punching the air, racing to the finish line! After 146 days on the trail, I was almost there, and yet, I couldn't move a muscle. I considered for a second whether I was still dreaming. Perhaps this was one of those recurring dreams you have where you're trying to run away, but you find that you can't move.

I knew that low tide was at 8 a.m. It made sense to get on

the beach at bang on low tide to give me the pick of the best sand to run on. I'd discovered on the previous day's 14-km run from Ahipara to the holiday park that there was a certain strip of sand that was optimum to run on. Too close to the sea and it became either too hard, and then sloppy and sodden; too close to the dunes and it became too soft and absorbed every ounce of effort.

I looked at my watch. It was now 7.30 a.m., and I lay in bed contemplating the day ahead for longer than intended. 'I'll leave in an hour,' I told myself. At 10 a.m. I was still at the park indulging in an advanced course of Grade-A faffing. 'Well, maybe I should have a shower?' I thought. I mean, I won't have a shower for the next few days. I should definitely have a shower. And so I had a shower. Then it was late morning and, well, I hadn't eaten much so I thought I should probably eat something warm before I left. I mean, I didn't want to run on an empty stomach. Yes, yes, best eat some pasta. At 11 a.m. I stood over my bags and exploded at myself in rage at the ridiculous pattern in my behaviour: 'For God's sake, Anna! Get moving. Move!' I yelled at myself.

Truth be told in that room I was lonely, but all at once I didn't want to leave it because I knew that the days ahead would be lonely too. Perhaps it was better to at least be lonely in the vicinity of others than on an expanse of beach by yourself? I realised I was nervous because I didn't know how I would react up on that beach alone, and I didn't know if I had the mental strength to deal with the loneliness anymore. I was mentally tired. So very tired, and as a result I was well and truly dragging my heels.

Ninety Mile Beach Holiday Park was now 17 km behind me and I was, in runners' terms, on fire! My mind may have been tired, but my body must have had a good night's sleep and it was in charge. I knew only too well that the mind had the power to override the body, but today the opposite had happened. In getting out there on the trail, and letting my body do what it had trained for almost six months to do, I'd found a new well of energy. I bounded gleefully along the beach, listening to the remainder of Michael McKintyre's audiobook. When that finished, I flicked on to Julie Walters' autobiography. There had to be some kind of sick irony in choosing to listen to comedians in arguably the most painful and complex section of the journey, but I found solace in both their very British voices, in their honesty, their own struggles, and their ability to transport me from the beach entirely.

A dark shape loomed into view on the beach up ahead. I squinted. Was that? Yes! A sea lion! There was a sea lion hanging out on the beach up ahead. It didn't look to be moving, but it was upright. Surely it couldn't be upright and dead? Did sea lions get rigor mortis when they died? I read a story about a bear who went to sleep standing up once, but I'm pretty sure it was a made-up one. As I got closer I saw it was, in fact, moving. A live sea lion – a frickin live sea lion! Just hanging out at the side of the trail.

Now, it's a well-known fact that sea lions are cute, docile, lovable, huggable friendly creatures – or at least that's what the cartoons and movies tell us. Long eyelashes and awkward arm/fin things, which look like they may break at any moment. Just adorable. The last time I'd seen a sea lion it'd popped up alongside me in the water off the coast of Vancouver. I remember being mesmerised by the darkness of its eyes. Each one a world of galaxies. That sea lion had been friendly, and so I had no reason to believe that this one would behave any differently.

I approached it and spoke in perfect sea lion: 'Hey, buddy. How you doing?' No reply. I stepped closer still. I wasn't entirely sure what I intended to do once I reached it… pet it? Shake its fin? Hand it a beach ball and expect some tricks? But for some reason, I felt compelled to move closer. It was facing sideways on to me and craned its neck around to look directly at me. And when it did I detected something. Attitude. This sea lion had bags of it, and it wasn't afraid to show it. I took another step, which was evidently a step too far.

The sea lion launched forward, hissing with a face like Satan himself. Mouth wide open, eyes glaring, teeth bared. 'WOOOAAAAHHH!' I yelped, immediately retreating up the beach. My heartbeat hit the roof, before it returned to baseline and allowed me to laugh at my own stupidity. Of course this sea lion wasn't going to welcome me with open arms. What a muppet I was.

By mid-afternoon I'd run out of water, and the stream beds running from the dunes to the beach were dry. An hour or so on I managed to follow a small stream to a pool in the dunes that looked clean enough to drink. Gasping, I knelt down beside it and began to lap it up like a crazed cat. It tasted a little like dirt and left an odd milky aftertaste, but it wasn't the worst water I'd tasted. As I finished drinking it and pulled out the hydration bladder to fill up, I realised how much I enjoyed these moments. The constant need to think and seek out the basic things in life – food, water, shelter, even people.

A few miles later my legs grew heavy and the light began to fade. It was time to search for a spot to pitch the tent. I followed a stream away from the beach and into the dunes. The wind was up so I took a while to find an area that had enough shelter. I mean there were a number of suitable spots, but most of them were covered in horse poop. In fact, there were horse droppings everywhere. Many people had told me about the wild horses that roamed the dunes of Ninety Mile Beach, but I thought it was a myth. The horses had been living wild up here for over 100 years and it was estimated that there were around 300 of them in existence, so a sighting was quite rare.

I found a suitable poop-free spot behind a larger bit of scrub and threw my pack on the floor. Checking the map, I calculated that stopping here meant that I had 52 kilometres left to run. I'd planned to finish the day after tomorrow, but two 26-km days seemed a bit, well, soft. I knew 52 km was something I could run in a day; I'd done it once before, albeit without a backpack.

I sat on my pack and, gazing into the forest behind the dunes, considered why I was waiting to arrive at the finish line so gently? That didn't seem like something I would do, and yet here I was, planning to play it safe and slide in gracefully. I thought about the person I knew myself to be. The me who relished a challenge, usually so full of energy. She was buried under weary legs, a fuzzy mind, sore shins and an aching back, but she was there somewhere.

I didn't know what lay ahead, and most importantly I didn't know whether the tide would allow me to run 52 km in one go or whether arriving at the lighthouse when the sun was going down was especially wise. But screw it; this run had started in the knowledge that I may not make the finish, and I would begin tomorrow in the same way.

From that point on, everything became special. This was my last camp. This was the last time I'd eat noodle surprise for dinner. This was the last time I'd dig a hole and deposit the previous night's noodle surprise in it. This was the final time I'd find it acceptable to crawl into bed at 5 p.m.

The seed was planted. I would finish tomorrow.

31

The Lighthouse

I woke in the morning to find that my confidence from the night before had faded. Could I run 52 km today? Did I want to run that far today? What would happen if I didn't make it before sun down? If I got there so late, and there was no one around? I decided that none of these doubts were reasons not to give it a go.

Besides, I needed this challenge. Finishing with certainty, grace, ease and dignity didn't seem appropriate for a journey that had pushed me to the edge. No, I wanted ugly. The narcissist within me craved pain and one last test. And at last I felt ready to rise to any test; rising to it was something I was strong enough to do today. Best of all, the thought of waking up the next morning and not having to run another step was just too tempting to ignore.

Packing up the tent, I noticed that my hands were shaking. Why the heck were my hands shaking?! I realised I was nervous. I rolled my eyes at myself. I had experienced my fair share of anxiety since leaving Bluff, so this really should have come as no surprise. I continued to pack away what had been my home and haven for the past five and a half months, before deciding to closer examine the root cause of my nerves. It was then I realised that I didn't know what lay beyond that light-house. For months I had thought of nothing but the finish line. I had never imagined making it there, let alone my life beyond it. In fact, there was nothing beyond it but a black void. And I was about to start running towards that void. Who was I at the end of all of this? What would I do? What did it all mean?

I pulled myself together, back to the present and the task at hand. 'Come on, Anna, it's just a 52-km run for goodness' sake.' My mind was a certifiable mess. I couldn't think of the possibility of finishing, and yet, I could think of nothing else.

Backpack bulging once more with all of my worldly pos-sessions, I took a deep breath. I spun 360 degrees, taking in the sight of the forest at the edge of the dunes, and the three wild horses grazing nearby. They seemed to sense me looking and lifted their heads to stare back. 'Time to take this thing home, boys,' I announced, much to their bemusement. I continued my 360 view and paused looking out toward the sea.

Shutting my eyes, I listened to its roar, and felt each and every grain of sand that moved across my face, carried by the wind. A lump swelled in my throat, but I swallowed it down. Not yet. I wasn't ready to let go yet. I took one last breath and found the emotion I was looking for. A tiny bubble of excitement started at the soles of my feet, and forged its way upwards through my calves, thighs, stomach – when it hit my chest, I was ready. I pulled the straps of the pack tight, turned my back on the horses and took off like a woman possessed.

I couldn't tell you what I thought about the first hour of the day. My shoes swayed wildly from the back of my pack as I ran barefoot again, and my toes spread upon each and every contact with the sand. I was in a trance, and a welcome one at that. I slotted back into a routine that had become so familiar now, concentrating on one hour at a time, and thinking of nothing beyond it.

Forty kilometres to go.

The tendonitis, which had been mild in my left foot yesterday, had by now become a little too much to bear. Running barefoot felt incredible, but my feet weren't used to the slightly altered action it required, nor my calves to the extra strain it seemed to place on them, and both were starting to complain. I stopped to inspect the extent of the damage and scrunched up my toes – the tendons creaked and groaned. I decided to put my shoes back on for a little while, and see how that went.

I sat on a pile of rocks opposite a small rocky island, dusted off as much sand as I could from my feet, and pulled on my shoes. I stood upright again and was just in the middle of bending down to go for a wee, when something told me to look to my left. I'm not sure why. I hadn't seen anyone since leaving the holiday park, but I did know that tour buses ran up and down the beach at low tide, and it was bang on low tide now. Just as I was poised, mid-squat, a tourist bus came whizzing past, brimming with faces squashed against the glass. They waved vigorously at the odd-looking girl now perched in an awkward half-squat at the edge of the beach. I played it cool, pretended I was just 'readjusting' and looking for shells all at once, and waved enthusiastically in return to throw them off the scent.

Twenty-four kilometres to go.

The mind games had worked a treat. Putting on the shoes, however, had not. On account of the wet and the sand, blisters started to form between my big toe and second toe on both feet. These were only the third and fourth blisters I'd had in the whole trip – and the first ones since just before Wanaka.

Eighteen kilometres to go.

The blisters were getting sore now, and we had another guest at the blister party, rapidly forming under the ball of my left foot. This one I figured was on account of my awkward gait to protect my shin, which was now emitting a constant, searing pain. As the trail exited the beach and started up over a headland, I stopped to inspect the damage. Straining my muscles and in some odd kind of backwards lotus-flower yoga move, I studied the bottom of my feet. I was expecting some small raw patches, perhaps a little red, but what I found was one enormous blood blister which extended between my toes and onto the bottom of my foot, and two other similarly flu-id-filled blister-beasts at the prime of their life. Crap. I'd hoped to take the shoes back off and return to going barefoot, but running on those things, with nothing between them and the sand, was a sure-fire way to disaster. I wound some surgical tape around them as best I could, hoping I wouldn't cut off circulation to my toes, and pulled my socks and shoes back on.

Standing up I winced as the weight went back onto my toes. I inspected the trailhead sign. It said 6 hours to Cape Reinga. I checked my watch – I had 4 hours until the sun went down. That should be okay, providing the trail didn't throw up any more surprises. But I was becoming increasingly aware of the fact that the tide was now coming back in and I had no idea what the trail did beyond this point. The sign gave me a clue: 'Some sections of this trail are not passable at high tide – please check the tide times before starting.' Which sections were they? How long would it take me to get to them?

Ten kilometres to go.

Ten kilometres, Anna! Come on! You've got this. You're going to make it. And with that, the blister on my right foot gave off a sharp sear of pain, as I felt the warm liquid once contained within it seep into my socks. Half a kilometre later and one on the left foot did the same; its now raw flap of skin beginning to rub against my sock.

I stopped for a moment to take in everything I could see. The landscape was wild, open and windswept. It was a mix between the west coast of Wales and pretty much all of Cornwall. Scrub tumbled over orange sandy clifftops, which plunged steeply onto the beach below. Looking back I could see for miles; almost all the way back to where I had come from. The spray from where each wave crashed onto the beach was throwing up mini rainbows across the horizon. I realised I was in no man's land, and it was beautiful. I was somewhere between a race to the finish line and a desire for this to never end. I felt like I was running to the end of the world.

At the end of Twilight Bay, the trail left the shoreline, and turned into an undulating bush track, alternating between small sections of knee-high scrub, and head-high bushes at intervals. I ran freely now, following the narrow sandy trail as it twisted and turned, and feeling my own focus narrow too. My adrenaline levels were reaching a critical mass and so I opted to blast euphoric dance tracks into my ears to reflect my own mood. I turned up the volume as loud as I could bear and concentrated on nothing beyond the pounding of my own feet. I flitted between watching my red trainers 'Live' and 'Life' strike the ground in front of me and looking ahead for the next turn. I leapt down the short steep hills and blasted up the other side, sometimes scrambling on all fours. I was a woman possessed, upping my cadence and moving faster and faster with every track that played. My lungs burned and my legs screamed in pain, but I kept upping the pace. I shoved all thoughts aside. I didn't want to think anymore, I just wanted to let my body do what it was built to do: run!

Five kilometres to go.

The trail opened out again, and emerging from the bush, breathing hard and beginning to taste blood I found myself at the crest of a rocky hill. I followed the coastline with my eyes, and then I saw it. The lighthouse. That lighthouse. The lighthouse that I had seen a thousand times in my dreams. It was beautiful. Like a lone soldier it stood precariously perched on the edge of the land. It was waiting. It was waiting for me.

My bottom lip wobbled, and the tears began to flow. Five and a half months' worth of emotions tumbled down my cheeks and into the corners of my mouth. 'I would have taken that lighthouse over all of the money in the world at that moment. Because all of the money in the world couldn't have made me feel the way I did in the hour that followed. Money buys you material things which can be taken away. And no one could take away the way I felt today.

Through tears and smiles, I kept pace. Every five steps I would look back up, just to check the lighthouse was still there. As if it were cruel prank and could disappear at any moment. And all I could think is 'That's it. That's where I can stop.' I was so nearly there. Had someone happened upon me at the moment, I would have been the perfect example of the blubbering idiot. I kept running, sobbing, and repeating: 'I can see it! I can, actually see it!' And then 'OhMyGosh' (intake of breath). I'm not sure I made much sense, because nothing really made sense and so I just kept running.

Two kilometres to go.

I crested a small hill and spotted the final beach, but it wasn't long after then that I spotted a problem at the end of that final beach. I couldn't see where the trail went – it seemed to just disappear into the rocks at the end. I could see that I was supposed to run along the beach, and then I could see a trail wind steeply up the headland in the distance, and along toward the lighthouse, but I couldn't join the dots between the two. There seemed to be a big black rocky outcrop smack bang in the way. Then it dawned on me – the Tasman Sea was now almost in, and it could well be covering a section of beach below it, and the missing section of trail.

'Crap!' I exclaimed out loud. Had I missed the tidal window to complete the trail? 'You've got to be kidding me.' There was no way I was making it within 2 km of the lighthouse and not finishing this thing today. I looked down along the beach and saw the footprints of two people. They must have walked back up to the lighthouse recently, and that gave me hope. I ran down to the beach and along it in sheer panic, desperately trying to get to the end of it as fast as I could. With every wave that landed on the sand, those footprints began to disappear further.

At last, making the end of the beach, I stopped at a wall of black rock. Now that I was closer, it looked more like a set of jagged, uneven steps, steps that I could perhaps use to edge around and connect with the next section of the trail. I stood contemplating my options for a few moments, watching the waves crash onto the section of rock at intervals. In relation to how far I had come, this was the smallest of obstacles. Between where I stood, and the trail that I knew was on the other side of the rocks couldn't have been more than 30 metres. But those rocks looked intimidating, slippery, steep and not a place for a lone runner to be scrambling along at dusk. I concluded that I still had just enough time to make it round the rock face to the final section of the trail the other side, but it would be tricky. So with waves crashing over me at intervals, I clung tightly to the black rock. Waves threatened to suck me into the foaming sea as I edged slowly around; adrenaline pumping through my veins, I barely remembered to breathe. Jumping down onto the sand the other side I whooped and cheered at the triumph. 'Yes!' I hollered, before retracting my elation and remembering that I was actually quite scared. 'Easy now, Anna, easy… almost there…' I told myself.

After clambering up a set of steep steps and running along a grassy ridge, I rounded the final bend of the trail and everything suddenly became very real. The surface underfoot had now turned into a tarmac walkway, lined with stone walls. Lookout benches were dotted along the walkway and there was no way that the lighthouse was a figment of my imagination now. I floated the final 50 metres to the circle of stone which the lighthouse stood in the centre of. Running three paces past it, I at last stopped. I looked up and ran my fingers over the cold metal of a signpost, which said: 'Bluff – 3,000 km'.

Standing at last at the edge of the wall in front of the lighthouse, I looked out from the most northerly point of land. In the distance I could see a jagged line of white waves where the Tasman Sea and Pacific Ocean collided. From here on my land perch the blue ocean looked vast, and I felt very small.

Waves slammed into the rocks below and the wind swirled around my head, blowing strands of hair in front of my eyes. A few seagulls swooped to and fro, going about their business as if today were a day like any other. I shut my eyes and listened: the crash of the waves, the wind rushing past my ears, my own breathing. My mind was racing, but I could feel my heart begin to slow. I breathed in and exhaled slowly. I could go no further. Physically it was impossible, and to know that brought a huge wave of relief. For someone who was so hard on themselves, who moved through life wondering whether they could perhaps 'be' something a little more than they were – there was nothing more I could be in that moment. Nothing more I wished to be. No one else on the planet I would rather be. There was no striving. No belief that the grass was greener. No envy, jealousy, no discontent, no ungratefulness. It was like nothing else I had ever experienced before. It wasn't elation. Nor joy. In fact, I wasn't entirely sure what the emotion was. And then I recognised it. It was contentment. And with every inhalation it nourished me. All that mattered in the world, mattered now. For those 5 minutes staring out from the lighthouse at Cape Reinga, I was enough.

Epilogue

Isn't it amazing how often we work tirelessly for something, only to reach it and find it's nothing at all like we expected?

For six months I dreamt only of that finish line. Of what that would feel like. I'd well up even imagining the day I could finally stop running, but when I got there I found that I wasn't overwhelmed with a sense of elation, or of achievement. Instead, I experienced that deep sense of contentment and I discovered that contentment is better than any form of ecstasy. Elation excites; contentment nourishes. It is the rarest feeling of all, and one to be cherished.

On that day I finished at the cape, I didn't go buck wild and party. I didn't drink a drop, in fact. (I'd have passed out for a start.) Instead, I hitched a ride south to the nearest big town of Kaitaia. I checked into a hostel where I knew no one. I contacted my parents, then Jamie, sent a few messages, and stood in a hot shower for a very long time before hobbling out to get a curry. Returning, Peshwari naan in hand, I sat on a tattered sofa in the hostel and watched *The Terminal*. When the German backpacker next to me asked me what I was doing in New Zealand, I spooned some more pilau rice into my pie hole and said, 'Oh, you know, just travelling around.'

I decided that heading straight home from New Zealand

was a sure-fire way to disaster and so instead I went to catch up with some friends in Sydney for a few weeks. Sitting on the shores of an estuary with a former work colleague, the conversation naturally turned to Jamie.

'He sounds like your flicker flame,' my friend Kat said.

'My what?! What in the heck is a flicker flame?'

'Someone who is…' There was a long pause.

'Do you love him?' she asked.

'No.'

'Are you sure?'

'I don't feel like I know him well enough to love him. I think he's a bit of a lad.'

A few days after I landed back in the UK, I met up with Jamie. A 45-minute coffee turned into 5 hours of chatting and laughing in Hyde Park. Just as I was beginning to wonder for the hundredth time what it was we were 'doing', Jamie crawled across the 2 metres between us, and kissed me. What followed were a few serious conversations, one freak out (which I have heard is customary for the male counterpart in any new relationship) and the proclamation of us as an item a week later, about three years since I'd first sent him an email as he ran across Canada.

So it turns out that I was lying to Kat on that day at the estuary. Well, not about the lad part, Jamie is definitely a lad, but I do love him with every battered bone in my body. I love him more than I have ever loved anyone in my life. And as an unexpected bonus, he loves me too. He looks at me like I'm made of pixies and stardust, and that's how any girl deserves to be looked at.

We now live together in his home town of Gloucester, where the Cotswold Way is our playground and there's Barton Street piri-piri chicken on tap. He's my best friend and I cannot imagine life without him in it. We're going to have adventure babies one day and EVERYTHING. Who knows what the future holds? I'm sure there'll be adventures apart and adventures together, but by God there'll be adventures.

As for the members of my beloved 'pack'... I managed to catch Mav (Peter) and Goose (Andrew) for one final beer in Auckland before I left. They'd finished a week earlier than me and were now preparing for the next phase of their own lives. Peter was continuing on with a round-the-world trip with a girlfriend from home joining him, before returning to his job working for NASA, and Andrew was heading right back to San Francisco to resume normal life. I have great plans to go over and visit them one day soon.

Finny and Fi have remained in their native and beloved Palmerston North. Most weekends they can still be found out tramping and laying out traps for stoats in their local Tararua Range. They have hatched a plan to walk the North Island's 'spine'– a gruelling three-month tramp through some of the

North Island's gnarliest mountain ranges.

Coach Ron spent a year looking after his parents in Canada before returning to the trail at Lake Sumner to complete the remainder of the South Island, and the North Island section. Ron entertained fellow trampers with his songs at night again, continued to send me updates from his GPS device and even hiked sections of the trail with an inflatable kayak on his back, which he used to descend the Whanganui River. In between tramping he proceeded to fix up signs, cut steps and replace markers as he went along the trail, making sure things were spick and span for other trail users who came behind him.

A visit to my chiropractor confirmed that there were a few 'kinks' that needed to be ironed out in my body. My lower back had become so tight that it'd set my pelvis off at an angle, making my left leg shorter and placing a lot more strain on my left side, which explained the pain I suffered in my calf and shin in the final month. Of most concern was the slight curve I'd developed in my lower spine – a result of running with an off-set pelvis and a heavy pack. The chiropractor said it may take some time for my spine to return to normal, but it shouldn't be long lasting. Phew.

My right shoulder was sitting out of place on account of the fall I had after Bog Inn Hut, but that just needed a quick snap back into position, and some scar tissue had formed on my right ankle – a memento from the Deception River day-from-hell – that would take some time to heal. The best news was that nothing I had done to myself was irreparable; a fact which made me very happy. I plan to keep using this body for a long time yet after all.

I'll confess that I was slightly rocked by my mental state on a number of days during the run, especially when it came to hallucinating and imagining other people, or animals, on the trail, and so I did a little research. I learned that hallucinations and delusions are not uncommon in times of great challenge and it seems that imagining there is some kind of 'unseen presence' next to you is a natural way to attempt to ease the trauma. These sightings are even something that one of the greatest explorers in history documented. In Sir Ernest Shackleton's book *South*, he wrote: 'During that long and racking march of thirty-six hours over the unnamed mountains and glaciers of South Georgia, it seemed to me often that we were four, not three.' I am in no way comparing my endeavours to Shackleton's – they are not a patch – but it is a theory that could help to explain some of the bizarre games my mind played on me in the bush after days out there alone.

Over the course of the run, I managed to speak to over 4,000 kids in schools, something which kept the cheerleaders in my mind well-fed all the way along. The younger children reminded me about a world without limits – one governed by music, art (pipe cleaners and Pritt Stick), running around barefoot and whatever adventure their imagination could conjure up that day. In the older kids, I saw the early seeds of self-doubt begin to form, and watched as these young adults grappled to build a solid foundation for their fragile roots, which would one day allow them to stand tall and proud. I was always struck by how the teenagers seemed to be consistently exploring what it meant to be 'them', what it was that gave them a sense of identity and purpose – a search we give up all too easily in adult life.

I was completely blown away by the kindness shown to me by the entire Kiwi population. I took extra special joy from those who shared their life stories with me, or chose to run alongside me for a kilometre or two. It was through these encounters that I realised that we are all one and the same after all. There will always be times in our lives when we are frightened, lonely and filled with self-doubt. My adventure took place on a trail through New Zealand's backcountry, but the journey through these emotions can happen anywhere, for anyone. I'm sure that you have your very own country to run.

I will be forever grateful to the Te Araroa Trail. Taking the first few steps along it in Bluff, I was a girl who was too afraid to read the trail notes, forgot to pack a GPS, had no idea how to cross a river and had never heard the word 'saddle' in relation to a mountain before. Under the Te Araroa's guidance I was transformed into a woman with a deep appreciation and respect for New Zealand's harsh and beautiful backcountry environment, a woman who could run 52 km in a day with a 14-kg backpack and still be smiling at the end. Alone on the Te Araroa, the only person I had to rely on was myself, and so it didn't matter if others thought that I was able to get myself out of a fix, I truly had to believe it too. Of course, it always helps if you have a few magic tricks up your sleeve – some cheerleaders, a stuffed kiwi bird and unicorn pants, for example.

The trail took me right to the jagged edges of what I believed I was capable of, and it will take me some time before I want to go to those edges again, but return I will, because I know that when the cobwebs cling to the dusty pages of this tale, all of the hardships will fall away. All I will know is that I have placed myself in a state most fragile, so that I might see the world at its most beautiful, and its people at their most kind. All I will know is that I have played an irreplaceable part in a great adventure, and that I have truly lived.

Author Note

I really hope you've enjoyed reading this book as much as I did writing it. I would love you more than I love Whittaker's chocolate (and Fanta) if you could go on to Amazon and leave a review right this very moment. Even if it's just a one sentence comment, your words make a massive difference.

Amazon reviews are a huge boost to independently published authors like me who don't have big publishing houses to spread the word for us. I'll never fully understand Amazon algorithms but it's safe to say - the more reviews up there, the more likely it is that this book will land in other people's laps.

If you'd like to be kept up to date with future book releases and adventure shenanigans - then you can join my mailing list here. No Spam, just awesomeness - that's a pinky promise.

www.annamcnuff.com/McNewsletter

If social media is more your kind of fandango, you can say hello here:

On Twitter: **@annamcnuff**

On Facebook: **'Anna McNuff'**

On Instagram: **@annamcnuff**

Or if social media is your idea of hell, I can also be found here:

www.annamcnuff.com

anna@annamcnuff.com

Failing that, send me a pigeon.

Thank You's

The Book People

To my draft readers: Chrisy Fox, Ailsa Stewart and

Naomi Hoogesteger. Your honest words and willingness to read a gigantic 130,000 word manuscript will never be forgotten. I will repay you over time in smiles and cake. Also thanks to Mum, who tried to read the draft, but got too frightened by my stories and so decided to wait for the finished version. Wise move, Mum.

To my primary editor, Debbie Chapman— an angel of the travel writing world. This book would be a hot mess without your input. I still cannot believe you agreed to take it on as a side project in your spare time! I have learnt so much under your counsel and I had no idea that reading comment boxes could be so much fun. Thank you for answering my sometimes ridiculous and endless rookie book questions, for your essay like email replies and for commenting on the bits you love, as well as the parts that needed 'work'. I have found not only a wonderful editor in you, but also a friend, and that truly rocks.

To Sophie 'hawk eyes' Martin for your swift copy-edit. For keeping the story on track when I wanted to do things like talk about how horses are going to take over the earth and that'd I'd like to knit a small bobble hat for my perpetually cold nose. You taught me when to use semi-colons and why stars are naughty and should be banished. Thank you too for letting me keep in stories about pyramids of poo, dancing on mountain tops and many (many) other asides. Any clunky language that remains in this book is my own doing, and not yours.

The Wise People

It seems that I am bound to take advice only from those with red hair. Although, you all vary from the windswept strawberry blonde to the full blown red bombshell. To Dave Cornthwaite for your friendship and endless and ongoing support, and for loaning me your incredibly savvy business brain from time to time. To Alastair Humphreys for your guidance and advice, and for keeping my feet on the ground when my head is in the clouds. I love nothing more than a bullet-pointed email from you. To Sean 'lion-locks' Conway for your imparted wisdom about the pros and cons of traditional vs self-publishing. And to Lois Pryce, largely just for being Lois Pryce, but also for taking time out of editing your own book to talk to me about running the book publishing gauntlet. Heart felt thank you's all round.

The UK Charity People

To the Superhero Foundation team: Kev Brady for your enthusiasm and persuasive skills at the start of the run. Rich

Leigh for your ridiculously talented PR brain. Jody Gooding, for welcoming me into the fold and for just being... The Jode. Ed 'Arch' Archer. For showing me what it truly means to be strong like a bull, and equipping me with exercises that would stave off injury (if only I'd kept them up). And lastly to 'The Wend' and Nigel, for supporting the foundation at every turn.

To Outward Bound UK, Isabel Berry especially —for all of your hard work and for giving me the opportunity to see first-hand how the money raised was put to good use with a visit to the Aberdovey Outward Bound Centre. What you and the charity achieve on a daily basis really does change lives. I feel honoured to have been even a small part of it.

The Body Guardian

To my long-suffering Chiropractor, Matthew Clifton-Hadley at Waldergrave clinic. For patiently greeting me with a smile each time I enter your treatment room and regale you with a new plan for a crazy adventure. And for welcoming me home with open arms when I return to the UK a broken mess. I almost had to leave you out of the thank you's for fear that other people will discover your talents and steal you from me, but that would have been a crime in itself.

The Kiwis

Oh my, there are so, so many of you! I started writing a few sentences for each person, but the book reached encyclopaedic length, so here are just your names instead. And I am sure I have forgotten some people, please take that more as a complete failing of my brain than your ability to be memorable.

For cheering me on, hosting me, feeding me, treating me like a long lost daughter or running alongside me:

South Island: Alex and Allison Kidd; Graeme and Jan Appleby; Kevin Hawkes; Scott, Chantal, Ava, Iris and Zach Hindrup; Barbara Swan (along with Ann and Joe); Raewyn and Michael Fleck (as well as Toby and Jack); Duncan, Michelle and Coll Stewart; Liana Poole; Mike and Louise Neilson; Graeme Murray; Mal Law; Syd Woods and Kevin Johnston; Hollie, Boo and Hamish Woodhouse; Paul and Sheila Johnson; Olivia and Gareth Dalley; Zoe and Ben Moulam.

North Island: Paul and Lindsey Frampton; all of the Welly Warriors (especially Sue!) Juls, Mahe (and SpiderPig) Drysdale; The O'Brien family; Hannah Cleland; Gerald and Davina Mannion; Viv and Ken Eastwood; Rob Wakelin (and family); Natasha Furness; Sonja Austin; Stephen Prendergast and Kara-Lee Combes; Stef Menashe and James Gibbings;

Kirsty Hamlin (and family); Hilton and Melva Ward, Linda Donaldson and Jim; Victoria and David at Hone Heke Lodge; Matthew, Tracey, Luke and William Hare; Graham Simpson.

Plus, a gigantic thank you to all of the Outward Bound Gang in New Zealand, both at the HQ in Wellington and also at Anakiwa. You lot are my kind of crazy.

The Pack

To Finny and Fi, Mav and Goose (also known as Peter and Andrew), and of course to Coach Ron. I will never be able to tell you how much each of you added to life on the trail. You are my brothers from another mothers, my sisters from another misters, and in Ron's case — just one very righteous dude. Thank you for the music, shared food, kindness, belly laughs and endless evenings of storytelling.

Family

To Mum and Dad, for a wonderful childhood in a stable, loving home, and for offering a caring ear through my various meltdowns, bright ideas and changes in life direction. Extra special thanks to Mum for going on a one-woman crusade to fill me with the confidence you have always felt you lacked. Self belief truly is the greatest gift you two could have given me. To my brothers Jamie and Jonty, as well as their wives Sarah-Jane and Kate for your understanding and support in everything I do — even when I miss your wedding because I'm pedaling up mountains!! Sheepish face.

Friends

To Jon Beardmore for whipping me into shape with my plans before the run, especially for convincing me to run the trail northbound. And also for flying down to wave me off at the start — it wouldn't have been the same without you.

To my wonderful friend Emma Frampton for being my 'phone a friend' back home in the UK and for injecting a modicum of calm when I needed it most. Also for ferrying me around in Auckland before the start, buying all those essential last minute bits and pieces. I will never forget the great hunt for the camera lens cover.

To Kate O'Leary for the boost in Queenstown and for managing to be physically present on all of my adventures so far, no matter where in the world they are. Where will we go next?!

To Becky Weeks for offering up her home in Mission Bay as a base in Auckland over those 6 months. I know we've changed a lot since we were 16 years old and trying to sneak into nightclubs in Kingston, but you will always be one of my dearest and oldest friends. Thanks of course to your man Nick, Billy (who was a bump then) and Winston the dog too.

To my Uni gang: Ed, Jess, Joyno, Tom, Lyds, Lizzy, and Cam. For your support from afar and ongoing messages and calls when on the road. I count myself so very lucky to have grown up alongside you all. It's been a long time since we stopped dancing on tables in Fulham on Sunday nights and dragged ourselves to rowing training at 6.30am the following morning, but nevertheless the bond remains strong.

You, My Adventure Army

To every single person who has followed, liked and commented on the blog or on social media, but especially to you for buying this book. They say that life should be spent being out in the world creating stories, or staying at home and telling them. Storytelling wouldn't be nearly as much fun without such a loyal adventure army to listen in. Some of you have been with me right from start of my adventurous journey through the 50 states of the USA, others have sent me money for a coffee or beer on the road, and all of you have offered much needed words of encouragement on the darkest days. I can't tell you how much your support means to me, and how you have guided me in chasing a life fuelled by passion.

And Finally...

To my McMan, Jamie. For being a knight in shining armour. Although you came dressed in a hoodie and board shorts instead of chain maile, and atop a £50 bike you bought online as opposed to a white horse — you are a fairytale character in this book, and in my life, nonetheless. As a girl who does her best to hold it all together, I can't tell you how wonderful it is to be able to fall apart once in a while, and to still feel so loved. Thank you for believing in me, and for consistently telling me I am 'AMAZING'.

Praise for Anna McNuff: Speaker

Anna has delivered motivational and inspiring keynote talks for schools, corporates, not-for-profits and after dinner events all around the world.

"Absolutely fantastic!"

HRH Prince Edward

"In the same way Jamie Oliver has a kind of innate and interminable positivity that makes cooking and food seem like the best thing ever, adventurer Anna McNuff manages to do that about life."

Stylist Magazine

"You made a huge impact in such a short space of time!"

English Institute of Sport and the GB - Archery Team

"Full of guts, energy, determination, stamina and vision, you placed us right in the heart of the action, and encouraged each and every one of us to try new things and push ourselves more. We can't wait to hear what you get up to next!"

Barclays

"It really felt like we experienced the journey with Anna. Her drive to encourage others to do make the most of life shone through from start to finish."

Cancer Research UK

"Anna is as brave as a wolf and a fire dragon. She is an awesome person because she helps kids around New Zealand. The more money she raises, the more kids get to go OUTSIDE. She is a blue eyed, blonde haired superhero!"

Leonard, aged 7, Deanwell School, New Zealand

"The whole school was buzzing for days after you left!"

The International School, Geneva

"After listening to you speak I just know that I am made for bigger things. I'm now super motivated to work towards doing something really meaningful with my life."

Katie, aged 15, Hamilton, New Zealand

"Great motivational speakers are hard to find. Anna was infectiously positive, and with a real story to tell. Exactly what the kids needed as they head into taking their GCSEs."

Head of Progress, Icknield Community College

Find out more about Anna's speaking at

www.annamcnuff.com/speaking

or email: **speaking@annamcnuff.com**

Also by Anna McNuff

A life-changing journey by bike through every state of America

THE
UNITED STATES
OF ADVENTURE
ANNA MCNUFF

The United States of Adventure is a down-to-earth, heartfelt and hilarious account of an adventure through a country well-known, but far less well-understood. It is a stunning tale of self-discovery told through the eyes of a woman who couldn't help but wonder if there was more to life, and more to America too.

Also by Anna McNuff

WINNER of the 2020 Amazon Kindle Storyteller Literary Award

"Llama Drama is simply hilarious. If anyone wants something witty and moving at the same time. Also, something empowering, then this is the one for them. I literally inhaled it."

- Claudia Winkleman, TV Presenter and Author

Armed with a limited grasp of Spanish and determined to meet as many llamas as possible, Anna and her friend Faye set off on a 6-month journey along the spine of the largest mountain range in the world – the Andes.

Join the Adventure Queens

Founded by Anna McNuff and her Kiwi best-bud Emma Frampton, Adventure Queens is not-for-profit women's adventure community – set up with the aim of delicately smashing down the barriers that prevent women from heading off on adventures.

We provide practical information, tips and advice on all things; camping, adventure and the great outdoors.

Little by little, bit by bit, Adventure Queens is helping women from the UK and beyond have the confidence to get out there and get WILD.

Website: www.adventurequeens.co.uk

Mailing list: www.adventurequeens.co.uk/joinin

Email: hello@adventurequeens.co.uk

About Anna McNuff

Anna McNuff is an adventurer, endurance athlete and professional speaker. Once upon a time she represented Great Britain at rowing, but after retiring from the sport, she began darting around the world on the hunt for new and exciting endurance challenges.

Named by The Guardian as one of the top female adventurers of our time, Condé Nast Traveller have also included her in a list of the 50 most influential travellers in the world. She is also the UK Ambassador for Girl Guiding.

Aside from running the length of New Zealand, she has ridden a beautiful pink bicycle through every state of the USA, and more recently spent 6 months cycling up the peaks and passes of South America's Andes Mountains. She has also cycled across Europe directed entirely by social media, run the length of Hadrian's Wall dressed as a Roman Soldier, and the length of the Jurassic Coast, dressed as a dinosaur (as you do).

She is relentless in her search for a decent cup of coffee and will never turn down a good slice of lemon pie.

www.annamcnuff.com

In memory of Matthew Hare
a legend of the Te Araroa trail, and loved by so many.

Made in the USA
Monee, IL
15 December 2022

21682555R00256